JESUS AND DIVORCE

JESUS AND DIVORCE

Towards an Evangelical Understanding
of New Testament Teaching

William A. Heth
and
Gordon J. Wenham

HODDER AND STOUGHTON
LONDON   SYDNEY   AUCKLAND   TORONTO

British Library Cataloguing in Publication Data

Heth, William A. and Wenham, Gordon J.
  Jesus and divorce.—(Hodder Christian
  paperback)
  1. Divorce—Religious aspects—Christianity
  I. Title   II. Wenham, Gordon J.
  261.8'3589   BT707

ISBN 0 340 35542 5

Contents

Preface

Joint authorship is unusual: rare indeed are works written by two authors living in different continents who have never met. Yet this is how we wrote this book. For several years Bill and I corresponded, before he suggested that I collaborate with him in writing a book about Jesus' teaching on divorce. This I was glad to do, since he had already done most of the work: my role has been essentially that of editor and amplifier.

Our subject is an ever topical and sensitive one. Both of us were brought up in what we call the Erasmian tradition which holds that in certain circumstances both divorce and remarriage are justified for Christians. Both of us flirted with various modern alternative interpretations of Christ's teaching before reaching the conclusion that the view of the early church has most to commend it.

Nevertheless we are somewhat diffident about our attempt to defend this view because we realise that many of our readers will have been taught that the Erasmian approach is the only tenable one. Furthermore if we are right, we who dare to call ourselves evangelicals have been guilty of the kind of mistake for which Christ castigated the Pharisees, namely 'invalidating the word of God for the sake of our tradition' (Matt. 15:6b; cf. 22:29b). The very suggestion will raise hackles. But we would echo Wilberforce's plea to the House of Commons when he introduced measures to abolish the slave trade:

> I only ask for their cool and impartial reason . . . I mean not to accuse anyone but to take the shame upon myself, in common indeed with the whole Parliament of Great Britain, for having suffered this horrid trade to be carried on under their authority. We are all guilty – we ought all to plead guilty, and not to exculpate ourselves by throwing the blame on others.

So we beg you to read what follows not simply as an interesting piece of theology, but prayerfully. We believe our conclusions are of vital concern to the individual Christian, the church and the whole of society. May God give all of us the grace to know his will and to live by it.

Finally we should like to thank all those friends and critics who have helped us by reading and commenting on the manuscript at various stages, specially Mrs Everdell Atkins, Professors Don Carson and John Grassmick, Dr David Preston, my father the Revd John Wenham and my brother, Dr David Wenham.

Gordon Wenham

Introduction

The Problem with the Evangelical Consensus

For centuries New Testament scholars have wrestled with the content and form of Jesus' various and apparently contradictory pronouncements on marriage and divorce.[1] Within evangelical circles, however, there is a near consensus on how these texts should be harmonised. In the Western church this interpretation was first propounded by Erasmus in 1519, it was subsequently adopted by many of the Protestant Reformers and was later enshrined in the Westminster Confession of Faith in 1648.

But by non-evangelical scholars this Erasmian interpretation is not even considered as a viable option.[2] In recent scholarly literature at least four other interpretations have been advocated which harmonise the gospel divorce texts more credibly than the Erasmian view and have the added bonus of being compatible with the early church's understanding of these texts. Regrettably these alternative interpretations are hardly acknowledged by modern evangelicals.[3] It is the aim therefore of the present study to expound the various alternatives and offer a constructive critique of them so that the Christian who wants to be loyal to his Lord and keep His commandments may know what He taught.

The problem in harmonising Jesus' teaching on divorce may be illustrated by the following summary of the New Testament evidence.

1 God intends marriage to be an indissoluble union. 'What God has joined together, let no man separate' (Mark 10: 2–9 = Matt. 19: 3–8).[4]
2 Divorce followed by remarriage constitutes adultery (Matt. 5: 32b; Mark 10: 11–12; Luke 16: 18).
3 Married couples should not separate or divorce (1 Cor. 7: 10).

4 In cases of separation or divorce, those involved must remain single or be reconciled (1 Cor. 7: 11).
5 Divorce is a kind of adultery and leads the woman to commit adultery, except in the case of unchastity (Matt. 5: 32a).
6 'Whoever divorces his wife, except for immorality, and marries another, commits adultery' (Matt. 19: 9).

Statements 1 to 4 are in obvious harmony. Particularly interesting is the way Paul's summary of the Lord's teaching (statements 3 and 4) fits in with the remarks attributed to Jesus in the Gospels (statements 1 and 2). If marriage is indissoluble (1), this means spouses should not separate or divorce (3). Further, if marriage is indissoluble then a second marriage must count as adultery (2). Elsewhere Paul seems to echo the gospel terminology of statement 2 more closely when he says remarriage before the death of one's spouse is adultery (Rom. 7: 2–3; cf. 1 Cor. 7: 39).

Only statements 5 and 6 – the two clauses in Matthew 5: 32a and 19: 9 – appear to conflict with statements 1 to 4. On further consideration there need be no conflict between saying 5 and sayings 1 to 4. If lust is seen as a breach of the seventh commandment, 'adultery in the heart' (Matt. 5: 27–30),[5] it is not surprising to find divorce condemned in similar terms (Matt. 5: 31–2). The divorce saying in Matthew 5: 32, 'Every one who divorces his wife, except for the cause of unchastity, makes her commit adultery; and whoever marries a divorced woman commits adultery', is one of the six antitheses in the Sermon on the Mount (5: 21–48) in which Jesus contrasts His teaching with what was said to the men of old. Matthew apparently wants us to understand that Jesus' sayings in the second and third antitheses (5: 27–30, 31–2) are both concerned with thoughts and actions that violate the spirit of the seventh commandment, 'You shall not commit adultery' (v. 27).[6] We shall develop this point at the end of chapter 2. Here we merely wish to make two observations about the meaning of Matthew 5: 32a. First, the statement that divorce will cause the woman to become an adulteress is simply another way of condemning the second union she will most probably be obliged to contract in her situation (cf. statement 2). Second, the 'except for unchastity' clause, as many have suggested in previous studies,[7] may mean no more than the fact that divorcing an unchaste woman would not *make* her an adulteress, for she probably is *already* an adulteress, adultery being the most common type of sexual offence covered by the term 'unchastity'.

It is really statement 6, with the exception clause inserted in the middle, that causes problems in the harmonisation of the New Testament teaching on divorce and remarriage. Numerous early Christian writers held that 'except for immorality' allowed a man to divorce his wife for this offence, but did not allow him to remarry. In this way their exegesis was in harmony with statements 2 and 4, which may envisage separation, but certainly exclude remarriage after divorce for whatever cause. Some modern exegetes[8] follow this view, but more prefer to regard the clause as stating grounds why the first marriage ought never to have taken place.[9] 'Immorality' (Greek *porneia*) however interpreted is understood as a ground of annulment rather than divorce, for a legitimate marriage has never occurred. If the nullity view is correct, it would still follow that in case of postmarital offences such as adultery, for which divorce was mandatory in the early church period, a Christian man might have to separate from his guilty wife but would not be allowed to remarry. In other words the consequences of the nullity view of the exception clause would be the same as the early church view in adultery cases.

Now the Erasmian view is quite different. This holds that 'except for immorality' qualifies not only the opening clause of statement 6 ('whoever divorces his wife'), but also the second clause, 'and marries another'. This means that in cases of sexual immorality the innocent spouse may not only divorce the guilty party but may remarry without being stigmatised as adulterous. This interpretation is clearly in conflict with statements 2 and 4, which insist that remarriage after divorce is adultery and that separated or divorced spouses should remain single. However, defenders of the Erasmian view contend that adultery was such a serious offence in ancient times as well as today that this exception was simply understood by the other evangelists and Paul. They too, it is argued, would have allowed remarriage after divorce for adultery because everyone knew that adultery meant the termination of a marriage. While this view has a semblance of plausibility if 'immorality' (*porneia*) is equated with 'adultery' (*moicheia*), it becomes less likely if 'immorality' is understood to cover a much broader range of offences.[10] We should also mention that this possible means of harmonising the New Testament teaching assumes what it desires to prove. To insist that the other gospel writers assumed the implicit operation of Matthew's exception clause (and the Erasmian interpretation of that exception!) in addition to what they have clearly written in their accounts, is hardly the proper approach to the synoptic differences in the divorce sayings. And the only divorce which Paul mentions did not permit the Christian to marry another (1 Cor. 7: 10–11).

To sum up, there are currently seven major interpretations[11] of the meaning of the exception clauses as they now stand in Matthew's Gospel, but only one of these allows remarriage after divorce on the ground of a serious sexual sin: the Erasmian or contemporary evangelical interpretation.[12] All the other views affirm unanimously that in the teaching of Jesus, remarriage after divorce for whatever cause amounts to adultery.

The Purpose of This Study

The purpose of this study is threefold. First, the current interpretations of Jesus' divorce sayings, complicated by the troublesome Matthean exception clauses, will be set forth and critically examined. Our desire for the reader is that he or she may be able to grasp fully the particular nuances of each view as they have been defended by various exegetes. Often one view is summarily dismissed as being less probable than another because it was only superficially understood to begin with. This study will enable the reader to evaluate for himself or herself each view on the basis of its own strengths and weaknesses.[13]

Second, we hope to demonstrate that the Erasmian exegesis of the exception clauses, originating in the sixteenth century, is beset with numerous exegetical problems. Employing proper exegetical method at the textual, grammatical, lexical, biblical-theological, contextual and historical-cultural levels, we will present an alternative view that does not create nearly as many problems as does the Erasmian approach. John Murray's book, *Divorce*, which first appeared in six issues of the *Westminster Theological Journal* from 1946 to 1949, remains to this day the standard defence of the Erasmian interpretation. This is evidenced by the fact that the more recent works defending the Erasmian exegesis continue to appeal to portions of Murray's book, in particular his treatment of the syntax of Matthew 19: 9, in support of their opinion that divorce *and* remarriage are permitted to the innocent party in the case of the genuine exception.[14] Yet Murray is not at his best when it comes to the syntax of Matthew 19: 9, nor has he properly understood significant Old Testament texts which bear on the interpretation of the New Testament data. This, in part, accounts for why four chapters of this study are given to explaining the history of the Erasmian exegetical tradition, modern day arguments in defence of this view and, most importantly, the exegesis of the Old and New Testament texts which we feel Erasmians improperly cite in favour of their view.

Finally, the implications of what we believe to be a proper understanding of the New Testament teaching will be considered. It is our opinion that the rising problem of divorce and remarriage among evangelical Christians today is largely the result of misinformed counsel that arises out of an inadequate exegesis of the biblical data. We sincerely hope that this analysis of the current interpretations of Jesus' divorce sayings will provide the reader with a framework from which to understand God's perspective on the marriage union and the words of Jesus who said, 'What God has joined together, let no man separate.'

CHAPTER ONE
The Early Church View

We begin our study of the New Testament teaching on divorce and remarriage with the earliest interpretations of the texts available. These are found in the writings of the early church Fathers, namely those Christian theologians who wrote in the first five centuries of the Christian era.

The Value of Consulting the Church Fathers

Every generation of New Testament exegetes inevitably must approach the Scriptures with cultural, sociological, philosophical and other personal limitations. Thus one of the values of consulting the commentary tradition in various eras is the realisation that one or more of our personal limitations will have been another man's strength in another generation. One writer goes so far as to warn Protestants, who are often eager to repudiate tradition in favour of *sola scriptura*, of unwittingly subjecting themselves to a self-deception.

> For their interpretation is, for the most part unconsciously, conditioned to a large extent by the Christian education and environment from which they come – that is, by the tradition (here used in the customary meaning of the word) of their particular denomination. A great part of the differences in exegesis among them is to be explained by different doctrinal presuppositions.[1]

We, like the early Fathers, have been conditioned by the environment in which we live. We should do what we can to overcome the limitations that possibly may be influencing our exegesis of the biblical text.

Now in beginning with the views of the early church, we are not attempting to suggest that their interpretation has final authority. Only Scripture deserves that honour. Though we have found certain features of the Fathers' teaching on divorce and remarriage compatible with our own understanding of the New Testament texts, there are other features in their writings which go beyond Scripture. This is true of many matters of New Testament doctrine and practice on which they speak. So unless a practice or doctrine can be demonstrated from the Bible itself it should not bind the Christian conscience. This Protestants have always affirmed.

Nevertheless there are good reasons for paying special attention to the early church's interpretation of Scripture. The early readers of the New Testament had a built-in cultural, social, and linguistic grid in their thinking which the twentieth-century reader must labour to reconstruct if he wants to interpret the Greek New Testament accurately. Being closest in time to the composition of the Gospels, the Fathers are most likely to have understood the original intentions of the writers in matters of Greek grammar and syntax,[2] an important consideration for anyone's interpretation of Matthew 19:9. The Greek-speaking Fathers obviously wrote in their mother tongue with a fluency no modern scholar can hope to attain. Hence what may seem confusing to today's exegete may well have been perfectly plain to them.

Furthermore on a matter so intimately affecting the daily lives of Christians as marriage and divorce there must have been clear traditions in the church as to the standards expected of believers. theological, contextual and historical-cultural levels, we will pre-marriage, for on this point the church maintained a view which differed sharply from the prevailing views, both in Judaism and in the Greco-Roman world around it. This personal transmission of views down the generations in the early church suggests we ought to give some of the Fathers' interpretations of Scripture a strong claim to authenticity. This, of course, is not to say that the proximity of these early writers to the New Testament age guarantees the correctness of *everything* they say. Yet on the subject of divorce and remarriage their unanimity is remarkable.

Finally we should note that respect for the teaching of the early church Fathers' views has always been characteristic of main-line Protestant theology. The aim of the Reformers was to restore the church's doctrine and way of life to conform with those early centuries. For example Calvin in the Prefatory address to his *Institutes* writes: 'But we do not despise them [the Fathers]; in fact, if it were to our present purpose, I could with no trouble at all prove that the greater part of what we are saying today meets their approval.'[3] In the next few pages alone of his *Institutes* he notes the opinions of at least seventeen early Fathers as he seeks to demonstrate that his interpretations of Scripture are more consonant with early Christian teaching than the views of his opponents. Martin Bucer, the great Strasburg Reformer, was even more emphatic about the value of the primitive church. In his *Commentary on the Four Gospels* (1536) Bucer argues that 'nothing should be hastily repudiated that is commended to us by holy antiquity or by the public consensus of the faithful during so many centuries'. Again he writes: 'I judge that those most holy ancient Fathers should be regarded with the highest esteem and singular reverence paid to the doctrines they taught and the customs they observed . . .'[4] Similarly John Jewel in his *Apology in Defence of the Church of England* (1564) asks rhetorically, 'O immortal God! hath Christ Himself, then, the Apostles and so many fathers all at once gone astray?'[5] It is his claim, backed up by many quotations from Scripture and the early church, that the reformed Church of England has 'returned again unto the primitive Church of the ancient fathers and Apostles.'[6]

To this day evangelical Protestants accept the definitions of the person of Christ and the doctrine of the Trinity found in the early creeds as accurate and valid interpretations of the New Testament data. Yet these were doctrines over which there were long and bitter disputes in the early church. In contrast, on the subject of divorce and remarriage there was practically no dispute in the early church: for the first five centuries there was virtual unanimity on this issue from one end of the Roman empire to the other. Again, we would not suggest that this consensus automatically makes their interpretation correct any more than we would argue for the correctness of the Erasmian view in the light of the present-day evangelical consensus. For example, the Fathers' understanding of monarchical bishops and the eucharist as a sacrifice appears to differ from the New Testament teaching on these subjects. For this reason we would have difficulty in following their views here. The various issues which these early Christian writers address, even certain particulars within a given doctrine, must be placed alongside the teaching of the New Testament and evaluated by it. Where the Fathers' witness is massive and consistent, as it is on their attitude towards remarriage after divorce, and it agrees with the *clear* teaching of the New Testament on this point, we shall have to be offered overwhelming evidence to adopt an interpretation of the debated text – Matthew 19: 9 – that is incompatible with it. In fact, four of the views we shall examine are quite compatible with the early church view: only the Erasmian view flatly contradicts the patristic interpretation.

Let us begin then by summarising the early church view on divorce and remarriage and then set forth some of the evidence for it.

The Statement of the Early Church View

The author of the most comprehensive study ever written on this subject contends that in the first five centuries all Greek writers and all Latin writers except one agree that remarriage following divorce for any reason is adulterous.[7] The marriage bond was seen to unite both parties until the death of one of them. When a marriage partner was guilty of unchastity, usually understood to mean adultery, the other was expected to separate but did not have the right to remarry. Even in the case of 1 Corinthians 7: 15, the so-called Pauline privilege which later Catholics held to permit a believer deserted by an unbeliever to remarry, the early church Fathers said that the deserted Christian had *no* right to remarry.[8]

Furthermore the Fathers followed the New Testament in insisting that there should be equality of sexual rights in marriage, in contrast to the Old Testament, Jewish and Roman law which gave more freedom to married men than married women. Put simply, a man under Old Testament law could have more than one sexual partner without being guilty of adultery against his first wife, whereas a married woman had to be totally loyal to her husband. Extramarital affairs always counted as *adultery* where a wife was involved, but a husband was only guilty of *fornication* if his lover was unmarried. These attitudes were common throughout the ancient world before Christ came.[9] Thus the Pharisees approved of polygamy, and Roman men could have concubines as well as a wife. The early Christian teaching on the equality of sexual rights in marriage is evidently based on Mark 10: 11 which introduced the notion that a man can be guilty of adultery against his *own*[10] wife and 1 Corinthians 7: 3–4 where Paul insists that husband and wife have exclusive rights to each other's body. The Fathers repeatedly stress this aspect of equality, contrasting Christian attitudes with pagan ones. This demand for total and mutual fidelity between man and wife is of course also expressed in the patristic refusal to countenance remarriage after divorce.

The Teaching of the Fathers

Hermas

The earliest Christian teaching on divorce, written well within a century of the Gospels themselves, is found in *The Shepherd of Hermas*. Scholars have long disputed the date of this work, some favouring a date at the end of the first century, others dating the work about 140–50. It is possible that Hermas, a resident of Rome, wrote this composite work over a period of thirty to forty years. Interesting is the point that Irenaeus, Clement of Alexandria, Tertullian and, apparently, Athanasius in his earlier years, all regarded the work of Hermas as quasi-canonical.[11] His treatment of divorce and remarriage is clearly not the scholarly opinion of an individual Father, but witnesses to a practice in the church characteristic of the whole period before the Council of Nicaea in 325.[12]

Hermas represents himself as questioning his heavenly guardian about what a man should do if he learns that his wife is guilty of adultery and persists in it. The account in *Mandate* 4.1.4–10 is as follows:

> 4. I said to him, 'Sir, permit me to ask you a few questions.' 'Speak,' he said. 'Sir,' I said, 'if a man is married to a woman faithful in the Lord and he finds her involved in some adultery (*en moicheia tini*), does he sin if he continues to live with her?'   5. 'As long as he knows nothing of it,' he said, 'he does not sin. But if the husband knows of her sin and his wife does not repent but persists in her immorality (*epimenē tē porneia autēs*) and the husband continues to live with her, then he

becomes guilty of her sin and a partner in her adultery (*koinōnos tēs moicheias autēs*).' 6. 'What then,' I said, 'sir, shall the husband do if his wife persists in this passion (*epimeinē tō pathei toutō*)?' 'Let him send her away (*Apolysatō autēn*),' he said, 'and let the husband remain single (*eph' heautō menetō*).[13] But if after sending away his wife he marries another, he also commits adultery himself.' 7. 'If then,' I said, 'sir, after the wife is sent away the woman repents, and she wishes to return to her own husband, she will be taken back won't she?' 8. 'Indeed,' he said, 'if her husband will not take her back he sins and brings upon himself a great sin. Rather one must (*dei*) take back the one who has sinned and the one who repents, but not often, because there is only one repentance for the servants of God. Therefore, for the sake of repentance the husband must not (*ouk opheilei*) marry. This is the proper course of action (*hē praxis*) for wife and husband. 9. Not only,' said he, 'is it adultery if anyone defiles his flesh, but also whoever acts as the heathen do commits adultery. So if anyone persists in such actions and does not repent, then depart from him and do not live with him, otherwise you also are sharing in his sin. 10. This is the reason why you were commanded to remain single, whether husband or wife, because in such cases repentance is possible.'[14]

In this passage Hermas makes the following points. First, a husband may not go on living with a wife he knows to be adulterous. He must put her away (vv. 4–6).

In prescribing the dismissal of the adulterous wife, Hermas is in agreement with the *Lex Julia de adulteriis* which stated that a husband must, within sixty days, send away a wife guilty of adultery. In Roman Law, a husband who keeps an adulterous wife is guilty of *lenocinium*, of connivance in the wife's adultery.[15]

Second, the husband must remain single: to remarry would be to commit adultery himself. By not remarrying the door is left open for repentance (vv. 6–7). Third, if the adulterous wife repents and returns to her husband, he must take her back (v. 8). On these last two points of forbidding remarriage and making it a duty to receive back a repentant wife Hermas is in direct opposition to the civil law of Rome. Fourth, the same principles apply in the case of an innocent wife with a guilty husband (vv. 9–10). We can be confident that these last three points have been influenced by the early Christian ethic of marriage and divorce.

Most of this, as Henri Crouzel observes, is 'an exegesis of Mt.

5: 32 and 19: 9, in the very terms it employs, looked at in the light of Mk. 10: 11, Lk. 16: 18 and 1 Cor. 7: 10–11. It is based on Scripture, but simultaneously offers a witness to church custom.'[16] However in stating that an innocent wife should likewise separate from a guilty husband, Hermas is going beyond the explicit remarks of Matthew 19, which only envisage an innocent husband's putting away a wife for immorality. But in view of Mark 10: 12 and the reciprocity of rights taught by Paul (1 Cor. 7: 3–4) and endorsed by most of the early church writers, Hermas' application appears justified.

The most interesting development compared with New Testament teaching is Hermas' insistence that a Christian ought to separate from a spouse guilty of adultery. This was indeed compulsory under Roman and Jewish law, but the New Testament texts dealing with divorce do not insist on separation. They simply allow it, while forbidding remarriage (as we hope to clarify later). It is possible that we have here a conflict between the laws of men and the laws of God (Matt. 22: 21; Rom. 13: 1–7) on the crucial issue of remarriage after divorce for adultery. More probable is Crouzel's suggestion that Hermas' teaching at this point is not based on Roman practice, but on 1 Corinthians 6: 15–17 which insists that Christians must never have sexual relations with a prostitute (*pornē*): it is incompatible with union with Christ. Jerome, Ambrose and Basil also cite the 1 Corinthians 6: 16 text in this connection, and Crouzel[17] suggests that Hermas is doing the same. It would certainly be natural for Christian expositors to link the Matthean exception texts and the Corinthian text because both contain the same root word (*pornē/porneia* = prostitute/immorality), and both the Gospel and the Corinthian texts quote Genesis 2: 24: 'The two shall become one flesh.' Paul had also told the Corinthians not to associate with any immoral Christians (1 Cor. 5: 9–11).

Hermas has also gone beyond the New Testament teaching in suggesting that a repentant adulterer may be received back only once. This is not the standard of forgiveness taught by the parables of the prodigal son (Luke 15: 11 32) and the unmerciful slave (Matt. 18: 21–35).

A few writers have suggested that Hermas' opposition to remarriage after divorce is occasioned by his theme of repentance which happens to be allowable only once. Thus in the case of a recidivist adulteress the reason for his prohibition of remarriage –

so the adulterer could repent and return (vv. 8b–10) – would cease to be valid. The argument from silence is that no other reason is given to prevent remarriage to the innocent husband. Hermas lived in a world where it was common practice in case of infidelity for an innocent husband to divorce an adulteress and by so doing have the right to remarry. If he opposed this practice why did he not make his opposition clear?'[18]

On the contrary, verse 6 makes it quite clear that the man commits adultery himself if he remarries after putting away a wife who continues in her adultery. The exhortation to remain single in this verse is immediately founded upon the statement that remarriage after divorce is adulterous. And with this statement we are closest to the teaching common to all the synoptic Gospels.[19] The reader should note that Hermas' questions (vv. 4, 6a, 7) advance the discourse and provide the occasion for the teaching of his heavenly guardian (vv. 5, 6b–d, 8–11). With each question a different emphasis is introduced. It seems obvious that Hermas' third question introduces his favourite subject of repentance as it relates to the foregoing ethical problem. This does not mean, however, that the teaching of verse 6 is null and void. The heavenly guardian teaches that not only is it adultery for a man to remarry after divorce, it also removes the possibility of the all-important aspect of repentance.

To sum up, the main question Hermas was treating was not whether a spouse might marry again, but whether it was sinful to live with an unfaithful spouse. The question of remarriage had been settled by the sayings of Jesus. Hermas felt no need to put this in the foreground. If he was acquainted with the exception clauses in Matthew's Gospel, which are not to be regarded as a command so much as a permission to separate from an unfaithful spouse, then the new element in his treatment was the teaching that it was the duty of the husband to leave an unfaithful and unrepentant wife. This would reconcile, for him, the prohibition of divorce with the prohibition of intercourse with immoral persons.

Justin Martyr

Justin was converted to Christianity in about AD 130 after searching for the truth in various pagan philosophies. Shortly after his conversion he moved from Ephesus to Rome where he opened up a Christian school of philosophy from which he fearlessly defended the Christian faith until his martyrdom in about 165. A.J. Bellinzoni, in his study on *The Sayings of Jesus in the Writings of Justin Martyr*, writes that 'In his role as a Christian apologist Justin wrote for those inside the church as well as for those outside to whom many of his writings were formally addressed. His work, therefore, certainly had a catechetical as well as an apologetic purpose.'[20] Bellinzoni's analysis of Justin's *First Apology* (*c.* 150) suggests that chapters 15–17, the section which contains Justin's condemnation of second marriages after divorce,

> . . . is probably based on a primitive Christian catechism in use in Justin's school in Rome, and it is likely that this same catechism or a similar catechism was known to Clement of Alexandria, Origen, and to the author of the Pseudoclementine *Homilies*. This catechism was based primarily on the text of the Sermon on the Mount with the addition of related material from Mark and Luke and from other parts of Matthew.[21]

In chapter 15 of Justin's *First Apology* he gives examples of Christian teaching on matters of sexual morality and quotes Matthew 5:28, 29, possibly verse 32b or Luke 16:18b and Matthew 19:11–12. Following these quotations he says 'Those who, according to human law, contract double marriages (*digamias*), are sinners against our master (*didaskalō*).'[22] Four possible meanings have been suggested for Justin's statement: (1) it forbids bigamy; (2) it calls successive bigamy or remarriage after the death of a spouse sinful; (3) it forbids remarriage after divorce; or (4) the phrase covers remarriage of any kind. Though a case can be made for the fourth option we feel a better case can be made for the third. Justin has just quoted Matthew 5:32b/Luke 16:18b which state that whoever marries a divorced woman commits adultery. Each of his Scripture quotations, with the possible exception of Matthew 19:11–12, focuses on the sin of adultery committed through action or intention. And immediately following the double-marriages statement Justin says Jesus 'condemns not only the man who commits the act of adultery, but the man who desires to commit adultery, since not only our actions but our thoughts are manifest to God.'[23] Finally, Justin's mention of what was right according to Roman law seems to allude to the legality of remarriage after divorce in the society around him. Though a general disapproval of remarriage after the death of a spouse can be found in the writings of the Fathers, possibly influenced by the writings of Paul himself (cf. 1 Cor. 7: 1–9, 39–40; 1 Tim. 5: 11–15), Justin appears to be forbidding only remarriage after divorce.

In his *Second Apology* (2.1–7) Justin confirms Hermas' teaching that Christians must separate from adulterous spouses. He describes the case of an immoral woman living with an immoral husband, both pagans. After the wife's conversion, her life style changed and she also tried to reform her husband. She eventually desired to divorce him because of his immoral life style, but remained with him after friends convinced her that there was hope that he might change his ways. But when her husband went to Alexandria and she heard that his conduct was worse than ever, she gave him a bill of divorce (Latin *repudium*) and left him. Although she availed herself of a bill of divorce under secular law, Justin does not say that she remarried. This account shows, as with Hermas, that the Christians of this era recognised that the woman, like the man, could separate from a persistently immoral spouse.

Athenagoras

Around 177 Athenagoras addressed his *Supplication for the Christians* to the Emperors Marcus Aurelius Antoninus and Lucius Aurelius Commodus. In this defence of Christianity he says the Christian way of life demands that a man must either

> . . . remain as he was brought into the world, or else . . . abide in one marriage and no more, for a second marriage is a fair-seeming adultery. *Whosoever shall put away his wife,* Scripture says, *and shall marry another, committeth adultery.* It does not allow him to divorce the one whose maidenhead he had [ended], nor to bring in another wife beside her. One that robs himself of his first wife, even if she be dead, is a covert adulterer, thwarting the hand of God – for in the beginning God made one man and one woman – and destroying the unity of flesh that was meant for the propagation of the race.[24]

Athenagoras cites literally either Matthew 19: 9, omitting the exception clause, or Mark 10: 11, leaving off the last two words (*ep' autēn* = against her). If Athenagoras knew of the exception clause it is very probable that he omitted it because he felt it applied only to the first part of the conditional clause about the dismissal of the wife, and not to the second part regarding remarriage. The sentences just before and just after the citation clearly indicate that Athenagoras is talking about a second marriage after separation. In order to contrast the high standards of Christians with the Roman way of life, he states that a second marriage is 'fair-seeming adultery'. This is because Roman society permitted such a thing, but the Scripture does not.

The line that begins with 'One that robs (*apostereō*, cf. 1 Cor. 7:5) himself . . .' is certainly obscure. The vast majority of commentators understand our converted Athenian philosopher to mean that he opposes any form of remarriage, even after the death of a spouse.[25] Crouzel, however, argues that this is not certain, for how can one 'rob himself' of his first wife if she is dead? Attempting to grapple with this difficulty, Crouzel suggests three possibilities: (1) Athenagoras condemns only remarriage after divorce; (2) he deprecates any remarriage, including widows'; or (3) he condemns any remarrriage. A fourth could be added: if there is a divorce and the woman dies, the spouse must not marry someone else lest he become a 'covert adulterer'. After a long discussion emphasising Athenagoras' moderation and general conformity to New Testament teaching, Crouzel concludes: 'Our preference is for the first: this text is only concerned with remarriage after divorce.'[26]

Crouzel's interpretation of this passage may well be the correct one. We are certainly not the expert he is on problems of interpretation raised by the Father's writings. Yet we do note Athenagoras' stress on 'one marriage and no more' and that in his opinion the essential purpose of marriage is procreation. It is also worth mentioning that it is a *consummated* marriage which Athenagoras regards as a bar to divorce. The reason (*hoti*) he gives for his statement that 'One that robs himself of his first wife, even if she be dead, is a covert adulterer', is that 'in the beginning God made one man and one woman'. This recalls the texts upon which Jesus based His teaching of the indissolubility of marriage: Genesis 1:27; 2:24. Is it possible that this Eastern Father viewed the creation basis of marriage as a near-everlasting relationship binding partners whether alive or dead? An aversion to second marriages could well be the outcome of the stress laid on the Gospel sayings prohibiting remarriage after divorce: 'the

marriage bond was so indissoluble that, even though one partner
was dead, he still remained the legitimate husband (or wife) in the
life beyond and the other party was still *married*'.[27] Whatever
the solution to this problem might be, the covert adultery of a
second marriage when the first wife is dead does not appear
obvious.

We have briefly mentioned the aversion towards remarriage
after the death of one's mate. This is indeed evident to varying
degrees in the early Fathers.[28] But note the direction of the
teaching that has gone beyond Scripture in our analysis of
Athenagoras. His possible aversion to remarriage after the death
of a spouse stems from Jesus' prohibition of remarriage after
divorce and not the reverse. Some writers feel confident that the
near-unanimous opposition of the early Fathers to remarriage
after divorce for adultery is merely the result of a growing
asceticism in the early church, and not a reflection of what Jesus
actually taught. But this solution assumes far too much even if
our analysis of Athenagoras is faulty. For G.H. Joyce and others[29]
have pointed out that the Western church never allowed itself to
be drawn into the much stronger opposition to second marriages
after the death of a spouse that characterised the Eastern tradition. Yet it was the Eastern church in the sixth century that
opened its doors to remarriage after divorce and not the Western.
The Fathers' opposition to remarriage after divorce for adultery
most probably derives from the teaching of Jesus Himself. The
asceticism explanation assumes far too much.

In short, there can be hardly any doubt that Athenagoras
asserts without hesitation that Jesus absolutely prohibited remarriage after divorce: it is a contradiction of the ordinance of
creation.

Theophilus of Antioch

According to Eusebius, Theophilus was the sixth bishop of
Antioch. He is recognised as the first Father to state clearly the
inspiration of the New Testament and the first to use clearly the
exception clause of Matthew 5: 32. Around 180 he wrote a defence
of Christianity to his friend Autolycus, probably in response to
disparaging remarks which Autolycus made about his Christian
faith. In this work Theophilus remarks:

The gospel voice provides a stricter teaching about purity when it says, 'Everyone who looks upon another person's wife to desire her has already committed adultery with her in his heart' [Matt. 5: 28]. 'And he who marries', it says, 'a woman divorced by her husband commits adultery, and whoever divorces his wife except for fornication makes her a partner in adultery' [Matt. 5: 32].[30]

Theophilus has done one of two things here: he may be citing only Matthew 5: 32 and in citing this text he inverts the two clauses of the sentence. Some writers have suggested that he did this to eliminate any ambiguity in what Christ taught: Jesus' prohibition of remarriage is absolute though separation for adultery is conceded. Or Theophilus first quotes Luke 16: 18b in a word order parallel to Justin's text in his *First Apology*,[31] and then places Matthew 5: 32a alongside it. Whichever option is chosen it looks as though Theophilus interprets Jesus' conditioned saying about divorce (Matt. 5: 32a) in the light of the unconditional and absolute saying about marriage to a divorcee (Matt. 5: 32b/Luke 16: 18b).[32] If remarriage to anyone divorced for whatever reason amounts to adultery then marriage is truly indissoluble. Though adultery may lead to separation and disruption of conjugal life it does not seem to 'dissolve' the marriage union.

Irenaeus

Born in Asia Minor between the years 140 and 160, Irenaeus was raised in Smyrna where he claims to have seen and heard Polycarp, the disciple of the apostle John.[33] In his famous work *Against Heresies* (c. 185) he briefly reiterates Jesus' remarks that divorce was simply given because of men's hard-heartedness and implies that it is incompatible with God's original law.[34] Like Athenagoras, Irenaeus adds that from the beginning God made them male and female, the text which along with Genesis 2: 24 served as the basis for Jesus' pronouncement on the permanence of the marriage relationship (Mark 10: 6-8; Matt. 19: 4-5). For both Irenaeus and Athenagoras the writings of Justin Martyr were an important source for many of their ideas.

Clement of Alexandria

Moving into the third century we come to the great Alexandrian theologians Clement (c. 150-215) and Origen (c. 185-254). In opposing various heretics who devalued marriage, Clement and Origen expound the Christian view of marriage with quite detailed comments on the Gospel divorce texts.

Clement states: 'Now that Scripture counsels marriage, and allows no release from the union, is expressly contained in the law, "You shall not put away your wife, except for the cause of fornication;" and it regards as fornication, the marriage of those separated while the other is alive.'[35] This passage is clearly a quotation from memory which combines both forms of the Matthean divorce passages.[36] It is even more interesting for its explicitness in insisting that fornication (*porneia*) is the only permissible ground for separation and that it does not entitle either party to remarry. Remarriage during the lifetime of a previous partner is clearly excluded. Clement even says that the marriage of those separated while either partner is alive is not marriage but 'fornication'. Origen, Clement's pupil, expresses himself in a similar fashion in his *Commentary on Matthew*:

> But as a woman is an adulteress, even though she seem to be married to a man, while the former husband is still living, so also the man who seems to marry her who has been put away, does not so much marry her as commit adultery with her according to the declaration of our Saviour.[37]

Of particular interest for our study is Clement's way of relating the eunuch-saying in Matthew 19: 12 to the preceding context in which Jesus prohibits divorce and remarriage. Matthew 19: 12 was one of the 'proof texts' employed by the Gnostic heretics in support of their misogamy. These heretics argued that marriage was fornication, that Jesus Himself was single and that he advocated celibacy in Matthew 19: 12. In response to this Clement quotes Matthew 19: 11–12 and then states that the Gnostics

> . . . do not realize the context. After his word about divorce some asked him whether, if that is the position in relation to woman, it is better not to marry; and it was then that the Lord said: 'Not all can receive this saying, but those to whom it is granted.' What the questioners wanted to know was whether, when a man's wife has been condemned for fornication, it is allowable for him to marry another.[38]

Quentin Quesnell[39] has argued quite persuasively that Clement is showing how the heretics have misconstrued the context of Matthew 19:12: the eunuchs who have made themselves eunuchs for the sake of the kingdom of heaven are those divorcees who refrain from remarriage in obedience to Christ's precept in verse 9.

There is no doubt that Clement understands some kind of relationship to exist between those separated for immorality in verse 9 and the eunuchs in verse 12. Clement talks about 'eunuchs' some five or six times in his writings and speaks of them in connection with his discussion of 'self control' or 'continence'. He uses these terms 'in their widest sense of a discipline of one's whole life and conduct rather than in the narrower sense of abstinence from coitus . . .'[40] Clement is not concerned with the precise exegesis of Matthew 19:10–12 as he refutes the heretics. For him Jesus' condemnation of divorce followed by remarriage to another contains Jesus' high view of the marriage relationship. In fact, it would be to Clement's disadvantage to interpret Matthew 19:12 clearly as a call to singleness for the sake of serving the Lord. This could be used by the heretics against him.

How are we to explain the close connection of the eunuch-saying with Jesus' statement in Matthew 19:9 that Clement thinks is so obvious? Clement is perhaps suppressing the invitation to singleness for those who are so called (v. 12c–d). Instead he focuses on the parallel invitation in verse 11, 'Not all men can accept this statement', where 'this statement' refers to the hard saying on divorce in verse 9 to which the disciples have just objected (v. 10). On this understanding, Jesus, as if to demonstrate that continence in a broken marriage is possible, presents the most convincing example: 'not only is this continence possible, but there are some who have renounced the possibility of marriage altogether for the kingdom (v. 12)'.[41] Those who remain single and continent after divorce are in no worse a position than those who remain continent while single for the sake of serving the Lord. God will give the grace to do what He commands.[42]

Finally, it is worth noting Clement's attitude to the remarriage of widows and widowers. Clement's teaching goes somewhat beyond Paul's (1 Cor. 7:8–9, 32–5, 39–40). He says that ideally widows and widowers should not remarry. But if they lack self-control, they may marry again. Clement adds that in this case the man

... does not commit any sin according to the Old Testament (for it was not forbidden by the Law), but he does not fulfil the heightened perfection of the gospel ethic. But he gains heavenly glory for himself if he remains as he is, and keeps undefiled the marriage yoke broken by death, and willingly accepts God's purpose for him, by which he has become free from distraction for the service of the Lord.[43]

Yet even in these words Clement's asceticism is evident. 'While St Clement does advocate abstention from too many marriages . . . , on the whole one may say that St Clement tends towards moderation in continence rather than moderation in marriage. In this he is consonant with St Paul in 1 Cor. vii.'[44]

Origen

Origen was not only one of the most influential theologians in the early church but also was one of the most prolific commentators on Scripture. In many passages he expounds the Christian doctrine of marriage, like Clement before him defending marriage against ascetic denigrators. Over and over in his *Commentary on Matthew* Origen states that to act contrary to the teaching of the Saviour, to act contrary to what is written, is acknowledged by everyone as impiety. He quotes Romans 7: 3 as proof that it is adultery to remarry as long as one's former spouse is alive.[45] Like Hermas, he insists that separation is obligatory where the wife is guilty of fornication (*porneia*; Matt. 19: 9).[46] The reason he says this is perhaps found in his commentary on the words of the Pharisees in Matthew 19: 3, where they ask if it is lawful for a man to put away his wife for any cause at all:

And I think that the Pharisees put forward this word for this reason, that they might attack Him whatever He might say; as, for example, if He had said, 'It is lawful,' they would have accused Him of dissolving marriages for trifles; but, if He had said, 'It is not lawful,' they would have accused Him of permitting a man to dwell with a woman, even with sins.[47]

Origen also argues that 1 Corinthians 7: 3–4 means that husband and wife are equal when it comes to conjugal rights.[48] He boldly states that the husband who withholds himself from his wife and does not satisfy her desires is perhaps more culpable for making his wife an adulteress than is the man who puts away his wife for a reason other than fornication: poisoning, murder or the like. And it is always adulterous for a divorced woman to remarry (Matt. 5: 32).[49] But nowhere in all his long discussion of Matthew 19 does he discuss the case of the innocent husband separated from an adulterous wife. Arguments from silence are of course doubtful. However, in view of his repeated clear-cut remarks that remarriage of divorcees is adulterous, his use of Romans 7: 3, and his reliance on earlier writers such as Hermas and Clement, it seems likely that Origen thought as they did, namely, that innocent divorced spouses could not remarry.[50]

Tertullian

In Carthage at the turn of the second century we meet Tertullian (c. 155–220), the first great Latin theologian.[51] The writings in which he treats of the permanence of marriage may be placed in three periods of his life: *Ad Uxorem*, written about 203 during what may be called the orthodox period; *Adversus Marcionem* (c. 208–11) and *De Exhortatione Castitatis* (c. 206) may be placed in the semi-Montanist period of his life; and *De Monogamia* (c. 217) in the Montanist period. In his earlier writings Tertullian 'wrote as a private individual expressing a private conviction'; but in *De Monogamia* 'he writes as the representative of a group, expounding sectarian dogma'.[52] As a Montanist he went even so far as to maintain the persistence of the marriage bond after the death of one of the partners. Tertullian's works are nevertheless of great value as source material, with certain reservations, for ascertaining the early church's view of the permanence of marriage.

In one of his early writings he envisages Christian partners separating and living in a state akin to widowhood if one of them is adulterous. His hope is that the guilty party will repent. He writes:

> But, however, since Patience takes the lead in every species of salutary discipline, what wonder that she likewise ministers to Repentance, (accustomed as Repentance is to come to the rescue of such as have fallen,) when, on a disjunction of wedlock – for that cause, I mean, which makes it lawful, whether for husband or wife, to persist in the perpetual observance of widowhood – she [i.e., Patience] waits for, she yearns for, she persuades by her entreaties, repentance in all who are one day to enter salvation? How great a blessing she confers on

each! The one she prevents from becoming an adulterer; the other she amends.[53]

In other words, the innocent party is prevented from committing adultery by abstaining from remarriage, and the guilty party is brought to repentance. When Tertullian speaks of 'a disjunction of wedlock' he does not mean the dissolution of the marriage bond that unites husband and wife. He holds that this is indissoluble in common with nearly all the early Christian writers. Even after a separation for immorality the couple remain husband and wife. He does not mention the possibility of remarriage for the innocent party because whatever happens the individuals remain husband and wife.

In *Ad Uxorem* (*To His Wife*) Tertullian takes up two subjects: the first book speaks to the question of remarriage after the death of a first husband, and the second book treats the unlawfulness of Christians marrying pagans. The second book touches on the subject of remarriage after divorce and begins as follows:

> I have just finished describing, as well as I could, my dearest companion in the service of the Lord, the manner of life a Christian woman should embrace when, for one reason or another, her marriage is brought to an end. Now, recognizing the fact of human frailty, let us turn our attention to an alternative course of action. We are led to do this because of the conduct of certain women who, when given an opportunity of practicing continence by reason of a divorce or the death of a husband, not only rejected the opportunity of living so good a life, but, in contracting a second marriage, were not even mindful of the prescription that they should *above all marry in the Lord*.[54]

It appears at first glance that Tertullian treats death and divorce on an equal footing as ways of terminating a marriage.[55] But this is a dubious conclusion once everything else that Tertullian has written on this question is taken into consideration. One also should not attempt to determine a writer's views about an issue he is not addressing and where his language is descriptive (not prescriptive). As one reads on it becomes quite apparent that Tertullian is not recommending remarriage in either case but is appalled that these women are not marrying 'only in the Lord' (1 Cor. 7: 39). The whole section speaks to the issue of marrying in the Lord, and there are no direct allusions to the permissibility of remarriage after divorce. There is, however, an allusion to

Tertullian's understanding of the permanence of marriage even
with non-Christian partners (cf. 1 Cor. 7: 12–16), a testimony
unfavourable to the practice of the Pauline privilege among
Catholics and Protestants today. The question he answers is this:
If a Christian is defiled by contact with unbelievers, why is it that
the man who is converted by the Lord after he has already
married a pagan is commanded to persevere in such a marriage,
but one who was a Christian at an earlier date is forbidden to
marry a pagan wife?

> In the first place, let me emphasize that the Lord much prefers that a
> marriage be not contracted at all than that, once contracted, it be
> dissolved. For He commends continence, while divorce He absolutely
> forbids, except for adultery. Therefore, the one man has the duty of
> preserving his marriage intact, while the other has the liberty of not
> marrying at all.[56]

The 'rightly dissolved' marriage which Tertullian speaks of
elsewhere is almost certainly that marriage which is dissolved by
the death of one of the partners. He states plainly that Christ did
not forbid divorce absolutely but permitted it in cases of adultery.
Yet this divorce permitted by Christ was qualified by the fact that
a man could not put away his wife *and* marry another.[57]

Tertullian also clearly presupposes that husband and wife
enjoy equal rights when it comes to separation. Though in his
later writings he talks of adultery terminating a marriage as death
does, it is mistaken to conclude that he would have allowed
innocent spouses to remarry after divorce. The fact that divorcees
could not remarry is the basis for his later Montanist view that
neither should widows do so.[58]

Summary of the Fathers' Testimony

Later Christian writers up to the end of the fifth century continue
the same tradition of interpretation of the Gospel divorce texts
found in the earlier authors we have looked at. All the relevant
texts have been exhaustively and carefully studied in H.
Crouzel's monumental work *L'église primitive face au divorce*
(1971). To list those who hold that remarriage after divorce is

contrary to the gospel teaching is to call a roll of the best-known early Christian theologians. Besides those already examined in some detail, they include Basil of Ancyra, Basil of Caesarea, Gregory Nazianzus, Apollinaris of Laodicea, Theodore of Mopsuestia, John Chrysostom, Theodoret, Epiphanius, Ambrose, Innocent I, Pelagius, Jerome, Leo the Great, and Augustine. In all, twenty-five individual writers and two early councils forbid remarriage after divorce.[59]

Crouzel, however, has identified one exception to this general picture. Ambrosiaster, so-called because in the Middle Ages he was wrongly identified with Bishop Ambrose of Milan, did allow remarriage after some divorces. We know nothing about the identity of Ambrosiaster save that he wrote commentaries on the Pauline epistles sometime between 366 and 383. In his commentary on 1 Corinthians 7 he argued that divorce was legitimate in cases of fornication and that an innocent husband could remarry in such circumstances but not an innocent wife. The reason: for 'the man is not bound by the law in the same way as the woman; for the man is head of the woman'.[60] He also allowed a Christian husband or wife deserted by a pagan spouse to remarry (the so-called Pauline privilege).

In three aspects Ambrosiaster stands alone among the early Christian writers. First, in permitting remarriage to deserted Christians. Second, in permitting remarriage to innocent husbands in adultery cases. And third, in discriminating against women in such situations: the doctrine of male headship was of course accepted by other early church Fathers,[61] but they did not appeal to it to justify giving men more licence than women. Here Ambrosiaster is apparently rejecting the normative Christian position that husbands and wives enjoy equal and exclusive rights in regard to each other's sexuality (cf. 1 Cor. 7:3–4). In this regard he may have been influenced by Roman law, but at any rate he is here 'in complete contradiction with the spirit of Christianity'.[62] It would seem too that in allowing divorcees to remarry he was also a stranger to the dominant Christian attitudes of the early church.

An Alternative Interpretation of the Early Church Evidence

In 1967 Victor J. Pospishil tried to turn this picture of the early church's attitudes inside out. *Divorce and Remarriage* is a fairly short, light-weight work full of special pleading in which Pospishil asserts that 'a distinct majority of the Fathers and ancient ecclesiastical authorities permitted the remarriage of husbands of adulterous wives, while generally denying it to all wives, even the innocent'.[63] In other words, Ambrosiaster represents normality, and the rest of the Fathers are out of line!

Pospishil's approach to the problem of remarriage after divorce in our day is as follows: (1) the meaning of the Old and New Testament teaching on this subject is not clear; (2) because the Fathers are not unanimous on the meaning of the relevant Scripture passages we must accept that it will never be possible to settle the problem by reference to Scripture and tradition alone; (3) thus the final judgment on this matter belongs to the Catholic Church with her unlimited power of the keys: the authority to grant total divorce and permit the remarriage of divorced Christians. Pospishil's study is suspect from the start for his exegesis of the biblical passages is determined by a hypothesis that does not emerge from the texts themselves but is imposed on them from the outside. Adopting the ideas of W.R. O'Connor,[64] Pospishil believes that marriages are *intrinsically* indissoluble (i.e., marriage cannot be broken by the will of the partners alone) but *extrinsically* dissoluble (i.e., the Church with its authority may grant dissolution). The reader, he says, will not be able to interpret the biblical passages accurately unless he first makes this distinction! As an example of his method, he argues that the main reason why Jesus' exegesis of Genesis 1:27; 2:24 in the Matthew 19 passage *cannot* refer to the absolute indissolubility of marriage, is that the Catholic Church today permits the complete dissolution of some marriages! No wonder Professor J.A. Fitzmyer, commenting on Pospishil's interpretation of the biblical passages, aptly noted: 'Whatever else is to be said about the merits or demerits of this book, the treatment of the biblical passages is unspeakably bad.'[65] Pospishil's book did have one good effect though. It provoked the eminent patristic scholar

Crouzel to produce his definitive study we have already mentioned.[66]

Basically Pospishil can only defend his interpretation of the early church statements by supposing that the Fathers used terms in the same sense as modern canon lawyers do. When canonists speak of a marriage being 'broken' they imply that those involved may contract new marriages. However, when the early Christian writers speak of marriage being 'broken' ('dissolved' or similar terminology) by adultery, they do not thereby mean that those involved may remarry. They simply mean that partners should separate and refrain from conjugal relations. An author like Pospishil thus approaches the ancient texts in quite the wrong way: he 'judges the text according to what the author ought to have said by the logic of the interpreter, without putting himself into the author's frame of mind, without taking into account his intentions and the problems that interest him, or the documents for study at his disposal'.[67]

In Crouzel's work, on the other hand, we are offered a comprehensive, detailed, and scrupulously fair treatment of all the relevant texts, which has been accepted by scholarly reviewers as the authoritative modern treatment of the subject. One such reviewer writes:

> It would be difficult to praise too highly Père Crouzel's scholarly study of the Church's teaching and practice with regard to marriage and divorce in the first five centuries. After an opening chapter on the relevant NT passages we are led through detailed analyses of patristic teaching, as well as conciliar legislation, in both East and West. The penultimate chapter of some forty pages is devoted to St Augustine, and the author summarises his conclusions in a valuable final chapter. These correct many widespread opinions as well as the claims of certain modern writers to have discovered in the early centuries significant evidence of a tradition permitting remarriage after divorce during the lifetime of the first spouse. In fact the evidence for such a tradition is so meagre as to be virtually negligible.[68]

As for Pospishil's primary objective in writing his book, a glance at his bibliography will indicate that his chief concern was with the moral and psychological problems that arise from broken marriages. Solutions offered for these problems are of course gladly welcomed but not when they fail to have their roots in a careful exegesis of the biblical texts. In both Catholic and

Protestant circles today the general trend is to move too quickly from a less-than-adequate exegesis of the relevant texts to an overly humanistic concern for the temporal happiness and well-being of the individuals involved.[69] In our opinion Professor Geoffrey Bromiley is correct when he says that 'Happiness, when it is attained, is a gift from God and it cannot be attained, nor human life be fulfilled, where there is conflict with God's stated will or a defiant refusal to see that true happiness and fulfilment lie in a primary commitment to God's kingdom and righteousness.'[70]

The Practice of the Early Church

Our concern in this chapter has been with the early church's interpretation of Christ's teaching, with what the theologians thought He meant. In every age, though, there has been a discrepancy between practice and theory, between what the leaders teach and what the people do, between what people indeed know to be right and what they actually achieve. Problems are even greater where the standards and accepted customs of society are at variance with those of the Gospel: the modern secular and permissive society creates great tension for any church or individual believer who wishes to remain loyal to Christ.

Similar difficulties faced the early church. Roman and Jewish law considered that divorce legitimated remarriage, and set higher standards for married women than married men. Infidelity by married women counted as adultery, whereas a man's flirtations counted as fornication. Judaism allowed polygamy, and Roman law permitted concubinage alongside full marriage. Even the accession of Constantine, the first 'Christian' emperor, led to very few changes in Roman marriage law. Inevitably the early church faced problems about marriage, divorce and remarriage. Since full divorce was freely available, obviously some believers took advantage of it and subsequently remarried. We know from Augustine's (354–430) writings of a certain Pollentius who had some erroneous notions concerning divorce and remarriage and who wrote a letter to Augustine contesting the habitual practice of the church of his day. Apparently he was looking for ways to justify full divorce on certain biblical grounds. One of his arguments involved the following 'legal fiction': the adulterous partner should be considered *as* dead, and on the basis of 1 Corinthians 7:39 the innocent partner should be permitted to remarry.[71] So from the beginning the church faced pastoral problems and had to deal with them.

The early church did have a system of discipline which was often invoked. Serious sinners were excluded from participating in the Lord's Supper, indeed, expelled from the church at least until they repented. By the time of Basil, Bishop of Caesarea (370–9), there was quite a drawn-out procedure whereby penitents were restored to fellowship. For example, canon 58 of Basil reads:

> Whoever has committed adultery will be excluded from the sacraments for fifteen years: he must weep for four years [outside the door of the church during the service], then he must listen for five years [in the vestibule], be prostrated [among the catechumens] for four years and then stand upright [among the full congregation] for two years without receiving communion.[72]

Though this system of penance hardly parallels the words of Jesus to the woman caught in adultery ('Neither do I condemn you; go your way; from now on sin no more', John 8:11), the adulterer in the early church went through a long ordeal before being received back into fellowship.

Canon 77 of Basil is also interesting: though Jesus regarded remarriage as adultery, in fact the Cappadocian church only insisted on seven years of penitence: weeping one year, listening two years, prostrated three years, and upright but not communicating one year. And evidently the practice varied from place to place depending on local tradition and the circumstances of the case. If Basil shows that excommunication was customary in the Eastern church, Augustine indicates that it was accepted practice in the West too, though it is not clear how long a period was involved.[73]

At the one extreme it appears that some bishops in Egypt turned a blind eye to remarriage after divorce, for Origen states:

> Already *contrary to Scripture* certain church leaders have permitted remarriage of a woman while her husband was alive. They did it

despite what is written: 'A wife is bound to her husband as long as he lives' [1 Cor. 7: 39] and: 'She will be called an adulteress if she lives with another man while her husband is alive' [Rom. 7: 3]. However, they have not acted entirely without reason. Probably this condescension has been permitted out of comparison with greater ills, *contrary to the primitive law reported in the Scriptures.*[74]

Despite saying three times that their action was contrary to Scripture, Origen admits that they may have had pastoral justification for their actions: it was a means of avoiding greater evils.

At the other extreme the council of Elvira (306) insists that women who desert their husbands without any reason and remarry shall never receive communion again, even on their death bed! And those who remarry because of their husband's adultery are barred from communion until their first husband's death (canons 8 and 9)! It would be a mistake to conclude that because these two canons are concerned specifically with women, men are excused from the prohibitions of remarriage after divorce. The historical context of this council indicates otherwise. In 293 Diocletian passed a law which permitted women to dissolve their marriages simply by writing a bill of divorce without even giving it to their husbands or even telling them about it. These canons are an attempt to counteract the civil legislation.

Furthermore, the council of Arles (314) makes it clear that husbands who have left adulterous wives are forbidden to remarry. Canon 10 states:

As regards those who find their wives to be guilty of adultery, and who being Christian are, though young men, forbidden to marry, we decree that, so far as may be, counsel be given them not to take other wives, while their own, though guilty of adultery, are yet living.[75]

This canon affirms unequivocally the doctrinal position of the early church: remarriage after divorce for adultery is forbidden. The canon then goes on to adopt a more flexible pastoral attitude. Roman public opinion in 314 was still governed by pagan standards, and the only natural course of action in such a situation was remarriage. Young Christians might find the teaching of Christ unreasonable, abandon the faith and return to their old life style. This canon simply forsees that it will not be an easy task to enforce the Christian marriage ethic and advises Christian leaders not to be too strict.

Some of these penalties seem exceptionally harsh to our age partly because discipline has virtually disappeared in many parts of the modern church. Excommunication, however, was a regular feature of the New Testament church for various sins (cf. Matt. 18: 15–18; 2 Cor. 2: 5–11; 2 Thess. 3: 14) including sexual offences (1 Cor. 5: 1–13).[76] We do not know how long such a sentence would have lasted, though presumably it could not have been revoked until the offender showed signs of repentance (cf. 2 Cor. 7: 7–13; 2 Tim. 2: 24–6).

The demand for repentance is what makes the discipline of the remarried divorcee so hard. That bishops of the early church did often put a time limit on the excommunication of remarried divorcees, shows that they were well aware of their obligation not only to uphold Christ's standards but to declare His forgiveness of sin. The vitality of a Christian community was and still is dependent upon its ability to deal with those who seek to justify rather than repent of their sin (cf. 1 Cor. 5: 6). At a practical level too, extending Christ's love and forgiveness toward repentant sinners is different from giving approval to what they have done. But whatever variations there were in the practice of the early church with regard to divorce and remarriage, the Fathers were clear about what Christ had taught. Upholding the Saviour's principles, they exercised a discipline that attempted to express His love for sinners. May the modern church do likewise.

CHAPTER TWO
The Early Church View:
Modern Exposition[1]

Modern treatments of Jesus' teaching on marriage and divorce differ markedly in style from the discussions we have met in the writings of the early church. Whereas the early Fathers tend to focus on the application of Scripture, what it meant for their congregations, modern expositors tend to be much more historically minded: what did these sayings mean for the first-century Jews or Christians? How the biblical evidence should be applied today is usually left to the discretion of professors of ethics or the preacher in the pulpit. This difference of approach makes the succeeding chapters quite different from the preceding one. We shall be examining the divorce sayings against the background of first-century Judaism, their setting within the Gospels, and within the early church. Despite this change of mood though, most modern scholars agree with the early church that Jesus *never* allowed divorce with the right of remarriage. It is simply on the interpretation of the Matthean exception clauses that scholars cannot agree: Are these giving grounds for separation only? for nullification of the 'marriage'? avoiding a direct answer to the Pharisees' trick question? or do they represent Matthew's modification of Jesus' teaching?

The early church view that the Matthean clauses are giving grounds for separation only, not total divorce, has been most fully defended in recent years by Jacques Dupont, *Mariage et divorce dans l'évangile* (1959). Combining crystal clear exposition with tremendous thoroughness, a fine sensitivity to literary and legal formulations, and a high degree of critical acumen, this book must stand as one of the best treatments of our time.

Most of Dupont's exegesis would be accepted by most New Testament commentators, though few draw out their implications as acutely as he does. We will therefore begin by summarising briefly this standard modern interpretation of Matthew 19: 3–9 and its parallels, and then expand more fully Dupont's more controversial reading of Matthew 19: 10–12. We shall conclude this chapter with a new look at the meaning of Matthew 19: 9 in the light of Matthew 5: 32.

Matthew 19: 3–9 and Parallels

Matthew 19: 3–9

According to Matthew, the Pharisees asked Jesus if it was 'lawful for a man to divorce his wife *for any cause at all*' whereas in Mark this italicised phrase is missing. In Mark, then, the question is simply about the general legitimacy of divorce. Matthew's account makes the issue more specific. Jesus is asked for His opinion on one of the big moral issues of the day: how should Deuteronomy's law of divorce be interpreted. The Pharisees who followed Shammai held that divorce was only legitimate for serious sexual offences such as adultery, whereas the more liberal followers of Hillel argued that any misdemeanour, even spilling food or talking too loud, justified divorce.[2]

But Jesus rejects both positions. Quoting Genesis 1: 27; 2: 24 (vv. 4b–5) He says that marriage is indissoluble: 'What therefore God has joined together, let no man separate' (v. 6b). Neither the conservative Shammaites nor the liberal Hillelites are right in permitting divorce and remarriage. 'God joins the wedded couple together, for ever and ever, and does not allow men to put apart what he has made one . . . Jesus restores to force God's will for paradise as the divine law of the new age, as he declares that marriage is indissoluble.'[3]

Like modern scholars, the Pharisees see these remarks as an apparent rejection of Moses' permission for divorce, and so they shift their line of attack by immediately quoting Deuteronomy 24's provision (v. 7). But Jesus stands by His position. Divorce was a concession introduced by Moses because of Israel's obdurate sinfulness ('hardness of heart'). In other words divorce is sin. God did not intend to allow it when He created man: 'from the beginning it has not been this way' (v. 8).

Up to this point in the dispute Jesus has not yielded an inch to the Pharisees over the legitimacy of divorce, and so it makes excellent sense to take verse 9 as a last clinching remark by Christ rebutting the Pharisees' position. 'And I say to you' (cf. 5: 22, 28, 32, 34, 39, 44, etc.) suggests that some authoritative dominical remark is about to follow: 'Whoever divorces his wife . . . and marries another commits adultery.' If divorce is against God's creative will, then remarriage after divorce is even worse, namely adultery.

Now this is more or less how the narrative concludes in Mark 10: 11–12. Jesus addressing His disciples says: 'Whoever divorces his wife and marries another woman commits adultery against her; and if she herself divorces her husband and marries another man, she is committing adultery.' Luke 16: 18b// Matthew 5: 32b add another striking remark: 'And he who marries one who is divorced from a husband commits adultery.' Even without the dispute with the Pharisees to explain them, these legally formulated sayings from Mark 10 and Luke 16//Matthew 5 enshrine a revolutionary view of the marriage bond. This appears if we examine the two cases covered: (1) the situation of the divorced wife; and (2) the situation of the husband who divorces his wife.

The Situation of the Divorced Wife

Luke 16: 18b and Matthew 5: 32b, condemning marriage with a divorced woman as adultery, deal with the first situation. 'In order to grasp the paradoxical character of the declaration it is necessary to take account of what the Jews understood by divorce.'[4] The essence of a Jewish divorce was the declaration to the woman, 'Behold, thou art permitted to any man' (*m. Giṭ.* 9: 3). Thus the essential aim of a bill of divorce was to permit the woman to remarry; at the moment he divorced his wife the husband put in her hand the legal document attesting the dissolution of the marriage.

But by this statement Jesus does not simply condemn divorce as wrong: He says the legal procedure does not work. Remarriage despite the legal form of divorce is adultery.

Note the way Jesus puts it. He does not say in a general abstract sort of way: 'divorce does not dissolve the marriage'. He describes a concrete situation, that of a divorced woman, and declares to him who wants to marry her that this marriage is adultery. The affirmation is so much more striking in going right to the consequences. This woman whom a divorce has liberated is not free. Contradictory? Not at all, but a way of making us feel more vividly a quite new teaching, which deprives divorce of its essence. Jesus keeps the term, but changes the content. This freed woman is not really free: the dissolved marriage still exists. In speaking as he does, Jesus makes his hearers realise that divorce has no effect on the marriage bond; although separated, the spouses remain united by the marriage. That is why a new marriage would be adultery.[5]

The Situation of the Husband Who Divorces

The situation of the husband who divorces is summed up in Mark 10: 11 and Luke 16: 18a: 'Whoever divorces his wife and marries another commits adultery.' It should be observed that in this statement it is divorce followed by remarriage that constitutes adultery, not the divorce by itself. It is characteristic of legal statements first to give the circumstance(s) in the first verb(s) and then state the decisive point in the second verb. This same phenomenon is noticeable in other gospel sayings. For example, in Peter's question, 'Lord, how often shall my brother *sin* against me and I *forgive* him?' (Matt. 18: 21) Peter is asking how many times he must *forgive*, not how many times his brother may *sin*. Co-ordination of verbs in this way is typically Semitic. A more English way of putting the divorce statement would be: 'If someone who has divorced his wife marries another, he commits adultery.'[6]

But there are three very striking novelties about this remark of Jesus to the husband who divorces. First, he says a man can commit adultery against his own wife. Under Jewish law a man was guilty of adultery if he took someone else's wife, but affairs with unmarried girls did not count as adultery against one's wife. Second, this statement effectively forbids polygamy, also practised by Jews until 1948 (Western Jews stopped in 1030). This is because if a second union *after* divorce constitutes adultery, then *a fortiori* second unions *before* divorce (which was designed to allow freedom to remarry) must be adulterous too. Thirdly, Jesus denies the effect of divorce as well: despite its claims it does not give freedom to remarry.

This short sentence . . . therefore constitutes a profound revolution in relationship to the Jewish conceptions of marriage. In the eyes of Jesus, the indissolubility of marriage is absolute. Not only does he forbid divorce, but he denies the power to break the marriage bond. Moreover, he conceives marriage as only monogamous, granting the same rights and powers to the husband and the wife.[7]

Dupont's Interpretation of the Exception Clauses

Up to this point the majority of modern scholars would be in general agreement. It is Dupont's interpretation of the exception clauses in Matthew 5: 32 and 19: 9 that is distinctive.

Dupont argues that the early church interpretation which permits separation but never remarriage is less complex than the other views: other explanations which he reviews and rejects are the preteritive, inclusive, rabbinic (or unlawful marriages view), Erasmian and traditio-critical interpretations. He believes that all of these views create greater problems than they solve. The early church view is the most natural reading of the text.

The first point to notice is that it is characteristic of Matthew's gospel to mention a topic twice, indeed to quote a saying twice. See, for example, 3: 2//4: 17; 3: 10//7: 19; 3: 12//25: 29; and 5: 29–30 //18: 8–9. The twin divorce pericopae in chapters 5 and 19 fit this same pattern. This suggests that the exception clause, 'except for immorality', ought to be understood in the same way in both passages even though the Greek is slightly different.[8] Furthermore, it is also significant that when Matthew repeats himself or takes material from another gospel or common sources, he tends to abridge so that some of his remarks can only be understood in the light of the fuller text.[9] Robert H. Gundry has brought some of these observations together when he comments on Matthew 5: 32 that

> In 19: 9 we will read, as here, the typically Matthean 'But I say to you' . . . instead of Mark's 'and he says to them'. This assimilation to 5: 32 shows that Matthew associates the two passages with each other and anticipates his later material in the present passage [5: 32]. The same conclusion follows from the occurrence of the exceptive phrase in 19: 9 as well as in the present saying . . .[10]

If 19: 9 must be read in the light of 5: 32 and vice versa, this makes certain views we shall discuss improbable, and also makes the Erasmian view very difficult to accept as well. Matthew 5:32 states: 'Every one who divorces his wife, except for the cause of unchastity, makes her commit adultery; and whoever marries a divorced woman commits adultery.' If with Erasmus we suppose that 'divorce' here means 'the complete dissolution of the marriage', the logic of this statement seems defective or at least unfair. For on this understanding Matthew 5:32a means that divorce with the right to remarry is only valid if the wife commits the particular sin of adultery.[11] Yet in other situations that result in divorce neither party can remarry as the unconditional statement of Matthew 5:32b declares. Now if the sin of adultery results in the complete dissolution of the marriage, that allows both parties, the adulterous wife *and* the innocent husband, to remarry! Dupont regards it as 'manifestly absurd' to allow a woman divorced for adultery to remarry, but to deny this right to a woman divorced for another reason.

This absurdity may be alleviated, as Dupont suggests, if one supposes that the divorced adulteress is refused the right of remarriage, but the innocent husband may remarry (= Erasmian view). But this is effectively to allow polygamy! For if the woman cannot remarry she is not technically divorced, but separated. The marriage bond with her husband still exists: that is why remarrying a divorced woman is adultery (5:32b). Thus her former husband is really becoming a bigamist if he takes a second wife since the marital bond with his former spouse has not been dissolved. The early church view, in contrast, leads to no such contradiction. In no case is there the right of remarriage. Immorality may justify separation but not remarriage: in every case remarriage involves adultery.

If the Erasmian view has an inherent illogicality about it in Matthew 5:32, this is even more true in Matthew 19:9. Exegetes agree that in verses 3–8 of Matthew 19 Jesus has slammed both the liberal Hillelite and the conservative Shammaite views of divorce by affirming the strict indissolubility of marriage. Then suddenly in verse 9, according to Erasmians, Jesus backtracks allowing real divorce for immorality just as the Shammaites would.[12] Tradition critics who assume the Erasmian interpretation argue that this is a glaring example of Matthew's lack of editorial ability. Dupont says it is surely preferable to credit Matthew with more understanding than this. It is most unlikely that Matthew would have allowed Jesus to contradict Himself so blatantly in adjacent sentences. If, however, Matthew understood verse 9 to allow separation but not remarriage, there is no contradiction between verses 3–8 and verse 9. Jesus was being much stricter than Shammai, so the disciples' astonished reaction in verse 10 is quite understandable.

Read in the light of Matthew 5: 32, Matthew 19: 9 is not necessarily ambiguous.

> 5: 32: But I say to you that every one who divorces his wife, except for the cause of unchastity, makes her to commit adultery; and whoever marries a divorced woman commits adultery.
> 19: 9: And I say to you, whoever divorces his wife, except for immorality, and marries another commits adultery.

If 5: 32 in its more natural interpretation excludes remarriage, it becomes easy to take 19: 9 as an abridged summary of the fuller remarks made earlier. It is also perfectly legitimate grammatically. Dupont[13] says that there is only one way of understanding the syntax of 19: 9: it is a double conditional clause in which an elliptical phrase is placed immediately after the first condition, 'to put away'. The elliptical phrase – 'except for immorality' – does not contain a verb, and one must be supplied from the context. The only verb which has already been stated for the reader to understand is the one immediately preceding the exception clause – 'put away' – the verb Matthew's readers just passed over. Matthew 19: 9 would then read: 'If a man puts away his wife, if it is not for immorality that he puts her away, and marries another, he commits adultery.'[14]

The exception clause is thus stating an exception to the first condition, 'If a man puts away his wife.' The question we must then ask is: does this exception also qualify the second clause, 'and marries another', as Erasmians argue? Gundry, like Dupont, feels this is very unlikely.

> Here [in 5: 32] Matthew writes nothing about the question of remarriage by the husband who has divorced his wife for unchastity. Luke gives an unambiguously negative answer . . . But it would be a mistake to think that Matthew allows the husband to remarry. To the contrary, his dropping 'and marries another woman' (so Mark and Luke) favors that in 19: 9 (where remarriage of the husband does appear) the exceptive phrase applies only to divorce. In the word order of 19: 9 the exceptive phrase immediately follows the mention of divorce but

precedes the mention of remarriage by the husband. Had Matthew been concerned to establish the right of the husband to remarry under the exception, he would hardly have omitted remarriage here in 5: 32 and then put the exception only after the matter of divorce in 19: 9. To be sure, the Jews took the right of remarriage after divorce as a matter of course. But it is not for nothing that Matthew's Jesus demands a surpassing sort of righteousness (vv. 19–20; cf. 1 Cor 7: 10–11).[15]

Dupont admits that it might be possible for the exception to qualify the second clause, 'and marries another'.[16] But he also says that it is not likely here because the precise question posed by the Pharisees is 'what reason justifies divorce?' The phrase 'for any cause at all' in Matthew 19: 3 anticipates the answer 'except for immorality' in verse 9, and both are peculiar to Matthew's Gospel. We should therefore have expected Jesus to reply to this issue eventually, and in a manner consistent with His earlier remarks in 5: 32. Thus 19: 9 could be paraphrased on this interpretation, 'No cause, save unchastity, justifies divorce, and even then remarriage is adultery.' This makes Jesus give an explicit reply to the Pharisees that is consistent with his earlier remarks allowing no real divorce but only separation.

In contrast, the Erasmian interpretation makes Jesus use the word 'put away' (apolyō) in two different senses. This makes Jesus enunciate two propositions in one sentence: (1) Putting away for unchastity plus remarriage does not equal adultery; (2) Putting away for other reasons plus remarriage equals adultery. In the first case, since remarriage does not constitute adultery, putting away obviously dissolves the marriage completely as traditional Jewish divorce always did. But in the second case 'putting away' cannot have this significance, for the marriage bond must still exist since remarriage involves adultery. The result is semantic confusion about the meaning of 'put away' when the Erasmian view is adopted.[17] On the early church view, however, the meaning is the same in both instances: 'put away' means 'separate,' not 'dissolve the marriage bond'. There is thus a linguistic problem in the Erasmian interpretation of 19: 9 like that already encountered in 5: 32.

This brings us to Dupont's controversial interpretation of Matthew 19: 10–12.

Matthew 19: 10–12

One of the most interesting differences in the controversy between Jesus and the Pharisees on the question of divorce is the way in which Matthew and Mark conclude their respective accounts. In Matthew (19: 9) Jesus pronounces in public to both the disciples *and* the Pharisees what Mark reserves only for the ears of the chosen disciples, 'the insiders'. The Marcan place of private instruction (cf. 4: 10–12, 33–4),[18] 'the house' (7: 17; 9: 28, 33; 10: 10), is present, indicating that for Mark this saying on divorce and remarriage has special importance. It is somehow an embodiment of the Christian mystery itself, an ethic to which Christ expects His disciples to conform. Mark's account makes it clear that Jesus reserves His explicit teaching on this subject only for His followers, the ones who are better disposed than the Pharisees to receive it.

On the other hand, in Matthew Jesus apparently has said everything He has to say about divorce in public (19: 3–9), and the private talk between Jesus and the disciples (19: 10–12) must now be on a subject other than divorce and remarriage (so it seems). Furthermore, whereas in Mark Jesus speaks enigmatically (i.e., in parables; cf. 4: 11, 33) to the Pharisees (10: 2–9) and clearly to His disciples (10: 10–12), it appears that in Matthew Jesus provides the Pharisees with a clear statement of His position (19: 3–9) and then speaks in riddles to His disciples by way of the eunuch-saying (19: 10–12). The question commentators have sought to answer is: what is the meaning and function of the eunuch-saying in its present context and within the framework of Matthew's Gospel as a whole?

Dupont argues in the long third section[19] of his book that the early church interpretation of Matthew 19: 3–9 is confirmed by the discussion about eunuchs that follows in verses 10–12. The eunuchs for the sake of the kingdom (v. 12c) are not those who have voluntarily embraced celibacy for the sake of the gospel but those who in obedience to Christ's word refrain from remarriage after divorce.

In order to set forth and evaluate Dupont's exegesis of Matthew 19: 10–12 we have divided the following discussion into three parts: (1) a brief overview of the traditional interpretation of Matthew 19: 10–12; (2) a development of the arguments presented by Dupont and others; and (3) finally, we shall evaluate and critique the 'refrain-from-remarriage-after-the-divorce view' and present our own understanding of the argument of Matthew 19: 10–12 in the context of verses 3–12. The passage to be considered here follows. We have appropriately included Matthew 19: 9.

v. 9 'And I say to you, whoever divorces his wife, except for immorality, and marries another commits adultery; [and whoever marries a divorced woman commits adultery].'[20]

v. 10 His[21] disciples said to Him, 'If the relationship of the man with his wife is like this, it is better not to marry.'

v. 11 But He said to them, 'Not all men can accept this statement, but only those to whom it has been given.'

v. 12 'For there are eunuchs who were born that way from their mother's womb; and there are eunuchs who were made eunuchs by men;[22] and there are also eunuchs who made themselves eunuchs for the sake of the kingdom of heaven. He who is able to accept this let him accept it.'

The Traditional Interpretation

The eunuch-saying in Matthew 19: 12 is normally taken as an independent saying regarding celibacy which Matthew has connected, by means of verses 10–11, to the somewhat related teaching on marriage and divorce.[23] W.D. Davies calls Matthew 19: 10–12 'a treatment of the renunciation of marriage', and D.R. Catchpole sees in these verses further evidence that Matthew's account is disjointed for 'nothing in verses 3–9 contains the slightest hint that avoidance of marriage is the best policy . . .'[24] The reasons for Catchpole's harsh words should become apparent as we set forth the common understanding of the interpretive problems contained in these verses.

Everyone agrees that the disciples' reaction in verse 10, 'If the relationship of the man with his wife is like this (houtōs), it is better not to marry', is an objection to Jesus' difficult teaching on divorce in verse 9. The problems begin when Jesus responds in verse 11a, 'Not all men can accept *this statement (ton logon touton).*' To what 'statement' or 'precept' (*RSV*) was Jesus referring when He responds in this verse to the disciples' objection in verse 10? Davies's first inclination is that 'this statement' refers back to

Jesus' own difficult saying in verse 9 (which he also understands
in an Erasmian fashion). On this understanding

> . . . the Lord takes the point of view of the disciples seriously and
> proceeds to temper his demand, modified as it already is by the
> exceptive clause treated above, still further. The words on marriage
> are not to be applied to all alike: in their utterly radical form (and this
> includes for Matthew the exceptive clause, be it repeated) they can
> only apply to him 'who is able to stand it' or 'to those to whom it is
> given to do so'. On this view those are to accept marriage on Jesus'
> terms who alone are capable of it: his prohibition of all divorce, except
> on the ground of adultery, cannot be made a fixed law for all.[25]

This would have been a legitimate interpretation of verses 9–11,
Davies states, had Matthew closed off the discussion at verse 11.

In the light of verse 12, however, Davies feels that the better
alternative is to understand 'this statement' in verse 11 to refer to
the words of the disciples in verse 10: 'it is better not to marry'.
Jesus picks up on the disciples' statement and says that this
principle does not hold true for all Christians, 'but only those to
whom it has been given ([houtoi] hois dedotai', v. 11b). Most
commentators compare these words of Jesus with Paul's words in
1 Corinthians 7: 7.[26] After expressing his desire for all men to
remain single as he is, Paul adds: 'However, each man has his
own gift (charisma) from God, one in this manner, and another in
that.' Thus the believers given something in Matthew 19: 11 turn
out to be those Christians to whom God has given the gift of
singleness (celibacy). This means that verse 12, the eunuch-
saying, must be understood as Jesus' explanation of what it
means not to marry. The 'eunuchs who have made themselves
eunuchs for the sake of the kingdom of heaven' (v. 12c) are those
Christians who have renounced marriage and taken up a life of
celibacy because of the claims and interests of God's kingdom.[27]
Jesus finally counsels or exhorts believers who have this gift to
live in accordance with it: 'He who is able (ho dynamenos) to accept
this let him accept it' (v. 12d).[28] This is the traditional understanding of the eunuch-saying.

It is interesting that many of the exegetes who eventually adopt
the traditional interpretation of this passage at first almost in-
tuitively understand Jesus' mention of 'this statement' (v. 11) as a
reference back to His teaching on the indissolubility of marriage

(cf. Davies and Catchpole). This has to be rejected, however, if the interpreter assumes that the two classes of people denoted by verse 11 ('Not all . . . only those') must both be Christian disciples. Though it is possible to think that Matthew presents the way of celibacy for some who have the gift, but not all, it is inconceivable that Matthew would suggest that Jesus' teaching on divorce and remarriage is for some of His disciples, but not all! In Gerhard Barth's words, 'discipleship is never in Matthew required of only a part of the congregation'.[29]

The traditional understanding of Matthew 19:11b–12 also stands in the way of W.C. Allen's suggestion that 'this statement' may possibly refer to the statement by the Lord on the indissoluble character of the marriage bond (vv. 1–9). If this is what Matthew intended,

> . . . the logical consequence of 'not all receive this saying (vv. 1–9) but those to whom it has been given', is *not* for there are some who abstain from marriage, *but* for there are some who recognize the sacred nature of the bond, and live married lives without recourse to divorce.[30]

Thus in the common interpretation of Matthew 19:10–12 it is more important to understand 'this statement' (*ton logon touton*) as referring to the comment by the disciples ('It is better not to marry') than to alter one's understanding of the two categories of believers mentioned in verse 11.

But there are strong indications in Matthew's gospel that 'the two categories of believers' understanding of Matthew 19:11 may have missed the mark and consequently caused traditional interpreters to make some unwarranted assumptions in other connections as well. This will become clear in Dupont's and Q. Quesnell's[31] exegesis of the passage.

The Dupont-Quesnell Interpretation

Dupont contends that the greatest difficulty posed by Jesus' seemingly enigmatic response in Matthew 19:11–12 is the problem of determining the relationship His words have with the context: 'is it a question of a simple extension on the teaching of indissoluble marriage, or is it necessary to understand it as a new teaching on the subject of celibacy?'[32] Unlike Davies, Dupont is not swayed by the presence of the eunuch-saying in verse 12 because its significance is dependent on one's answer to the preceding question put by Dupont. Nor should one necessarily draw a 'eunuch-celibacy' parallel from Jesus' saying in verse 12 and allow this to influence the interpretation of Jesus' words in verse 11. The first two classes of eunuch in verse 12, 'eunuchs who were born that way from their mother's womb' and 'eunuchs who were made eunuchs by men', are discussed in the Mishnah tractate *Yebamot* 8: 4–6. Both categories concern men incapable of procreation.[33] None of these men 'comparable to eunuchs' was incapable of marrying and many of them were already married before the circumstances or accidents leading to their impotency came about. So the import of the third and figurative category of eunuchs must be determined by exegetical considerations outside of verse 12.

'Not all men can accept this statement.' Dupont rejects the possibility that Jesus' mention of 'this precept' (*RSV*) refers to what follows in verse 12. This is grammatically unlikely,[34] and the conjunction 'for' (*gar*) at the beginning of verse 12 makes it into an explanation which carries on the assertion of verse 11, not an assertion on the contents of the 'precept' mentioned in this verse. Dupont also rejects the 'lost context' hypothesis advocated by A.H. McNeile and T.W. Manson.[35] This view emphasises that not only do verses 10–12 in Matthew have no parallel in the corresponding passage in Mark, but their supposed connection with Matthew 19: 3–9 creates almost insurmountable difficulties. It is suggested, therefore, that verses 10–12 originally stood in some other context, perhaps following some utterances on self-denial for the sake of the kingdom of heaven, which might include the renunciation of marriage (cf. Luke 9: 59–62//Matt. 8: 21–22; Luke 14: 26//Matt. 10: 37; Luke 18: 29//Matt. 19: 29).

We agree with Dupont that this is a desperate solution. Why would Matthew, who is so concerned elsewhere to preserve the teachings of Jesus, here produce a conclusion apart from the instruction which makes sense of it? Instead of hastily declaring that Matthew 19: 10–12 is not in the context where it should be, one should rather try to determine the connection it does have with the context in which it is found.[36]

Dupont allows only two possible antecedents for Jesus' mention of 'this precept'. It either refers to the disciples' comment, 'It is better not to marry' (v. 10b) – the traditional interpretation[37] we have just reviewed – or it refers to Jesus' condemnation of divorce followed by remarriage (v. 9). In the latter case the eunuch-saying prolongs Jesus' instruction on the indissolubility of marriage. This is the view which Dupont prefers.

Before looking at one of the most compelling reasons in favour of this understanding – the identity of individuals referred to in verse 11 ('Not all . . . only those') – it is instructive to examine a parallel situation.

The Young Rich Man Parallel. A number of writers[38] have observed a parallel between Jesus' interaction with His disciples after His controversy with the Pharisees over the question of divorce (Matt. 19: 3–12) and Jesus' interaction with His disciples after His discussion with the young rich man on the question of how one may obtain eternal life (Matt. 19: 16–30). After the departure of the rich man, the following conversation takes place:

> v. 23 And Jesus said to His disciples, 'Truly I say to you, it is hard for a rich man to enter the kingdom of heaven.'
> v. 24 'And again I say to you, it is easier for a camel to go through the eye of a needle, than for a rich man to enter the kingdom of God.'
> v. 25 And when the disciples heard this, they were very astonished and said, 'Then who can be saved?'
> v. 26 And looking upon them Jesus said to them, 'With men this (*touto*) is impossible, but with God all things are possible.'

The 'this' (*touto*) in verse 26 does not allude to the question of the disciples, 'Who can be saved?' but to whether or not it is absolutely impossible for a rich man to enter the kingdom.[39] Note that in both verses 9–12 and 23–6 of Matthew 19 'there is a harsh word from Jesus (vv. 9 and 23–4) followed by a stunned, human reaction from the disciples (vv. 10 and 25) resolved by a word from Jesus, referring back to his harsh statement, on the possibility of even humanly impossible things in a God-given situation (vv. 11 and 26).'[40]

This parallel suggests that it is more natural, as many at first glance have been led to believe, to refer 'this precept' in Matthew 19: 11 back two verses to Jesus' prohibition of divorce and remarriage. The foundational theme of discipleship, of obedience to the divine commandments, pervades the whole of Matthew 19.[41] And the way in which Matthew has composed verses 3–12 does not suggest that verses 3–9 contain one message about marriage and divorce for the Pharisees and that verses 10–12 contain another message for only certain disciples about voluntary celibacy. On the contrary, Jesus' response to His followers' objection to His ethic of 'no divorce followed by remarriage' suggests that because they are now Christians they have the 'graced ability' to live in accordance with Jesus' radical demands of discipleship.[42] If this is correct, then Matthew 19: 11, 'Not all men can accept this statement, but only those to whom it has been given', does not envisage some disciples who have not been given the gift of celibacy, on the one hand, and other disciples who have this gift, on the other; rather it views on the one side, the Pharisees and unbelievers who will not obey Jesus' new teaching on divorce and remarriage, and on the other side, the true disciples of Jesus who are able to obey His precepts because 'with God all things are possible.' But is this the import of verse 11?

'Only those to whom it has been given.' We have noted above the traditional 'two categories of believers' understanding of Matthew 19: 11, often compared with Paul's teaching in 1 Corinthians 7: 7. Yet there is an excellent parallel to the vocabulary and the teaching of this verse in Matthew's gospel itself. Dupont and many others[43] have noted the incontestable relationship that exists between Matthew 19: 11, 'Not all men can accept this statement, but only those to whom it has been given (*hois dedotai*)', and Jesus' words to His disciples in 13: 11, 'To you it has been granted to know (*hymin dedotai gnōnai*) the mysteries of the kingdom of heaven, but to them it has not been granted (*ekeinois de ou dedotai*).' The parallel in Mark 4: 11 is similar: 'To you has been given the mystery of the kingdom of God; but those who are outside (*tois exō*) get everything in parables.' The 'outsiders', those who have not been granted an insight into God's divine rule, are 'the broad mass of the people not amongst the disciples of Jesus'.[44] In other words, 'to understand' or 'comprehend' or 'gain insight' (*syniēmi*)[45] into the message of Jesus is a privilege accorded only to His disciples (cf. John 6: 65; 8: 43). This means that those who do not accept Jesus' teaching are the unbelieving outsiders. In Matthew 19: 11 they are set over against Jesus' disciples who *have* been granted this ability.

Dupont goes to great lengths to discuss all of the passages in Matthew and Mark that touch on this theme of the disciples' understanding.[46] Both Gospels emphasise that understanding is

a characteristic of Jesus' disciples, but whereas Mark emphasises the disciples' misunderstanding in certain circumstances,
Matthew over and over again stresses the disciples' comprehen-
sion of the truths revealed by Jesus (cf. Matt. 13: 51). The bringing
together in Matthew 19: 11 of those who do not 'accept' (chōreō)[47]
or make room in their hearts for Jesus' teaching and those who
have been accorded this privilege, once again reminds the reader
of this common gospel theme.

But just because the disciples have been given the grace to
perceive divine revelation (cf. Matt. 11: 25//Luke 10: 21; Matt.
16: 17) does not mean that they are exempt from making a
concerted effort to realise the fruit of such teaching in their own
lives. True discipleship involves conduct commensurate with the
believer's new relationship with God. This is the message of the
parable of the sower (Matt. 13: 3–9, 18–23). 'Therefore, a life
devoid of the conduct demanded reveals a life devoid of any
evidence of the new age, the presence of the Kingdom, and such a
life results in exclusion from the future Kingdom regardless of
one's claims and actions (7: 21–3).'[48] And where Jesus has spoken
a particularly difficult word and the disciples react as if not even
they could live up to such demands (as we react today to Jesus'
prohibition of divorce and remarriage), it would not be surprising
to hear Jesus exhort His followers to faith. This is precisely what
we find in Matthew 19: 12d: 'He who is able to accept (chōrein) this
let him accept it.' This does not mean that the acceptance of his
teaching is optional. This is the same sort of call for insight and for
fertile hearing found elsewhere in Matthew's Gospel. Sometimes
they have parallels in other Gospels: 'Let the reader understand'
(Matt. 24: 15//Mark 13: 14); and after the parable of the sower is
spoken to the multitudes: 'He who has ears, let him hear' (Matt.
13: 9//Mark 4: 9//Luke 8: 8). Then in Matthew's Gospel at the end
of the parable of the tares Jesus calls out: 'He who has ears, let him
hear' (Matt. 13: 43); and following Jesus' enigmatic words about
John the Baptist and Elijah: 'He who has ears to hear, let him hear'
(Matt. 11: 15).[49]

To sum up Dupont's arguments to this point, Jesus' words in
Matthew 19: 11 do not denote two categories of believers. They
denote the Pharisees and other unbelievers who have not been
given insight into the Messiah's revelation as opposed to Jesus'
true disciples who have and are thus expected to act in accordance with it. The primary reference of 'this statement' or 'this

precept' is thus not to the disciples' remark, 'It is better not to marry' (v. 10b), but to the precept on divorce and remarriage delivered by Jesus in verse 9, and secondarily, to the whole discussion in verses 4–8 which undergirds His final words to the Pharisees. The reason that scholars in the past have rejected this reference to verse 9 is due to the assumption that verse 12 is an independent saying on celibacy that has no intrinsic connection with Jesus' teaching on the permanence of marriage: that remarriage after any divorce is adulterous. This was sufficient justification for reading Matthew 19 as if a new section began with verse 10. But Q. Quesnell, taking the lead from Dupont, appropriately instructs his readers at the outset of his perceptive article on Matthew 19: 12:

> But in today's consciousness of the role of the redactor, of the evangelist as author, this has become simply impossible.
> It is now felt as necessary in every pericope at least to try to find the reason why it is in the position it is; and to try to find the flow of thought which the author (final redactor) expected to be produced in his readers by his composition when it was read consecutively as a whole.[50]

We now turn to three additional arguments advanced by Quesnell in favour of the interpretation that Matthew 19: 10–12 is primarily an extension of and conclusion to Jesus' teaching on the indissolubility of marriage.

The Function of the Disciples' Speeches. Quesnell states that it becomes very difficult to see verses 10–12 as a call to consecrated celibacy when one understands the roles played by the disciples' speeches in the gospel narratives.

> The ordinary function of the disciples' speeches in the gospels is to ask questions, to misunderstand or object, or simply to advance the action dramatically. They do not enunciate the Christian ideal for life. Their objections are not accepted and confirmed by the Master, but are refuted or made the occasion for stronger restatements of the original teaching.[51]

After systematically examining all the words of the disciples in Matthew up to this point, Quesnell notes that only once does a disciple give a statement of faith which is approved and praised: Matthew 16: 15–17. Peter says, 'Thou art the Christ, the Son of the living God.' But Jesus immediately assigns Peter's comment to its proper origin: 'Flesh and blood did not reveal this to you, but My Father who is in heaven.'

However, if Matthew 19: 10–12 are understood as a call to consecrated virginity they present a great anomaly: the disciples' objection in verse 10 to Jesus' teaching on the permanence of marriage (despite legal divorce) would result in a complete reversal of the argument of verses 3–9. The whole argument that has been developing in verses 4–8 is that man and wife are not to separate because God made the two 'one flesh'; and this union joined by God is not to be put asunder. This culminates in Jesus' precept that man and wife, if separated for some reason, are never to marry another (v. 9). Then in verse 10 the disciples reject this conception of life and marriage. Quesnell argues that if verses 11–12 really do constitute a call to celibacy, then Jesus suddenly backs off, agrees with the disciples' objection and begins to teach that it may well be advantageous not to marry; that it is a good thing to give up marriage for the sake of the kingdom. Let him accept it who can.

In light of the role which the disciples play in Matthew and in all the Gospels, Quesnell says 'Jesus cannot be intended to accept and approve this statement of theirs.'[52] If, however, the eunuch-saying is not a direct call to celibacy, but a challenging formulation of the state of the man whose wife has been put away on account of immorality, Jesus is forcefully driving home the whole argument which He has just built up in verses 4–9. Just as Mark shows the significance of Jesus' teaching (that divorce *and* remarriage *always* is adulterous) by placing it 'in the house' only for the ears of the disciples, Matthew has in turn employed another device for emphasis of his own. He makes the disciples object to the difficult saying of verse 9; then Jesus reformulates His teaching and restates His standard for indissoluble marriage even more forcefully. The condition of the husband whose wife has been put away because of her immorality 'can leave a man in a state comparable to that of those most pitiable of men – the eunuchs, born incapable of marriage or castrated by men so as to be incapable of marriage'.[53] In Geoffrey Bromiley's paraphrase of verse 12: 'For God's sake some people may have to forgo marriage, some may have to put it in a new perspective, and some who have broken their marriages may have to refrain from remarriage.'[54]

The Incongruity of a Call to Celibacy in Matthew. Quesnell also maintains that a call to celibacy would be especially incongruous in the Gospel of Matthew. This is because Matthew elsewhere omits all material of this sort which he shares with Luke and/or Mark.[55] Luke 18: 29, for instance, includes 'wife' in the list of persons and things which a disciple must be willing to leave for the sake of the kingdom. Matthew 19: 29 does not mention the wife, and neither does Mark 10: 29.[56] Luke 14: 26 also has: 'If anyone comes to Me, and does not hate his own father and mother and *wife* and children and brothers and sisters, yes, even his own life, he cannot be My disciple.' Matthew 10: 37 has: 'He who loves father or mother more than Me is not worthy of Me; and he who loves son or daughter more than Me is not worthy of Me.' Thus Luke has four items to be renounced which Matthew does not have here (brothers, sisters, wife, life). All of these do show up elsewhere in Matthew for explicit renunciation (19: 29; 16: 25; 10: 39) with one exception: 'the wife'.

Furthermore, Luke calls what Matthew terms 'a wedding feast' (22: 2–14) 'a big dinner' (Luke 14: 16–24). The invited guests give excuses why they cannot come: one has just bought a field, another just bought five oxen, and the third says, 'I have married a wife, and for this reason I cannot come' (Luke 14: 20). Matthew, once again, completely omits the suggestion that marrying a wife might interfere with following the call to the kingdom.[57]

Another interesting detail is the Matthean and Lucan treatment of the dispute about the resurrection (Luke 20: 27–40//Matt. 22: 23–33; cf. Mark 12: 13–17). Luke distinguishes two classes of men: 'The sons of this age marry, and are given in marriage, but those who are considered worthy to attain to that age and the resurrection from the dead, neither marry, nor are given in marriage' (vv. 34–5). Matthew, like Mark, omits, if he knew of it, the Lucan implication of two classes of men.

Finally, on the question of the seven husbands for the woman, Luke writes: 'Moses wrote us that "if a man's brother dies", having a wife, "and he is childless, his brother should take . . ."' (20: 28). Mark 12: 19 is similar: '. . . that "if a man's brother dies", and leaves behind a wife, "and leaves no child . . ."' It appears that both, especially Luke, leave room for the possibility that a man might die and not leave a wife. Yet Luke's 'having a wife' (*echōn gynaika*) suggests plainly that there are men who do not have wives. Matthew writes: 'Moses said, "If a man dies, having no children, his brother as next of kin shall marry his wife, and . . ."' (22:24). Quesnell believes 'The clear supposition is that though some men may not have children, all men have wives.'[58]

'*Concerning virgins I have no command of the Lord.*' The third problem Quesnell finds confronting the traditional interpretation of Matthew 19:10–12 is Paul's opening statement to the only other passage in the New Testament that is cited in support of the benefits of the celibate life: 1 Corinthians 7:25–35. Paul had earlier appealed to the authority of the Lord in support of what he had to say on the matter of divorce (vv. 10–11), and he will do so again on the legitimacy of ministers of the Gospel making a living from the Gospel (9:14). But when he turns to discuss the status of those who have never married, he states that he has no 'command' (*epitagē*) from the Lord on this subject (7:25). If Paul knew of the sayings now recorded in Matthew 19:11–12, it would have been to his advantage to appeal to them in support of his teaching on the benefits of the single life.

Quesnell is aware of the objection to his conclusions on this point: Jesus' words in Matthew 19:12 are not a direct *command* to embrace the single life but a *counsel* or encouragement addressed to those who are able to undertake a celibate life.[59] Quesnell responds that Paul knows of the rabbinic distinction between command and counsel, and uses it in 7:6: 'But this I say by way of concession (*syngnōmē*), not of command (*epitagē*)'. But this does not explain Paul's words in verse 25. Throughout chapter 7 Paul seems clearly to be speaking in favour of virginity and voluntary celibacy.

> He is trying to persuade his readers to this, by appeals to his own prestige (v. 7; v. 17; v. 25b; v. 40b); by arguments from reason (v. 26a; 32–5). Why should he weaken his persuasive case by saying, 'I have no command from the Lord but I give advice as one who has received mercy from the Lord to be faithful' (v. 25)? The unavoidable conclusion is that Paul knew of no such counsel from the Lord.[60]

This completes our survey of the arguments in favour of the interpretation that Matthew 19:10–12 is simply an extension and restatement of Jesus' teaching on marital indissolubility. In particular, the disciples object to Jesus' new teaching that legal divorce does not, under any circumstances, open the door for remarriage. Jesus responds that this is indeed a difficult path to follow, but His true followers have been given the divine resources to live up to it. They may be compared to eunuchs who have chosen to live a single life in faithful obedience to their Master's teaching because they have grasped the meaning of the Messiah's lordship over their lives.

Evaluation and Critique of the Dupont–Quesnell Interpretation

The Dupont–Quesnell approach to Matthew 19:10–12 has been favourably received in a number of recent studies.[61] We feel that the parallel established between Matthew 19:11, 'Not all men can accept this statement, but only those to whom it has been given', and 13:11, 'To you it has been granted to know the mysteries of the kingdom of heaven, but to them it has not been granted', can hardly be overlooked. This makes it most probable that Matthew 19:11 does *not* refer to two classes of believers, some who have not been given the gift of celibacy and some who have; instead it sets the Pharisees and unbelievers who have not been granted insight into Jesus' teaching against the true disciples of Jesus who have been granted this ability. If this is correct, the antecedent to 'this precept' in verse 11 cannot be to the disciples' words, 'It is better not to marry,' but must pick up once again Jesus' emphasis on the permanence of the marriage bond despite legal divorce.[62]

Some may object that the word for 'accepting' or 'understanding' (*chōreō*) Jesus' precept in Matthew 19:11, 12d is not the same word used in 13:11 (*ginōskō*). Does this suggest that Matthew 19:11 is not a true parallel to 13:11? This is unlikely for two reasons. First, a number of different words are used in Matthew's Gospel to communicate the common theme of the disciples' understanding.[63] Thus it is likely that the word used in Matthew 19:11 falls into the same category. Yet its lexical character suggests that it is chosen here because of the particularly difficult line of conduct Jesus has just required of all who claim to be his true disciples. This seems to be the significance of P. Schmidt's remarks about the word in our passage:

It means to receive or embrace the apocalyptic teaching of Jesus (Matt. 19: 11f., contained in vv. 9 or 10). The meaning corresponds to understanding and grasping the teaching of the parables (cf. Matt. 13: 11, 16f., 19, 23). In both instances Matt. stresses the understanding of the disciples. *chōreō* appears to go beyond understanding and points to the capacity to receive and act upon the teaching.[64]

Schmidt's words seem to allow for either the traditional interpretation of our passage – that Jesus picks up on the words of the disciples in verse 10b – or the reference back to verse 9, the extension or emphasis on the teaching of marital indissolubility. As we have argued, the parallel to Matthew 13: 11 and the theme of the disciples' understanding throughout Matthew's Gospel makes the latter more probable.

The second reason that Matthew 19: 11 is a true parallel to 13: 11 (thus carrying on the theme of understanding which marks off the true from the false disciple) may be observed in the way the two halves of the verse are laid out: 'Not all men can accept this statement [because it has not been given them to do so], but (*alla*) only those to whom it has been given [to accept it].' Matthew 13: 11 along with many other passages make it clear that certain people have not been granted insight into God's revelation: they are the unbelievers, those outside the circle of Jesus' true disciples. The response of this group – indifference and rejection – to God's word conveyed through the Messiah is seen again in Matthew 19: 11a.

We are, however, attracted to the suggestion that Paul, in chapters 6 and 7 of 1 Corinthians, seems to be aware of the whole synoptic context of the divorce debate found in Matthew 19//Mark 10,[65] including Jesus' saying about 'eunuchs who made themselves eunuchs for the sake of the kingdom of heaven'. In 1 Corinthians 7: 10–11 Paul undoubtedly reflects the various forms of the divorce sayings recorded to the synoptic Gospels: he intends a prohibition of remarriage along with his rejection of divorce. In 6: 16 Paul quotes a portion of Genesis 2: 24, 'The two will become one flesh' (cf. Matt. 19: 5//Mark 10: 8). Then in 7: 7 he speaks of singleness as a gift and then develops the reasons for and benefits of singleness in 7: 25–35. Paul also alludes to a saying of the Lord in 9: 14 which is found in Matthew 10: 10//Luke 10: 7. Since Paul was a missionary delegate sent out from the church of Antioch (Acts 13: 1–3; cf. 11: 19–30), and since many believe

Antioch was the most likely destination for Matthew's Gospel, 'we may suppose that this was primarily the tradition of the "words of the Lord" which he took with him, and it would explain the otherwise rather unexpected affinity in doctrine and in discipline between Paul and Matthew . . .'[66] All of this suggests that the source for Paul's remarks about celibacy may be his knowledge of a saying similar to that found in Matthew 19: 12.

Furthermore, the conjunction 'for' (*gar*) which introduces Matthew 19: 12 seems to suggest that a new idea forms the climactic conclusion to verses 3–12. In other words, verse 12 makes reference to a possibility that explains why Jesus' remarks in verse 11b are equally if not more possible (cf. Matt. 19: 26). We thus have reason to question the Dupont–Quesnell understanding that the third class of eunuchs is simply a figurative reference back to the state of those separated from their wives for immorality, in verse 9.

How are we to reconcile the results of our exegesis up to this point? Matthew 19: 11 almost certainly refers back to Jesus' prohibition of remarriage after divorce for whatever cause, yet the evidence from 1 Corinthians 7 leaves open the possibility that Jesus suggested that some of His followers may voluntarily choose not to marry at all 'because of the kingdom'. This last phrase is clearly a motive clause meaning that one should seek earnestly the divine rule,[67] and for some this may involve a life without ever marrying; for others it may involve a life of singleness after an unfortunate divorce and failure to achieve reconciliation with one's partner. What matters in any situation in life is obedience to the revelation of God. But how do those who live a life without ever marrying relate to Jesus' disciples who must never put away the wife they married or refrain from remarriage in the event of an unavoidable separation?

We believe that Jesus is using a common argument form that moves from the greater to the lesser. Let us explain. Jesus delivers His difficult precept that there must be no remarriage after divorce for whatever reason (v. 9). The disciples react in unbelief and object to this new teaching (v. 10). Jesus responds that His prohibition of divorce and remarriage is indeed a difficult precept to understand and to live by, but that His disciples have been given the ability to understand it and will be given the grace to live by it should they face a divorce they cannot prevent (v. 11). Jesus then explains how and why this is possible: not only is continence in a broken marriage possible, but consider those who may never marry because they are born eunuchs or made eunuchs by men; there are even some who have renounced the possibility of marriage altogether for the kingdom.[68] Upon introducing the possibility that some may never marry because of the claims and interests of God's kingdom, Jesus concludes with the call to faith: 'He who is able to accept this let him accept it.' This call is directed to those disciples who might dare to follow Jesus' suggestion that it is appropriate for some to forgo married life for the sake of more freely serving the causes of the kingdom.

Why did Paul not quote Jesus' suggestion in a more concrete fashion if he knew of it? Apart from the fact that it is the exception, not the rule, for Paul to say that he is citing Jesus, R. Balducelli notes the following about Matthew 19: 12:

> The grammar of the text is declaratory ('there are eunuchs . . .') not exhortatory or prescriptive. And the parting words, 'Let anyone accept this who can' (v. 12d), which are exhortatory, are not an exhortation to accept celibacy but to 'accept' what has been said about it ('this'), namely, that it has happened. This explains why Paul, who so outspokenly promotes his own appreciation of celibacy (1 Cor 7: 1, 7–8), is not in a position to canonize that appreciation by tracing it back to a direct endorsement ('disposition') of the Lord (1 Cor 7: 25). Jesus' restraint is not surprising. A direct exhortation to celibacy would have been wasted on people committed to a vertical legitimation of procreation.[69]

Though we have not been exhaustive in our treatment of Matthew 19: 10–12, we want to bring this discussion to a close. Jesus is arguing from the greater to the lesser in response to His disciples' objection to this new demand: if God enables some individuals to live continently apart from marriage, He can enable those married to stay married; and He can enable the separated partner to live continently in spite of a broken marriage. In this way the separated disciple avoids the sin of adultery that is committed by remarrying during the lifetime of the original spouse.

This, in our view, is the interpretation of Matthew 19: 10–12 that best accounts for the available data. It seems safe to say, moreover, that the considerations advanced here make improbable any understanding of Matthew 19: 9 which permits remarriage after divorce for immorality.

Matthew 19: 9 in the Light of 5: 32

Almost by way of postscript we should examine the most recent short article which has attempted to see Matthew 19: 9 as part of the evangelist's total message and to interpret verse 9 in the light of verse 32 of chapter 5. J.J. Kilgallen[70] accepts the early church interpretation, but he draws attention to a point usually overlooked.

Matthew 5: 32 reads: 'but I say to you that every one who divorces his wife, *except for the cause of unchastity*, makes her commit adultery; and whoever marries a divorced woman commits adultery'.[71] We made two observations about Matthew 5: 32a in the Introduction to this study. We first observed that the statement that divorce will cause the woman to become an adulteress is simply another way of condemning the second union she will most probably be obliged to contract in her situation. But even more obvious than this is Matthew's emphasis on the guilt of the husband who divorces for an unwarranted reason, as if exculpating the wife. There is complete consensus on this observation that Matthew's 'makes her commit adultery' points a finger at the divorcing husband and makes him morally responsible for making his wife and her second husband commit adultery against him.[72] In Gundry's words, 'Special emphasis falls, then, on the demand that a husband not contribute to the adultery of his wife, as would happen if she remarried because he had divorced her.'[73]

This consideration leads naturally to the second observation we made about Matthew 5: 32a. The 'except for unchastity' clause is 'simply a matter-of-fact recognition that if the wife has already committed adultery, her husband cannot be held guilty of driving her into it by divorcing her.'[74] *She* is responsible for the sinful adulterous connection, not he. This brings us to Kilgallen's important contextual observations.

Kilgallen argues that Matthew 5: 31–2 are part of Jesus' expansion and reinterpretation (or application) of the seventh commandment, 'You shall not commit adultery', which begins in 5: 27. Verses 27–32 are concerned with the law against adultery, that is, thoughts or actions that violate the spirit of the seventh commandment. Jesus gives two examples of such violations 'which His audience would never contemplate as adulterous':[75] lust (vv. 27–30) and divorce (vv. 31–2).

Thus in verse 32 we have two cases cited which violate the commandment against adultery:

1 Divorce (unless it be for unchastity) (v. 32a)
2 Remarriage after divorce for whatever cause (v. 32b)

In the first case the husband is guilty of violating the seventh commandment because in divorcing his wife unjustly he has become, in essence, the instigator of her subsequent adulterous 'marriage'. J.A. Fitzmyer writes that Matthew 5:32a 'relates divorce itself, and not divorce and subsequent marriage, to adultery . . . the Matthean form regards divorce itself as the cause of adultery'.[76] Thus Matthew 5:32 teaches that unwarranted divorce and remarriage after divorce are both violations of the seventh commandment and tantamount to adultery. The purpose of this teaching is not to clarify whether a divorce where there is unchastity is permissible or desirable. In the past this has been the perspective within which many have sought to understand this text. Rather the context suggests that the cases being considered are those which violate the seventh commandment, 'You shall not commit adultery.' If this is correct, then the one who attempts to determine if this passage permits divorce for unchastity (and the consequent freedom of the 'innocent' party to remarry) is looking for an answer to a question not addressed by Matthew 5:32.

All of this seems to indicate that Matthew knows of a saying of Jesus that placed most divorce actions (in the Jewish legal practice of Jesus' audience) in the category of violating the spirit of the seventh commandment. This is reflected in the context of Matthew 5:27–32 where he makes 'lust' and unwarranted 'divorce' tantamount to committing adultery.

Why then is divorce wrong if in some cases it is not adulterous in the sense of violating the seventh commandment? Kilgallen sees this as the chief point under discussion in chapter 19. The Pharisees ask Jesus about divorce clearly expecting Him to rule against it. He does indeed do so, grounding His objections in Genesis (Matt. 19:4–8).

> It is only after explaining His reason for not permitting divorce that Jesus repeats His statement in 5:32, that divorce is, in most cases, adulterous. Thus, in verse 9 He adds to the wrongfulness of divorce, in that He suggests that divorce is wrong, not only because man cannot sunder what God has joined together, but that in general divorce is an example of adultery.[77]

The context of the divorce-cum-exception sayings is above all else the indicator that, if there is a meaning to the exception, it is that not every divorce is necessarily adulterous; Jesus, therefore, does not offer the possibility of exceptions to His law against divorce, but only to the general rule that divorce is adulterous.[78]

Thus in Matthew 5:32 divorce is seen as a violation of the seventh commandment, and in Matthew 19:9 divorce is presented as incompatible with the union of husband and wife taught in the ordinance of creation.

Kilgallen's observations shed light on Dupont's insistence that 19:9 must be read in the light of 5:32 and that 19:9 is likely to be an abridgement of 5:32. From 5:27–32 three propositions about divorce can be deduced:

1 To divorce one's wife is tantamount to committing adultery (vv. 27–32a)
2 To divorce one's wife for unchastity is not tantamount to committing adultery (v. 32a)
3 To marry a divorced woman is to commit adultery (v. 32b)

As we noted earlier, proposition 3 is equivalent to (a) *Whoever divorces his wife and marries another commits adultery.* Whereas propositions 1 and 2 are equivalent to (b) *Whoever divorces his wife, except for unchastity, makes her commit adultery.* If (a) and (b) were combined in a single sentence the result would be 19:9: *Whoever divorces his wife, except for unchastity, and marries another, commits adultery.* The idea that divorce, except for unchastity, is tantamount to committing adultery is an idea peculiar to Matthew's Gospel. Mark and Luke always state that divorce followed by remarriage is adulterous. What we appear to have in Matthew 19:9, then, is a combination of the common synoptic principle with Matthew's special emphasis rolled together in a potentially ambiguous sentence. However, when 19:9 is analysed into its constituent parts, the ambiguity disappears and it makes a fitting punch line to the dispute with the Pharisees. They asked: 'Is it lawful for a man to divorce his wife for any cause at all?' Jesus replies: 'It is always wrong to divorce what God has joined together: what is more, divorce, except for unchastity, is adulterous; and remarriage after divorce is always so.' Naturally the disciples object: 'If the relationship of the man with his wife is like this, it is better not to marry.' Unabashed, Jesus replies in a vein reminiscent of His remarks about cutting off hand or eye to avoid committing adultery (5:29–30): 'You are able to live up to this teaching for there are some who are even able to become eunuchs for the kingdom of heaven.'

These, then, are the main reasons that have been put forward recently for maintaining the early church view. The objections to it will be reviewed in the succeeding chapters.

CHAPTER THREE

The Erasmian Interpretation: Early Exponents

The early Christian writers' interpretation of the divorce texts remained the standard view of the church in the West until the sixteenth century when Erasmus suggested a different view that was adopted by Protestant theologians. The next four chapters are devoted to the history of this exegetical tradition and a critique scrutinising it. We feel an extensive treatment of this nature is needed in the light of the popularity of the Erasmian view among evangelicals today. As in the study of any subject, a knowledge of its origin and subsequent development provides the necessary perspective for evaluating the feelings we may have towards it in the present. On such an emotional issue as divorce and remarriage this perspective is obviously helpful.

The Catholic Understanding of Marriage

During the Middle Ages a development transpired in the Roman Catholic understanding of marriage that must be noted if the reaction of both Erasmus and Luther to the practice of the Catholic church is to be understood. The Protestant reformers who follow Luther only develop the exegetical arguments originally set forth by Erasmus.[1]

Augustine's (354–430) understanding of the absolute indissolubility of marriage, which denied remarriage even to the innocent party after divorce, led him to view marriage as a sacrament. For Augustine marriage was a sacrament or mystery 'in the sense that it is a symbol or analogy of Christ's unity with the church, as expressed by the Apostle Paul' in Ephesians

5: 31–2.[2] This later became the interpretation of Luther. It was the scholastic doctrine of the sacrament of marriage that achieved its synthesis in Thomas Aquinas (1222–74) which became the source of contention for both Erasmus and Luther at the beginning of the Reformation period.

Aquinas treated marriage as a sacrament that 'transmits grace'. He viewed it as equal to the other six sacraments[3] as an instrument of God for the infusion of supernatural grace into the life of the recipient, and Ephesians 5: 32 was his textual foundation for this idea. 'What Aquinas thus taught became the perfect exposition of the doctrine of marriage within the Roman Catholic Church, and four centuries later the Council of Trent confirmed it to be an absolute truth of faith.'[4]

Erasmus, however, knew that neither Augustine nor Jerome called marriage a sacrament in the sense that it was later understood. So in his annotations to the first edition of his Greek New Testament (1516) he commented that the use of *sacramentum* in the Latin Vulgate did not imply the notion then commonly held by the church. In his second edition (1519) he stated further that the Greek 'does not actually signify a sacrament of the kind of which the Church has seven, but means hidden and secret . . .'[5] Luther used Erasmus's Greek text as soon as it was printed, and in *The Babylonian Captivity of the Church* (1520), where he replies to the seven sacraments of the Church of Rome, Luther said the Catholics could have avoided their false exegesis of Ephesians 5: 32 had they read the Greek text.[6] This understanding of marriage as a sacrament that transmits grace and the meaning of salvation in the Catholic church had a significant influence on Erasmus's as well as Luther's exegesis of the divorce texts.

Now although the Catholic church insisted on the indissolubility of marriage, that did not mean that divorce was not practised. It was merely understood and approached in a different way from the later Protestant reformers. Catholics differentiated between two types of divorce. The first was a separation from bed and board (*separatio a mensa et toro*), advocated by Augustine, Jerome and others. The other was an absolute annulment of the marriage tie by asserting that the marriage from the very outset had been unlawfully contracted. Erasmus lists and discusses some eighteen impediments advocated by the church as hindrances to contracting marriage. Not only did Erasmus consider these impediments contrary to the spirit and letter of New Testament teaching, but he also deplored the abuse into which their use had fallen. While divorce, in the light of Christ's words, was denied, Erasmus hoped that through canonical laws one might find ways and means to annul a marriage by *proving* it to be illegal from the start. Thus his interpretation of the divorce texts was not an academic exercise, but a practical application of a correct interpretation of Christ's words through which he hoped a higher moral standard might be achieved for the marriage relationship.

Erasmus's Approach to the Divorce Texts

In a brief survey of the life of Erasmus, T.F.C. Stunt speaks of him as 'a humanist *par excellence*' with a message that centred on Christianity as a quality of life rather than outward observances or doctrinal subscriptions.[7] Erasmus's humanistic concerns are evident in his approach to and exegesis of the divorce texts.

V.N. Olsen writes in his study of the interpretation of the New Testament divorce texts from Erasmus to Milton:

> In his interpretation of the New Testament logia on divorce Erasmus reveals himself as a Christian theologian who seeks to solve an ethical problem within Church and society by finding a solution based on Scripture and centered in Christ. No ecclesiastical institution should stand between the needy and the Good Samaritan. Erasmus appears not as an academic theorist but as a Christian pragmatist who is devoted to his Master in service for his fellow man.[8]

The main source of Erasmus's exegesis on the divorce texts is found in his *Annotations* on 1 Corinthians 7 (1519). He performs a theological and homiletical, not grammatical, exegesis of the chapter by making the text the basis for a long doctrinal and ethical discussion of marriage and divorce. The Protestant Reformers later imitate him with this same approach.

Erasmus's purpose is not to introduce any new opinion to cause contention, but to help those representing the pure and sound judgment of the church. He is aware of the common opinion which opposed remarriage after divorce for adultery, but he also knows that it lies within the hearts of good men to change their opinions in order to deal with a good cause. His conviction, evident throughout his approach, is that enlightenment would usher in a new era and bring reform within the church. 'Two basic propositions are laid down. It should be permissible to dissolve certain marriages, not fortuitously but for very serious reasons, by the ecclesiastical authorities or recognized judges, and to give the innocent party the freedom to marry again.'[9]

These two views were considered revolutionary and heretical by the theologians of his day. Erasmus knew it was wrong to cast doubt on fundamental Christian beliefs like the divinity of Christ, so in his opinion the question of divorce belonged to another category. Here rules could be changed as time and necessity required, even though formerly upheld by the authority of the church.

It should be noted that Erasmus's approach to divorce and remarriage was clearly influenced by an ecclesiastical system which firmly believed there could be no hope for salvation outside its doors and its sacraments. For Erasmus, of utmost importance was the need 'to procure the salvation of all men as much as possible and to succour the weak and sick members of the Church. In other words charity should come before any institutionalism . . .'[10] He held the opinion that if the many thousands unhappily coupled together (such that both partners perished) could be divorced and enabled to marry other partners they could be saved. Charity, he reasoned, sometimes does what it legally should not do, and it is justified in doing so. Since Christ sought the lost sheep, the church should seek the salvation of those who suffer. Erasmus believed that no human laws should be valued unless they were conducive to the salvation of men. This salvific context in which Erasmus sought to justify divorce and remarriage should not be overlooked. It is hardly parallel to the reasons for which most evangelicals seek to justify divorce and remarriage today.

It is also important to understand how Erasmus viewed those who are in the church. He believed that the Sermon on the Mount (including Matt. 5: 31–2) was not spoken to the multitudes but to the disciples who were the purest of Christ's body. These disciples belonged to the kingdom of heaven. Within the church, though, there is another group who do have need of laws, divorce, oath-taking and the like. These are the imperfect ones who are found in large numbers and constitute the kingdom of the world. For these people, Erasmus reasoned, it is not wrong to go to court, take oaths, and divorce. Christ restricted divorce to one cause, adultery, not because there was no more scandalous cause, but because it diametrically fights against the nature of marriage. Erasmus also believed that Paul enlarged this precept of the Lord.

Erasmus's Exegesis of the Divorce Texts

We present below a survey of Erasmus's interpretation of the New Testament divorce texts. This is deemed appropriate when one considers that the support which he offered for his interpretation has not changed to this day. His exegesis is for the most part identical with that offered by many modern evangelicals.

The Synoptic Accounts

In response to the Pharisees' question in Matthew 19:3, 'Is it lawful for a man to divorce his wife for any cause at all?' Erasmus said Moses permitted the letter of divorce because of the people's hardness of heart. Moses chose the lesser of two evils: the husband who hated his wife may do her great harm, even kill her, or this evil could be restrained if the letter of divorce were required. The problem in Jesus' day was the way the Jews used the bill of divorce to put away their wives for any trivial reason.

Christ pointed to Genesis 2:24 as the ideal of marriage where the two were made one flesh. He is said to be stricter than Moses in allowing only one reason for divorce, namely, adultery. Yet Erasmus also makes statements which seem to imply that there are other reasons. He understood Origen to contemplate other grounds for divorce besides adultery (i.e., parricide, poisoning, or witchcraft), and that Origen allowed the divorced person to remarry. This seemed evident to Erasmus since Origen did write about certain bishops who permitted some wives divorced from their husbands to marry again. He also believed that Tertullian and Ambrose allowed divorce and remarriage, and that Ambrose permitted a believing wife to remarry if she were divorced from an unbelieving husband.

Erasmus had two reasons for protesting against a divorce that permitted separation only and not also remarriage. First, Christ did not demand virginity of all his followers nor that a man should go against nature. He protested that a man separated from an unfaithful wife is excluded from entering the honours and privileges of the marriage relationship by human laws, but not by the law of the Gospel. In Erasmus's opinion it seemed cruel not to come to the rescue of these sufferers. Second, in view of the understanding of Christ's audience who knew only of a divorce with the right to remarry, he admits difficulty in reading the meaning of separation only into Christ's words in Matthew 5: 32 and 19: 9. He believed that since divorce without the right of remarriage seems to war against the equity of nature, 'it should be looked into if there may not be other interpretations which are to be read in the Gospels and Epistles'.[11]

Romans 7 and 1 Corinthians 7

Regarding Romans 7: 2–3, Erasmus states that Paul is not here reasoning about divorce. The Gospel has superseded the law of Moses, and since the Christian is married to a new spouse (Christ) he should no longer cling to the law. Paul uses a parable here, and a parable does not always fit on all points. If Paul really means to say that a second marriage is prohibited during the lifetime of either spouse, he would not have referred to the law. This is because Paul's readers knew of only one law, and it permitted a husband to divorce his wife by giving her a letter. This illustrates that a certain text should not be taken out of context and used to prove an already fixed precept. 'The Protestant theologians followed Erasmus's interpretation in their commentaries.'[12]

Erasmus also believes that Paul is not treating divorce in 1 Corinthians 7: 39, but just giving advice to virgins and widows.

Finally, in 1 Corinthians 7 he finds two different types of departing. The first is separation in verses 10–11, and the other is divorce in verse 15. Within this latter category is the case of an unbelieving husband refusing to live with a wife who has become a Christian, the crime of adultery, and similar or even worse cases.

The Results of the Erasmian Exegesis

The results of Erasmus's interpretation of the divorce texts began the process which gradually isolated him from the two camps during the Reformation. Olsen says: 'While Erasmus in his own mind sought to harmonize his loyalty to the Church with the results of his exegetical, doctrinal, philological and historical studies, the Protestant Reformers broke with the Church partly on account of these results, and the Catholic theologians opposed him for the same reasons.'[13] Indeed, the Protestant Reformers latched on to Erasmus's interpretation of the divorce texts and defended his exegesis from the moment they became known. When the Council of Trent met on November 11th, 1563 to discuss the sacrament of matrimony, the Protestant interpretation of the divorce texts had been crystallised.

> Trent thus expressed a clear denial of those exegetical results which had come from the pen of Erasmus fifty years earlier and were developed by the reformers into a part of Protestant belief and practice . . . Trent made its decrees on marriage and divorce very definite, and the history of Catholic interpretation of the New Testament logia on divorce may therefore be considered to end here.[14]

Luther to the Westminster Confession

Before considering the support for the Erasmian view as it is held today it is important to understand the original reasons set forth by Luther and others in favour of allowing the innocent party to remarry in cases of adultery and desertion.

Luther's Exegesis of the Divorce Texts

When commenting on Christ's words on divorce Luther states emphatically that Christ allowed divorce *only* in the case of adultery and desertion. The Christian who is deserted by an unbelieving partner may marry again as long as the future husband is a Christian. From this he concludes that the innocent party in *any* divorce case should be allowed to marry again, such as a wife whose husband deserts her or returns after ten years.

Elsewhere Luther contradicts his own remarks by allowing other reasons for divorce besides adultery. But there is a logical consistency in his position. His starting point is that only death can dissolve the marriage tie and leave the partner free to marry again. The act of adultery, however, makes the offender *as dead* in his relationship both to God and to his partner. He, like other Reformers,[15] knew that Moses demanded that the adulterer be put to death and he believed that the existing civil powers should do likewise. If this was not done, the adulterer was still considered as dead in the eyes of God.

This is why Luther allows the believing partner to remarry in the case of desertion by an unbeliever (1 Cor. 7: 15). He then takes this a step further in the practical application of his 'exegesis'. If a *Christian* husband is such a rascal that he leaves his believing wife and children, then he should be considered no better than a gentile or an unbeliever and deserves the punishment due to the adulterer. Since Paul, in Luther's view, permits the believing partner to marry again, Luther sees no reason why this should not be true in this case also.[16]

Somewhat similar is the case of the wife who, because of stubbornness, will not render conjugal duty (1 Cor. 7: 3–4). If she continues in her stubbornness after a warning, 'then the husband should let a Vashti go and take an Esther, just as King Ahasuerus did'.[17]

We are inclined to ask how Luther could categorically state that Christ allowed divorce *only* in the case of adultery and then go on to allow divorce and remarriage for impotence, and for a wife's refusal to render conjugal duty, as well as justify the annulment of a marriage for desertion and for ignorance of a former contracted marriage? Luther could do this because he viewed marriage as a *res sacra*, a most holy thing and a mystery, but not a sacrament in a *technical* sense. At the same time he also viewed marriage as a secular affair. Luther's interpretation of the divorce passages is influenced by his view that the state has the God-given power and authority that includes the right to deal with marriage problems.

Both Luther and Erasmus allowed other grounds for divorce and remarriage in addition to adultery because they, along with other Protestant Reformers who followed them, believed that God had ordained two kinds of rulership in the world just as there were two kinds of people: those governed by God's word and the Holy Spirit, and the unbelievers. Luther understood that under the New Covenant the government rules the secular world, and all ruling establishments are to be considered as God's servants. Thus the church should be obedient to the government. The believer, on the other hand, is not in need of a secular government because he lives within the realm of the Gospel in a spiritual kingdom. The unbeliever, though, needs the correcting and punishing sword of the secular power. The problem of divorce falls within this realm of the secular authority; and since Luther felt that the adulterer deserved capital punishment, the question of divorce must therefore be settled by the secular authority. God had not permitted the church to carry out this punishment. This concept of the 'two kingdoms', a spiritual and a secular, influences the interpretation of every one of the Protestant Reformers.

Other Protestant Reformers[18]

The exegesis of the Reformers takes a conservative turn with John Calvin (1509–64). His interpretation comes close to Luther, but the practical application of his exegesis is more rigid. Calvin brings his interpretation of Christ's exception for adultery in Matthew into line with his interpretation of Deuteronomy 24: 1 and Malachi 2: 14. He is more accurate in his approach to Deuteronomy 24: 1 than the other Reformers when he says that Moses did not lay down a law about divorces, but used the bill of divorce to restrain the wickedness of men. Calvin felt the bill which the husband gave to the wife would attest to her chastity. But at the same time this letter of divorce could not be separated from the probability that the man who divorced his wife had already entered conjugal relations with another woman. The husband who wrote the letter thus made himself an adulterer by signing it because he had dissolved a sacred and inviolable bond. This indicated to Calvin that even among the Israelites only one cause for divorce was allowed, namely, adultery. The covenant of marriage mentioned in Malachi 2: 14 refers to the original marriage state, the very basis for Christ's teaching. Therefore, the divorce which both Christ and Moses spoke about dissolved a sacred and inviolable bond.

It was left to Theodore Beza (1519–1605) to systematise and amplify the exegetical results of Calvin. Olsen summarises Beza's understanding of the divorce sayings:

The marriage tie is indissoluble and divorce is not allowed; however, an exception is made in the case of adultery because the civil authorities do not apply the law of capital punishment. Theoretically there is really no divorce, as the adulterer should be considered as dead.[19]

Like Erasmus and most of the other Reformers, Beza said 1 Corinthians 7: 11 does not speak about legitimate divorce. He also says that Paul does not express a second cause for divorce in 1 Corinthians 7: 15 – Paul adds nothing to the teaching of Christ who made adultery the only cause. Yet Beza expresses the same conclusion as Luther and Calvin that the innocent believer who is deserted may remarry! He can say this because, like Calvin, he cannot think of desertion without the deserter involving himself in relations with another, and this is adultery. Since adultery is involved, Paul does not add to the words of Christ.

The early English reformer, William Tyndale (d. 1536), interprets 1 Corinthians 7: 15 like Beza because he cannot conceive of desertion without adultery occurring. Tyndale's 'exegesis is a comprehensive usage of the basic arguments of Luther'.[20] It was through Tyndale that Luther's interpretation reached England in 1527, and from an exegetical standpoint the English Reformers (Tyndale, Cranmer and Hooper) do not add anything new when compared with the Continental writers.

Though the early Reformers followed Erasmus in allowing divorce and remarriage for various causes, even the relatively restricted views of Calvin did not succeed in becoming the official policy of the Church of England. For in the revision of canon law, published in 1603, only separation or annulment is authorised. Divorce with the permission to remarry is not. Canon 107 requires that separated partners 'shall live "chastely and continently", neither shall they, during each other's life, contract matrimony with any other person'. [21]

Finally, we come to the most liberal expositor of the divorce texts: John Milton (1608–74). One month after the Westminster Assembly had convened (July 1st, 1643), his first edition of *The Doctrine and Discipline of Divorce* was published with the hopes of effecting a more thorough reformation of the Church of England. Milton almost thinks of himself as a prophet within this reform movement which also called for a reappraisal of the marriage estate. Milton believed that Christ did not condemn all divorce but all injury and violence in divorce. He mentions the right of divorce by mutual consent, something which Calvin spoke against. His exegesis sounded radical and heretical to his contemporaries. Like Erasmus, he sought to synthesise the Reformation with humanism.

The Westminster Confession

Milton had addressed the Westminster Assembly in his divorce tracts. The Assembly, however, counteracted Milton's interpretation and confirmed the conservative Calvin-Beza exegesis. Chapter XXIV deals with marriage and divorce:

> Section V – Adultery or fornication committed after a contract, being detected before marriage, giveth just occasion to the innocent party to dissolve that contract [Matt. 1: 18–20]. In the case of adultery after marriage, it is lawful for the innocent party to sue out a divorce [Matt. 5: 32], and after the divorce to marry another, *as if the offending party were dead* [Matt. 19: 9; Rom. 7: 2–3. Italics ours.].
>
> Section VI – Although the corruption of man be such as is apt to study arguments, unduly to put asunder those whom God hath joined together in marriage; yet nothing but adultery, or such wilful desertion as can no way be remedied by the Church or civil magistrate, is cause sufficient of dissolving the bond of marriage [Matt. 19: 8–9; 1 Cor. 7: 15; Matt. 19: 6]: wherein a public and orderly course of proceeding is to be observed, and the persons concerned in it not left to their own wills and discretion in their own case [Deut. 24: 1–4].

The Westminster Confession has been influential in the beliefs and practices of Protestants ever since its emergence in 1648. It may be safely stated that the exegetical tradition started by Erasmus and amplified by Luther and other Reformers was confirmed by the above sections in this Confession of Faith.

Summary of the Reformers' Exegesis

This brief summary of the history of the Protestant interpretation of the divorce texts is crucial for understanding what undergirds the contemporary evangelical consensus on the subject of divorce and remarriage. It will become evident that one of the major problems in this exegetical tradition is the interpretation of Deuteronomy 24: 1–4 and the way in which this text is employed in the interpretation of Christ's teaching. Our impression after reviewing the Reformers' interpretation of Deuteronomy 24 is that none of them properly understands the intent of the legislation and what Christ thought of it. The proof texts given for the divorce and remarriage statements in the Westminster Confession reflect the opinion of John Lightfoot, author of *A Commentary on the New Testament from the Talmud and Hebraica.* It is known that Lightfoot took part in the Westminster Assembly, and in his writings he states clearly that he believes *porneia* (immorality, unchastity) in the Matthean exception clauses is equivalent to the 'some indecency' of Deuteronomy 24:1 which he thinks is adultery.[22] Though Matthew may well intend for his readers to note a veiled reference to Deuteronomy 24:1, especially in Matthew 5:32, it is nearly impossible to say that the 'some indecency' is adultery. The confusion over the meaning of the legislation in Deuteronomy 24:1–4 persists in contemporary defences of the Erasmian view.

Another interesting feature of the Reformers' exegesis is the justification given for permitting the innocent party to remarry after divorce for adultery or desertion. All the Reformers and the Westminster Confession indulge in a 'legal fiction'[23] by assuming that the adulterer should be treated *as if he were dead.* Romans 7:2–3 is used as the proof text for what in reality is not the case: the adulterer is *not* dead! It was Beza who argued, when commenting on Matthew 5:32, that the exception by Christ was added because at that time the punishment of death by stoning for adultery was not carried out among the Jews. He said that the Jews neglected this punishment, otherwise the exception would not have been added. This is basically the argument of R.H. Charles's 1921 treatise on the New Testament's teaching on divorce and remarriage, and he is followed in this by present-day writers like J.B. Hurley, Colin Brown, and others.[24] It appears that some evangelical interpreters believe that Jesus substitutes one form of the letter of the law (death for adultery) for another form of the letter of the law (divorce), rather than giving the spirit of the law, with its much higher standards of forgiveness and reconciliation, as Jesus does in Matthew 5:21–48. If it is true that the 'one flesh' bond of marriage taught in Genesis 2:24 is indissoluble during the lifetime of the partners, then no 'legal fiction' can change that fact.

Still another problem is the interpretation which the Reformers give to 1 Corinthians 7:15 and the use that some make of it to corroborate their view that Jesus was not speaking in absolute terms when He spoke of adultery as the only exception that permitted divorce and remarriage.[25] When Calvin, for instance, says that verse 15 teaches that the deserted believer is no longer bound to the marriage but is free to remarry, he introduces an idea foreign to the context. More will be said of this in chapter 6.

To summarise thus far: the differences between the Reformers' view and the early church's view of the divorce texts are as follows. The early church understood Christ's exception in Matthew in light of the clear teaching of Mark and Luke: that every divorce followed by remarriage is adulterous. Hence the exception in Matthew must apply only to divorce, not to the issue of remarriage. The Reformers, on the other hand, say that the shorter accounts in Mark and Luke must be understood in light of the more 'complete' account of Matthew which includes the one exception permitting divorce *and* remarriage in the case of adultery. Since the exception clause is not mentioned by Paul in 1 Corinthians 7:10–11, the Reformers make this passage apply to separation from bed and board which is a correct application for lesser offences than adultery. The early Christian writers, however, brought 1 Corinthians 7:10–11 alongside the divorce texts in Mark and Luke which mention no exception for divorce *and* remarriage in case of adultery. Thus there is reason to understand Matthew in light of the unanimous teaching of these other sayings. The Reformers next say that Paul's teaching in Romans 7:2–3 does not discuss divorce and its causes but teaches that a widow can with good conscience remarry. The same is true of 1 Corinthians 7:39. The Fathers, in contrast, said that these two passages were the only two texts that clearly specified when remarriage was permissible (after the death of one's partner) and that to understand them otherwise was to misconstrue their clear teachings. The Reformers bring 1 Corinthians 7:15 into relationship with the divorce texts in Matthew and assert that Mark and Luke should be understood likewise. The early Fathers, though, did not understand 1 Corinthians 7:15 to permit the deserted Christian to marry again, and they correlated this text with Romans 7:2–3, 1 Corinthians 7:39 and Christ's teaching on the indissolubility of marriage based on Genesis 2:24. The Reformers say the words 'What therefore God has joined together, let no man separate' (Matt. 19:6 = Mark 10:9) do not apply to divorce for adultery because 'the law of capital punishment and Christ's exception make God, and not man, the author of divorce for adultery'.[26] The early church, however, pointed to this verse in support of their belief that man and wife, joined by God in 'the law of marriage', became an indissoluble union that could be broken only by the death of one of them.

With this survey of the Protestant exegetical tradition completed, a more objective analysis of the Erasmian view as it is defended today is possible. If the Erasmian view has a stronger traditional than it does an exegetical base, then the foregoing summary of the Reformers' theological motives and concepts is critical in our evaluation of the support offered for the Erasmian view today.

CHAPTER FOUR

Modern Defences of the Erasmian View

Three Major Variations

Contemporary supporters of the Erasmian view that divorced Christians may remarry fall into several camps. First, there are those, like J. Murray,[1] who adhere to the view that only adultery or desertion justifies full divorce with the right to remarriage. Second, there are those, like D. Atkinson,[2] who claim that 'unchastity' (*porneia*) is a very much wider term than 'adultery' and therefore that Matthew 19:9 permits divorce and remarriage for a wide range of sins. Third, there is an older critical view[3] which argues that although the present text of Matthew permits remarriage after divorce, this was not Jesus' original intention. Jesus taught that marriage was indissoluble, but the evangelist Matthew modified this teaching to allow full divorce in some hard cases.

We shall postpone examining the third view because it only becomes viable if it can be shown that either of the other two views is correct. Although it offers a way of harmonising the New Testament divorce sayings, it does so at the expense of the unity of the message, setting the teaching of our Lord and of Paul against that of Matthew. This is somewhat improbable in itself, and the more so when it is considered that Matthew's Gospel was the most often read in the early church, yet the same church was firmly opposed to remarriage after divorce. It makes the evangelist Matthew very much the odd man out if he is sandwiched chronologically between Jesus, Paul, Mark and Luke before him and all the Fathers after him. Furthermore, as the more recent redactional critical studies have shown, it is most improbable that

Matthew 19: 9 should be understood in an Erasmian sense: the immediately following remarks in verses 10–12 show Matthew was not contemplating the possibility of remarriage after divorce. For these reasons we will concentrate our attention on the first two alternatives.

Indeed, most of our attention will be directed to the first view, namely, that Matthew 19: 9 permits divorce and remarriage for adultery alone: 'unchastity' (*porneia*) is taken as synonymous with adultery (*moicheia*). For although it seems likely that unchastity covers more offences than adultery, only proponents of the adultery view have really tried to prove that Matthew 19: 9 permits remarriage after divorce. And this is the key issue. As we have already seen, the early church permitted separation for adultery, but it did not permit remarriage. So whatever 'unchastity' covers, the point that modern Erasmians must demonstrate is that Matthew 19: 9 *demands* the right of remarriage for post-marital offences. If, however, supporters of the Erasmian view concede their view is *only one of a number of interpretations*, then it becomes highly improbable that it is the most primitive one, given the consensus of the rest of the New Testament and the views of the early church Fathers.

Contemporary Support for the Erasmian View

There are two pillars which support the superstructure of the Erasmian view today. The first is the belief that the divorce which Jesus spoke about was the Mosaic dissolution divorce, and the second is the understanding that the exception clause qualifies the entire protasis of Matthew 19: 9 (= 'Whoever divorces his wife . . . *and* marries another'), thus permitting both divorce *and* remarriage of the innocent party in the case of unchastity. This second argument appears to replace the exegetical basis for remarriage which the Reformers found in the legal fiction that the adulterer should be considered as dead. A discussion of the weaker lines of support will follow consideration of the two major pillars.

We should inform our readers here at the beginning of this presentation of the modern support for the Erasmian view that we shall be drawing largely on the work of Murray. For just as

Erasmus established the exegetical base that was later developed by the Reformers, so Murray's study laid the groundwork which more recent writers have built upon. What is said about Murray's interpretation for the most part may be said of the other writers who champion his understanding of the Matthean exception clauses.[4]

The Deuteronomy 24: 1–4 Dissolution Divorce

One of Murray's crucial arguments in support of the Erasmian view is that 'the dissolution permitted or tolerated under the Mosaic economy had the effect of dissolving the marriage bond'.[5] Since this is the divorce Jesus alluded to in Mark 10: 2–12, and especially in Matthew 5: 32 and 19: 9,

> . . . we are surely justified in concluding that the putting away sanctioned by our Lord was intended to have the same effect in the matter of dissolving the marriage tie. It should be appreciated that the law as enunciated here by Jesus does not in any way suggest any alteration in the nature and effect of divorce. The change intimated by Jesus was rather the abolition of every other reason permitted in the Mosaic provisions and the distinct specification that adultery was now the only ground upon which a man could legitimately put away his wife.[6]

Murray then concludes that if divorce involves the dissolution of the marriage bond we should not expect that remarriage would be regarded as adultery. Further support for this belief is that the word *apolyō* (let go, send away, dismiss) in the gospel divorce passages has turned up in the clear sense of 'divorce' in a Greek document of remarriage from Palestine.[7]

Murray is careful in his exegesis of Deuteronomy 24: 1–4 not to characterise the wife's second marriage as adulterous. For if the second marriage falls into the category of disapproval – the second marriage being tantamount to adultery – then he would have to carry into the New Testament this idea that a second marriage is adulterous despite the fact that a legal divorce has transpired. This would hint that remarriage after a legal or proper New Testament divorce (i.e., for immorality) is also adulterous. This is precisely what Murray argues against by bringing into the New Testament his conception of the dissolution divorce which he finds in Deuteronomy 24. Yet Murray observes the reason the divorced wife may not return to her first husband after a second marriage is that by her second marriage she has become 'defiled'. This defilement seems to be placed in a negative light.

Murray then brings to our attention the unique relationship that persists between the original couple even after divorce:

> The second marriage effects an unobliterable separation from the first husband. This implies a unique relation to the first husband and demonstrates that the marriage bond is so sacred that, although divorce may be given and a certain freedom granted to the divorced persons, yet there is an unobliterable relationship that appears, paradoxically enough, in the form of an unobliterable separation in the event that a second marriage has been consummated on the part of the divorced wife.[8]

Murray concludes his discussion of Deuteronomy 24 with a strong emphasis on what divorce does to the first marriage.

> The one insurmountable obstacle to the marriage of this particular woman with this particular man is not that the woman had been married to another man but simply that the particular man concerned is the man from whom she had been divorced. It is the fact of divorce that bears the whole onus of ultimate responsibility for the defilement that is sure to enter when the first marriage is restored after a second had been consummated.[9]

In other words, the divorce, not the second marriage, bears the whole blame for the defilement which takes place in the event the wife returns to her former husband.

What the Matthean Exception Clause Qualifies

Murray's second line of defence for the Erasmian view arises from his understanding of the function of the exception clause. He holds that it qualifies both what precedes it ('whoever divorces his wife') and what follows it ('and marries another'). His argument falls into two parts. First, he discusses the nature of exceptions to general statements in Greek syntax, and second, the need to maintain the co-ordination of divorce *and* remarriage if the sentence as a whole is to make sense. The latter point is the mainstay of the Erasmian view as it is defended today just as the

Reformers' belief that the adulterer should be considered as dead was the mainstay of their exegetical tradition.

Murray attempts to show that it should be obvious that the divorce in Matthew 19:9 clearly covers permission to remarry also; or at least that it is grammatically harsh to make the exception clause qualify only putting away the wife and not also the remarriage portion. He then allows that it is surely true that 'an exception clause is sometimes used in the Greek to intimate "an exception to something that is more general than that which has actually been mentioned"'.[10] Matthew 12:4, Romans 14:14 and probably Galatians 1:9 do this through the use of *ei mē* (except, unless).[11] In Matthew 19:9 this would mean that the negated prepositional phrase, *mē epi porneia* (not on the grounds of unchastity), would not be an exception to the principle that whoever puts away his wife and marries another commits adultery, but simply an exception to the principle that a man may not put away his wife – he may put her away for unchastity, but if he remarries he still commits adultery. Murray admits that this rendering makes good sense and solves many difficulties in harmonising Matthew with Mark and Luke, but he argues that there are weighty reasons for rejecting it.

To begin with, he observes that if the exception clause is

> . . . not an exception to that which is expressly stated but an exception to another closely related and more general consideration [i.e., connected only to 'put away' versus to 'put away *and* remarry'], then this is a most unusual, if not unparallelled, way of expressing it . . . In other instances the statement of that to which a more general exception is appended is given first in its completeness and then the exception in its completeness follows. But this is not the case here – the exception is inserted before the statement is completed. Analogy does not, therefore, favour this rendering.[12]

This concludes the first part of his defence. It will be shown in the critique of the above observations that the unusual construction Murray has noted in Matthew 19:9 actually argues *for* the very syntactical meaning he thinks it argues against! There are three possible positions the exception clause could have occupied in the conditional portion of Matthew 19:9 (= the protasis). When Murray notes that the exception clause is inserted *before* the statement of the protasis as a whole is completed, he intimates that something less than the whole is qualified.[13]

The second aspect of Murray's argument has to do with the logical sense the sentence makes depending on which words in the sentence the clause qualifies. He continues by saying that while it is true grammatically that an exception clause may modify one member of a sentence without modifying another, connecting it solely to 'put away' without reference to the remarriage clause results in

> . . . nonsense and untruth, namely, 'whoever puts away his wife except for fornication commits adultery'. In other words, it must be observed that in this sentence as it stands no thought is complete without the principal verb, *moichatai* [commit adultery]. It is this thought of committing adultery by remarriage that is the ruling thought in this passage, and it is quite indefensible to suppress it. The very exceptive clause, therefore, must have direct bearing upon the action denoted by the verb that governs.[14]

We should like to ask Murray at this point why he left out 'and marries another' after connecting the exception clause solely to 'put away'. It is his omission of 'and marries another' that results in a nonsensical statement, not the fact that the negated prepositional phrase may very well qualify only 'put away'. Dissecting the sentence to suit one's argument seems inappropriate at this point. Furthermore, it is quite clear in Matthew 5: 27–32 that divorce is seen as a breach of the seventh commandment: i.e., to divorce is tantamount to committing adultery. Once this is accepted it is surely not nonsense to say 'whoever puts away his wife except for unchastity commits adultery'.

Murray then says that the logion of Matthew 19: 9 must be clearly distinguished from the one in Matthew 5: 32 because in the latter passage only putting away is contemplated, whereas in Matthew 19: 9 it is putting away *and* remarriage. Thus Matthew 19: 9 must be placed in the same category as the sayings in Mark 10: 11 and Luke 16: 18 which also co-ordinate divorce *and* remarriage. This is all mentioned in support of his contention that putting away *and* remarriage must be dealt with in co-ordination. He concludes:

> The subject dealt with . . . is putting away and remarriage in coordination, and this coordination must not be disturbed in any way . . . It would be unwarranted, therefore, to relate the exceptive clause to anything else than the coordination. Furthermore, the exceptive

clause is in the *natural position* [italics ours] with reference to the coordination and with reference to the resulting sin to which it provides an exception.[15]

Other interpreters would agree with Murray that 'the natural meaning provides in the unfaithfulness of a wife an exception to what is said both of divorce and of remarriage'.[16]

Harmonisation with Mark and Luke

Murray resolves the apparent contradiction between the absolute prohibitions found in Mark 10:11–12 and Luke 16:18 and the exception in Matthew with three considerations. First, the burden of emphasis, he contends, in both Matthew 19:3–9 and Mark 10:2–12 is upon the abrogation of the Mosaic permission of Deuteronomy 24:1–4. Since there is no provision for divorce for adultery in the Mosaic law, Jesus must be annulling permission to divorce for other reasons introduced by Deuteronomy. Luke 16:18 may also be brought into the discussion, and it is clear that 'there is no exception to the abrogation of the permission implied in Deuteronomy 24:1–4'.[17] J. Job would add that in Luke 16:18

. . . Jesus is inveighing against the injustices of a man's world in which a wife could be lightly divorced. One who treated his wife in this way was not only committing adultery against her, but (ironically) encouraging some man to commit adultery against him. In other words, it is not the remarriage of the divorced woman which is condemned; all the fault and the folly lie with the man who dismisses his wife without a cause.[18]

Secondly, Murray notes the remarkable omission in Mark and Luke of the right of a man to put away his wife for adultery. However, there is no question about the propriety of such a dismissal which is clearly established by Matthew 5:32 and 19:9. Since one cannot suppose that Mark and Luke intend[19] to deny such a right, and they do not suggest it is illegitimate, their silence concerning this right does not in any way prejudice the right itself. Nor should their omission of the right of remarriage in case of divorce for adultery prejudice or deny that right.

Finally, 'since Mark and Luke do not refer to *divorce for adultery* they could not in the nature of the case refer to the *right of remarriage* in the event of such a divorce'. Their silence respecting divorce for adultery precludes any reference to remarriage after such divorce. Murray concludes 'that Mark and Luke are not envisaging the situation created in the event of adultery and are not reflecting on the rights of the innocent spouse in such a case.'[20]

C. Brown also observes that all three evangelists record the point that the man who divorces his wife and marries another commits adultery. In each case he feels it is not the divorce proceedings, but the action which constitutes the break-up of the marriage that is crucial in God's sight. 'In each case the starting-point is the marriage that already exists intact. What is condemned as adulterous is the action which causes the break-up of a marriage for the sake of contracting a new liaison.'[21] Thus Murray, Job and Brown all believe that the primary focus of Jesus' teaching was against the wrong of divorce and not the wrong of remarriage.

1 Corinthians 7: 10–11, 15

Present-day advocates of the Erasmian view harmonise Paul's words on divorce and remarriage to Christian couples in 1 Corinthians 7: 10–11 with Matthew's exception in the same way in which the Reformers did: a case of separation without the right to remarry is in view. Thus Paul is not here considering divorce for adultery.

1 Corinthians 7: 15, of course, is understood to permit remarriage to the Christian who is deserted by a non-Christian partner. It is usually observed that when Paul is speaking about divorce between two Christians (vv. 10–11) he makes it very clear that they are to remain single or be reconciled. But there is no such explicit command to remain single when the non-Christian partner has deserted the believer (v. 15).

The lexical arguments in favour of the view that the deserted Christian is permitted to remarry were first presented by R.H. Charles. He argues that a comparison of 1 Corinthians 7: 15 and 7: 39 suggests some parallel meanings between different words.

> Yet if the unbelieving one leaves, let him leave; the brother or sister *is not under bondage* (*douloō*) in such cases, but God has called us to peace (1 Cor. 7: 15).
> A wife *is bound* (*deō*) as long as her husband lives; but if her husband

is dead, she is *free* (*eleutheros*) to be married to whom she wishes, only in the Lord (1 Cor. 7: 39).

Charles feels that 'is not under bondage' in verse 15 has the same meaning as 'free' in verse 39. He then adds that 'free' has the same meaning in Romans 7: 2–3:

> For the married woman is *bound* (*deō*) by law to her husband while he is living; but if her husband dies, she is released from the law concerning the husband. So then if, while her husband is living, she is joined to another man, she shall be called an adulteress; but if her husband dies, she is *free* (*eleutheros*) from the law, so that she is not an adulteress, though she is joined to another man.

Charles concludes from the above analysis that 'is not under bondage' in verse 15 and 'free' 'appear to have the same meaning. This fact suggests that the right of remarriage is here conceded to the believing husband or wife who is deserted by an unbelieving partner.'[22] H. Ridderbos, in his excellent outline of Paul's theology, follows a similar line of reasoning.[23]

We want to point out, however, that whereas 1 Corinthians 7: 15 deals with a situation of *divorce* where the husband is still living, Romans 7: 2–3 and 1 Corinthians 7: 39 both refer to a situation of *death* which Paul clearly says 'frees' a person to remarry. Charles may well be mixing apples with oranges here.

Another lexical argument is sometimes advanced as evidence that Paul permits remarriage in the 1 Corinthians 7: 15 situation. Some writers have asserted that 'is not under bondage' (*douloō*) in verse 15 and 'is bound' (*deō* = 'of binding by law and duty')[24] in verse 39 have a common root and are therefore etymologically related.[25] Thus what is permitted in verse 39 – remarriage – is also permitted in verse 39. This seems confirmed by those who note that *deō* (v. 39) is 'a weaker word' than *douloō* (v. 15).[26] This is taken to mean that the freedom of remarriage given to the deserted Christian in verse 15 is equal to or greater than the freedom given to the Christian whose partner has died (v. 39).

G.L. Archer has recently addressed the problem of desertion in 1 Corinthians 7: 15. He feels that divorce is definitely not permitted on the ground of desertion alone. Archer, like Calvin and Theodore Beza before him, notes that when a separation of this sort takes place and continues for some time, the unbelieving mate will obtain a civil divorce and marry someone else. 'That, of course, would constitute adultery under the rule of Matthew 5: 32 and 19: 9; and the innocent party would then be free to marry again. But until that happens, no second marriage is possible without rejection of the authority of Christ.'[27]

Archer addresses a very important practical problem when he asks what the Christian should do if the unconverted partner goes on for years without sexual involvement with another. Suppose the children are at an age when they need a two-parent home in order to develop in a healthy and normal way? What if the option to marry another believer looks like the ideal situation? Would it not be best for the children if the mother or father remarried?

> The answer to this question is the same as in every other situation where it seems easier to solve a problem by doing what any unbeliever would do under the circumstances. The issue of full submission to the revealed will of God and complete trust in the faithfulness of God is really at stake here. Even more important than our achieving and maintaining the so-called happiness that worldlings consider to be the final yardstick of value is the test of faith and faithfulness to our Lord and Saviour, Jesus Christ.
>
> God has not called us to be happy, but He called us to follow Him, with all integrity and devotion. Hebrews 11: 35 honors the memory of those Old Testament believers who 'were tortured, not accepting their release, in order that they might obtain a better resurrection.' . . . None of them enjoyed what the world would call 'happiness', but they did obtain something far more important: the 'approval' of God. Surely this applies to living with the dismal disappointment and frustration of an unhappy marriage.[28]

1 Corinthians 7: 27–8

A relatively new argument which Erasmians are using to prove that Paul does not consider remarriage after divorce to be a sin stems from Paul's use of the word 'unmarried' (*agamos*) and a particular interpretation of 1 Corinthians 7: 27–8. Job, for instance, believes that it is clear from Paul's use of 'unmarried' in verse 8 and again in verse 11, where Paul instructs divorcees to remain 'unmarried' or be reconciled, that it not only signifies single people and widowers (v. 8), but that it can also include those whose marriages have been broken (v. 11). Paul thus brackets divorcees with widowers and single people in verse 8, but he deals particularly with the case of the divorced in verse 27.[29] The text of 1 Corinthians 7: 27–8 reads:

> Are you bound to a wife? Do not seek to be released. Are you released from a wife? Do not seek a wife. But if you should marry, you have not sinned; and if a virgin should marry, she has not sinned. Yet such will have trouble in this life, and I am trying to spare you.

Colin Brown sums up this new argument for remarriage after divorce when he says that Paul has in view here the single, widowers, widows and the divorced, 'but the particular argument [in vv. 27–8] is drawn from the case of the divorced'.[30]

How is this interpretation of 1 Corinthians 7: 27–8 to be reconciled with the lifelong purpose for marriage which Paul teaches in Romans 7: 2–3 and 1 Corinthians 7: 39? To answer this question, Brown first harmonises Paul and the synoptic Gospels by emphasising that whereas the act of adultery is sinful, the remarriage was not in the case of those whose partners had cheated and contracted sexual relations outside marriage. This is in keeping with his belief that what is condemned as adulterous is not remarriage but the action that causes the break-up of a marriage for the sake of contracting a new one. This understanding, he states, resolves the apparent contradiction between the divinely intended lifelong purpose for marriage taught in Romans 7: 2–3 and 1 Corinthians 7: 39 and the declaration in 1 Corinthians 7: 27–8 that remarriage is not a sin. It is the breach of marriage through adultery that is sin, and Paul discusses this matter in 1 Corinthians 6: 15–17.[31]

1 Corinthians 6: 15–17

Finally, we must note how contemporary defenders of the Erasmian view interpret Paul's words in 1 Corinthians 6: 15–17. Charles is convinced that this is where Paul treats 'the legitimacy or illegitimacy of divorce on the ground of unchastity'.[32] He writes:

> . . . if a married man joins himself to a harlot, he becomes one body with her and thereby severs at one and the same time the bond that unites him to his wife and the bond that unites him to Christ . . . The unity of the one body formed in marriage is destroyed by the union of

one or [the] other of the two spouses united in marriage with another person. Hereby arises a new body which displaces the old.[33]

Though few today would maintain that such a union could sever the bond that unites the Christian to Christ, Brown also feels that Paul discusses what breaches marriage in the two chapters preceding chapter 7, cases in which the issue is much deeper than that of separation. He reveals his dependence on Charles when he begins his discussion of 1 Corinthians 6: 15–17 by saying:

Paul then turns to the question of adultery, pointing out that the 'one flesh' relationship also applies to relations with prostitutes . . . It is because sexual acts establish relationships through the body that Paul distinguishes sexual immorality from all other sins (v. 18).[34]

Then later in his study on divorce, separation and remarriage, after stating again that the sexual relationship between a man and his wife establishes the marriage, he says: 'It is rather the physical union which makes marriage; and it is the contracting of a physical union outside marriage which breaks marriage.'[35]

This last point is very significant for the Erasmian understanding of Jesus' teaching on divorce and remarriage – perhaps the most important consideration of all the arguments we have discussed so far. Everyone agrees that Jesus' conception of the marriage bond is rooted in His understanding of Genesis 1: 27; 2: 24 (Matt. 19: 4–6//Mark 10: 6–9). Moreover, it seems that sexual union does play an important role in the formation of the marriage relationship denoted by 'one flesh'. Is it not possible, then, that sexual sin (*porneia*) is indeed a *de facto* exception to Jesus' teaching on the indissolubility of marriage – the Genesis 2: 24 foundation of marriage having been annulled by a violation of that upon which it is predicated? Erasmians state that this may not necessitate divorce; but permission for divorce and remarriage in the event of marital infidelity seems to be consistent with Jesus' teaching.[36]

Conclusion

The Erasmian view places great weight on their understanding that sexual sin is a *de facto* exception to Jesus' teaching on the indissolubility of marriage. There is a large gap to bridge, however, between the idea that marital unfaithfulness results in a disruption of the conjugal life (which may or may not be possible to forgive *and* resume), and the idea that the offended partner is now free to enter into another marital union. Jesus may have permitted the former and at the same time totally prohibited the latter. Genesis 2:24 does not give us any sure indication of whether or not sexual defilement of the 'one flesh' union thereby dissolves it. This must be determined from other aspects of the Old Testament legislation in which the holy and moral standards of our covenant-keeping God are reflected. We know of at least two other pieces of Old Testament legislation that are based on the Genesis 2:24 concept that man and woman become 'one flesh' through marital relations. Neither appears to lend any support to the contention that extra-marital sexual sins dissolve or obliterate the original 'one flesh'. The meaning of this 'one flesh' relationship is the primary consideration of our next chapter.

This exposition of the modern Erasmian case has already noted some tensions within the position and a certain hesitancy among its advocates to insist that theirs is the only possible reading of Matthew 19:9 even within the restricted context of verses 3–9. The major problems with this view will be noted in the next two chapters.

CHAPTER FIVE

A Critique of the Erasmian View: Old Testament Considerations[1]

It is very important in the study of the biblical perspective of marriage, and what, if anything, may dissolve this relationship, that we approach the subject chronologically, beginning with the creation ordinances in Genesis 1 and 2. One of the most serious errors in the contemporary evangelical approach to the divorce question is the failure to see the relationship between the meaning of 'one flesh' in Genesis 2:24, the Leviticus 18 legislation concerning forbidden unions, and the remarriage legislation of Deuteronomy 24:1–4. The significant connection between Genesis 2:24 and Leviticus 18 must be grasped before an interpretation of Deuteronomy 24 and its implications for New Testament teaching become clear. This is the most misunderstood factor in the history of the interpretation of the divorce texts.

Genesis 1 and 2

The first two chapters in the Bible present a theology of the marriage relationship that is crucial to the understanding of both Jesus' teaching in the New Testament and the Mosaic legislation soon to be considered. Genesis 1:27 indicates that intellectually, morally and spiritually, man has a relationship to God that is important and permanent. Genesis 1:27 is then amplified in 2:18–25. Here, in the context of the creation of the woman, whose nature, disposition and abilities supplied what was lacking in the man, lies the divine directive of verse 24: 'For this cause a man shall leave ('āzaḇ) his father and his mother, and shall cleave (dāḇaq) to his wife; and they shall become one flesh (bāśār '*eḥāḏ*).' The important concepts we need to understand in this verse are what it means 'to cleave' and the precise nature of this new 'one flesh' unit.

A. Isaksson, in his doctoral dissertation which he presented to the theological faculty at the University of Uppsala, makes this statement after his thorough analysis of Jesus' teaching concerning the marriage relationship: 'It is clear from the context of Mt. 19. 3ff. that Jesus was referring primarily to what is written in Gen. 2. 24 as proof that marriage is indissoluble . . .'[2] In the light of the importance which this passage plays in Jesus' conception of marriage (Matt. 19: 5; Mark 10: 7–8) and Paul's use of a portion of Genesis 2: 24 in the troublesome passage in 1 Corinthians 6: 16, the meaning of Genesis 2: 24 must first be established in its Old Testament setting. Only then will its use in the New be fully appreciated.

Isaksson's analysis of *dāḇaq* (to cling on to, to stick to someone) demonstrates that this word has no specific sexual significance, and this is 'probably also the case in Gen. 2. 24'.[3] The word is a technical term, prominent in covenant terminology in Deuteronomy (10: 20; 11: 22; 13: 4; 30: 20; cf. Josh. 22: 5; 23: 8). E. Kalland notes that in these verses where the Israelites are to cleave to the Lord in affection and loyalty, 'parallel words and phrases that describe this proper attitude to the Lord are: fear, serve, love, obey, swear by his name, walk in his ways, and keep his commandments'.[4]

What then is the meaning of this 'one flesh' that results in forming a unity that is far greater than the bond with their closest relations, father and mother?

To be someone's 'bone and flesh' (cf. 2: 23) was a common expression to denote kinship or blood relations (Gen. 29: 12–14; 37: 27; Judg. 9: 2; 2 Sam. 19: 13).[5] The two terms, 'flesh' and 'bone', are also used in each of these passages to speak about a person in his total relation to another.[6] 'Flesh' (*bāśār*) is a word that must always be considered in each individual context in order to appreciate its significance. Isaksson concludes that it is reasonable to translate 'flesh' in Genesis 2: 24 also by the word

> . . . 'relation', since in this context it is a question of how the original relationship between man and woman forms the explanation of man's strong desire to cleave to his wife. Since man and woman were originally of the same bone and flesh, a man leaves his father and

mother and cleaves to his wife, in order that they may become one flesh, i.e. together form a family.[7]

Some studies have implied that the phrase 'they become one flesh' (*RSV*) indicates a relationship that develops over time. While it is true that every marriage relationship takes time to develop, there is also that aspect of a relationship which involves its coming into being at a point of time. The latter appears to be the emphasis in Genesis 2:24.[8] The relationship which the 'one flesh' denotes does, of course, include the sexual aspect; but it includes far more than that. It signifies a couple bound in a covenant modelled after God's covenant with His people. This seems to be apparent in the admittedly difficult passage, Malachi 2:13 –14 (*NIV*):

> Another thing you do: You flood the Lord's altar with tears. You weep and wail because he no longer pays attention to your offerings or accepts them with pleasure from your hands. You ask, 'Why?' It is because the Lord is acting as the witness between you and the wife of your youth, because you have broken faith with her, though she is your partner, the wife of your marriage covenant (*berît*).

One writer contends that the divorce which God hates (Mal. 2:16) is not divorce on a human level, but the cultic crime of repudiating 'the covenant of our fathers' (v. 10), expressed symbolically as 'the wife of your youth' (v. 14).[9] To this we would respond with P.F. Palmer:

> Actually, there would be no symbolism unless two covenants are here discussed, Yahweh's covenant with Israel violated by Israel and the marriage covenant violated by the individual Israelite's infidelity to the 'wife of his youth.' Granted that the passage is the 'most difficult section of the Book of Malachi,' Grelot's judgment is more in accord with text and context: 'There is, however, no doubt that the fidelity of Jahweh [*sic*] towards Israel, whom he has joined with himself in a *berith*, is implicitly put forward as a model for husband and wife.'[10]

The man or woman in the Old Testament who made a vow or took an oath in the sight of God did so in all seriousness. For a man to break his word and promise was to imply that God Himself is not faithful. This is no less true of a man's word in his marriage covenant. Moreover, Jesus' exegesis of Genesis 1:27

and 2: 24 in Mark 10: 9, 'What therefore God has joined together, let no man separate', implies that there is more to this covenant than the husband and wife belonging to each other in mutual commitment: '. . . the third person negative imperative is used [in Mark 10: 9] and it formulates absolutely Jesus' prohibition of divorce itself. It involves God Himself in the matter . . .'[11] It is also interesting to note that Jesus' words on divorce and remarriage in the Sermon on the Mount are immediately followed by His discussion of oaths (Matt. 5: 31–7).

To sum up, the significance of the 'one flesh' union in Genesis 2: 24 is that God joins man and woman in covenant commitment with the result that a new kinship or family unit is formed. Before looking at how the legislation in Leviticus 18 and Deuteronomy 24 builds upon this kinship relation we should consider the essentials of marriage in the light of the biblical evidence.

The Essentials of Marriage

E. Neufeld, in his landmark study of marriage in the Old Testament, writes that marriage in its simplest form involves the following essentials:

. . . (a) an intention of the parties to enter into a binding marital union and (b) actual consummation. Neither the mere intention nor the sexual act was in itself sufficient. Intention would be indicated by conduct such as courtship or by promises or other expressions aiming at an immediate union.[12]

By bringing other biblical references together with Genesis 2: 24 it appears that marriage in the Bible consists of four elements (the second one being in question). First, marriage involves the consent and intent of the will between partners. Marriage is first and foremost a binding covenant. It appears that in the ancient Near East marriage agreements consisted of two parts: oaths (which may be subsumed under covenant stipulations) and witnesses.[13] Palmer interestingly notes:

Among ancient peoples the binding and inviolable character of covenants derived from the divine sanctions attached to the covenant agreement. Contracts have people as witness, and human or civil society as guarantor. Covenants have God or the gods as witness, but not in the sense that the gods or God simply vouch for the correctness of the agreement; they act as guarantors that the terms of the treaty, alliance, or covenant will be carried out. To borrow a phrase from the Akkadian treaties of the eighth century B.C., the gods are 'lords of the oaths,' favoring those who live up to the stipulations of the agreement and cursing or 'pursuing relentlessly' all who violate their oaths.[14]

Second, it appears that marriage should be ratified by the parents (cf. Eph. 6: 1–3; Gen. 21: 21; 34: 4–6; 38: 6; Judg. 14: 2–3; Josh. 15: 16; and 1 Sam. 17: 25; 18: 20–7). Third, marriage involves ratification before the public (witnesses). This would include the marriage licence and the social and legal customs of the day (cf. Gen. 29:25–6; 34:12). Finally, the physical consummation of the marriage should naturally follow.

Premarital intercourse (i.e., that between a man and an unbetrothed girl) is discussed in Exodus 22: 16–17 and Deuteronomy 22: 28–9. Four points are made in the law. First, the couple must marry: the Hebrew wording seems to underline the idea that marriage is the normal and right course of action (Exod. 22: 16–17). Second, the man must pay the appropriate bride-money: no sum is stated in Exodus, but Deuteronomy 22: 29 fixes it at 50 shekels. Third, the man may never divorce this woman (Deut. 22: 29). And finally, Exodus says that if the girl's father refuses to consent to her marriage, the man must pay the bride-money. In other words, as long as the girl's father approves of the match, premarital intercourse is hardly penalised at all. This sequence of events in Deuteronomy 22: 28–9 makes it clear that sexual relations alone do not make a marriage. This is also evident from the distinction in the Old Testament between a man's wife or wives, and his concubines (cf. Gen. 22: 24; Judg. 8: 30–1; 2 Sam. 3: 7; 5: 13; 1 Kings 11: 3).

We make the above points in view of the great emphasis placed on the consequences of sexual relations outside marriage by advocates of the Erasmian view of divorce and remarriage. This is especially true in their use of 1 Corinthians 6: 15–18 to support the idea that extramarital relations 'dissolve' the marriage bond. We find little Scriptural support for this notion.

Leviticus 18: 6–18

The proper understanding of the 'one flesh' relation in Genesis 2: 24 as denoting the establishment of a new kinship unit or family is elucidated in the biblical legislation concerning forbidden unions (cf. Lev. 20: 11–12, 14, 17, 19–21; Deut. 22: 30; 27: 20, 22–3). The various prohibitions in Leviticus 18 are based not only on literal blood lines but also on 'blood' relationships created through marriage. Leviticus 18: 7–8 teach that

> . . . marriage, or more precisely marital intercourse, makes the man and wife as closely related as parents and children. In the words of Gen. 2: 24, 'they become one flesh.' Marriage thus creates both vertical blood relationships in the form of children and horizontal 'blood' relationships between spouses.[15]

This is why, for instance, a son is commanded: 'You shall not uncover the nakedness of your father's wife; it is your father's nakedness' (v. 8). The phrase 'uncover nakedness' (*gillāh 'erwāh*) in this passage is a euphemism for sexual intercourse. The opening refrain directs: 'None of you shall approach any blood relative of his to uncover nakedness; I am the Lord' (v. 6). Here, 'blood relative' or 'close relative' (*šĕ'ēr bĕśārô*) is literally 'flesh of his flesh' (cf. Gen. 2: 23). These regulations interpret relationships of affinity (connection by marriage) in terms of the principle that man and wife are 'one flesh', that is, kin or blood relations.[16]

These regulations therefore define the limits within which a man may seek a wife. The moment a man married a woman she became an integral part of his family in the same way in which children born into that family did. Similarly he became related to her close female relatives, and should his wife die or should he divorce her, he could not marry them. The custom of Levirate marriage is the only exception to these rules (Deut. 25: 5–10). These rules are not concerned with prohibiting sexual liaisons with another party when that person is formally married, for this is covered by the prohibition of adultery (Lev. 18: 20; Exod. 20: 14). But 'Marriage after the death of the woman's first husband or after she has been divorced is what is prohibited here.'[17]

It is already clear from Old Testament regulations like these that there are limits placed upon one's right to remarry after divorce. 'The range of potential marriage partners was reduced as a result of the first marriage.'[18] On the other hand, divorce was a matter of private family law[19] and had few legal restrictions placed upon it. Nevertheless, the Mosaic legislation does record two instances which prohibit the right of a man to divorce his wife 'all his days'. One is the situation where the husband falsely accused his wife of infidelity during her engagement (Deut. 22: 13–19). The other concerns the man compelled to marry the woman he had seduced (Deut. 22: 28–9).[20] The prohibition of divorce may be both punitive – punishing the man for flouting social convention – and reformative – to curb his proven tendency to impetuous action with women.

The Old Testament presupposes the legitimacy of divorce but says little about its operation. Only one law gives any details, yet this law has nothing to do with *legislating* grounds for divorce. It, too, is a regulation like the rules of Leviticus 18: 6–18 limiting a man's right of remarriage after death or divorce. This is the Mosaic legislation found in Deuteronomy 24: 1–4. The understanding of Genesis 2: 24 as it relates to the legislation of Leviticus 18 is crucial to a proper understanding of the likeliest interpretation of Deuteronomy 24 thus far set forth.

Deuteronomy 24: 1–4

J. Murray, in his defence of the Erasmian view of divorce and remarriage, believes that the divorce reflected in this passage had the effect of dissolving the marriage bond. Therefore, he concludes that we should not expect remarriage after a proper divorce in Matthew 5: 32 and 19: 9 to constitute adultery. The only problem with Murray's exegesis and those who follow him is that the very opposite of what he states is true – namely, the regulation legislated in this passage is grounded upon the continuing existence of the 'one flesh' relation established via the first marriage. Divorces in the Mosaic economy did *not* actually result in 'the dissolution of the marriage bond', and to follow Murray's reasoning, the 'divorce' Jesus talked about likewise did *not* dissolve the marriage. As J.D.M. Derrett notes, 'Where the Jewish law went wrong was in the failure to perceive that the one flesh persisted after divorce . . .'[21]

The first thing to keep in mind about this passage is that it is really focusing not on divorce (as the conservative Shammai and more liberal Hillel later thought), but on remarriage after divorce. It is important to point out, as does P.C. Craigie, that

> . . . strictly speaking, the legislation relates only to particular cases of remarriage; the protasis [vv. 1–3] contains incidental information about marriage and divorce, but does not specifically legislate on those matters. The verses do not legislate divorce, but treat it as a practice already known, . . .[22]

Hence, the interpretation of 'some indecency' (*'erwaṯ dāḇār*)[23] in verse 1 is really not that important in this argument. Furthermore, it is almost impossible to suggest, as some Erasmians have, that Jesus gave an infallible interpretation of the Mosaic legislation regarding grounds for divorce, since there is, in fact, *no* legislation respecting grounds for divorce in Old Testament law! It is unlikely that Jesus would have given an interpretation respecting grounds for divorce to a piece of legislation which He knew was intended to regulate a specific case of remarriage.

Stated briefly, this remarriage regulation (v. 4) says that a divorced woman who has contracted a second marriage may never subsequently seek reconciliation with her first husband. The reasons given for this prohibition in verse 4 ('she has been defiled [*huṭṭammā'āh*] . . . that is an abomination [*tô'ēḇāh*] . . . and you shall not bring sin on the land . . .') have resulted in five different responses.[24] It may be mentioned at the outset that any suggested meaning of Deuteronomy 24: 1–4 that does not speak to the reason for the prohibition of the reunion of the original couple in verse 4 misses the intent of the legislation found in that verse.

The first and most commonly heard purpose of Deuteronomy 24: 1–4 is the one given by Murray, Atkinson, and others, that the law's intent was to discourage hasty divorce. Murray, giving these verses an interpretation based on New Testament assumptions, goes so far as to say that the divorce is what is wrong here and bears the whole onus of responsibility for the defilement that is sure to enter when the first marriage is restored after the consummation of a second![25] However, A. Phillips writes that

Deuteronomy 24: 1–4 cannot be taken as evidence that Moses sought to limit the husband's absolute right to divorce his wife whenever he wished and for whatever reason.[26] Furthermore, this Deuteronomic concession[27] would hardly deter an angry husband intent on divorcing his wife. When a man divorced his wife, he would not want her to return to him. Since the law accurately mirrors his feelings when he is giving the divorce it can hardly have discouraged him. Besides, '. . . probably the strongest deterrent to divorce in Israel and all over the ancient Near East was financial, since the husband had to forfeit the dowry and may have been involved also in other payments to his former wife'.[28]

The second suggestion is that this legislation in Deuteronomy 24 views the second marriage as adulterous. Craigie writes:

> . . . the language (*defiled*) suggests adultery (see Lev. 18: 20). The sense is that the woman's remarriage after the first divorce is similar to adultery in that the woman cohabits with another man. However, if the woman were then to remarry her first husband, after divorcing the second, the analogy with adultery would become even more complete; the woman lives first with one man, then another, and finally returns to the first.[29]

Yet in this statute the second marriage is regarded as perfectly legal. It is the restoration of the first that is prohibited (v. 4). Commentators advancing this position seem to be reading New Testament ideas back into the Old (cf. Matt. 5: 32). The language ('defiled') is suggestive, but that it anticipates the teaching of Jesus in the New Testament that remarriage after divorce is adultery is by no means certain. 'After she has been defiled'[30] could be paraphrased 'after she has consummated her marriage'. It is *possible* to read more into the language of 'defiled' than this and to see it as some sort of condemnation of the woman's second marriage, but it is a general principle of interpretation to accept the least semantic content in a word or phrase that makes sense of the passage. This would mean that if a woman legally married a second husband after being sent away by the first, but did not consummate the second marriage, she would not be prohibited from returning to her original husband.

The third suggestion with respect to the purpose underlying

this biblical rule is 'the Israelite view that a man must not have sexual intercourse with his wife after she has had it with another man'.[31] The Bible does evidence a deeply rooted view that a wife's sexual relations with her husband are defiled by intercourse with another man (Num. 5: 13–14, etc.; Jer. 3: 1; Gen. 35: 22 and 49: 4; 2 Sam. 16: 21–2 and 20: 3; Amos 2: 7). This view further claims that there is a 'natural repulsion' against taking back a wife who has cohabited with another man. This understanding, supported by Isaksson and Derrett, is somewhat defensible. One wonders, however, why any man in older societies would want to marry a divorced woman who had been defiled by another man. In addition, 'how is it that a "natural repulsion" has found expression only within one particular legal system?'[32] No other ancient Near Eastern legal system contains such a regulation preventing the renovation of broken marriages.

The fourth suggestion, that of R. Yaron's, is that Deuteronomy 24 should be explained *not* in terms of adultery but by reference to another sphere, namely, incest, and that the regulation aims at the protection of the second marriage.[33] Yaron has observed that the strong words in verse 4 are the same ones which appear in connection with the sexual/incest offences in Leviticus 18 and 20. He argues that incest laws are designed to protect the family and to insulate existing socially approved relationships from the disruptive influences of sexual tension. When a divorcee marries another man a 'triangle' of relationships arises. The first husband may want to go back to his wife, having repented of dismissing her, or the wife may draw comparisons between the two men unfavourable to the second one. The second husband may also be jealous and apprehensive, making life horrible for his wife. All these agonies and tensions are prevented if the reunion to the first husband is prevented.

However, there is one flaw in Yaron's argument. The reunion of the first couple is forbidden even if the second husband dies! Why protect the second marriage when death has ended it? Nor does Yaron's view account for the strong remarks in verse 4 and Jeremiah 3: 1.

Most recently Wenham has offered another explanation for this regulation that seeks to avoid the weaknesses of the others. Taking the lead from Yaron, he says that Deuteronomy 24 actually regards the restoration of the first marriage as a type of incest.

Through her first marriage the woman entered into the closest form of relationship with her husband . . . divorce did not terminate this relationship; she still counted as a very close relative. If a divorced couple want to come together again, it would be as bad as a man marrying his sister. That is why it is described as 'an abomination before the Lord' that 'causes the land to sin.'[34]

The result is paradoxical. A man may not remarry his wife because his first marriage to her made her into one of his closest relatives. Deuteronomy has taken the theological logic of Leviticus to its limit. It illustrates again the notion that underlies the incest laws and the laws on premarital intercourse. Sexual intercourse not only creates vertical blood relationships through the procreation of children, but horizontal ones as well: the partners to a marriage become one flesh. These horizontal relationships are just as enduring as the vertical ones.

In concluding this discussion of Deuteronomy 24, it seems evident that whether one understands the second marriage after divorce as adulterous[35] or remarriage to one's original partner (after she has consummated a marriage with another) as incestuous, one thing seems certain: the 'one flesh' bond of marriage is not dissolved by legal or customary divorce nor by sexual relations with a third party. Deuteronomy 24: 1–4 does not teach a dissolution divorce as Murray and so many others have wrongly taught and subsequently applied to the teaching of the New Testament. On the contrary, the passage seems to imply that to seek a divorce is to try to break a relationship with one's wife that in reality cannot be broken. Just as we cannot 'divorce' our children from being our own blood relations, no matter how disreputable they may be, so a man cannot 'divorce' his wife who is his own flesh and blood through marriage. Thus Deuteronomy 24: 1–4 understands the 'one flesh' bond of marriage to survive legal or customary divorce. Indeed, this 'one flesh' is the very basis for the legislation found in Deuteronomy 24: 4.

Conclusion

Why then does the Old Testament not ban divorce altogether? We are just not told. It is true that in ancient times divorce was expensive and infrequent; perhaps it was thought that it would make for greater social peace to allow divorce in a few cases rather than to ban it altogether. The penalties for adultery and divorce constantly reminded men and women that lifelong marriage was the norm. Remember also that under Old Testament law polygamy was permitted, so a man could have sexual relations with more than one woman perfectly legally. By forbidding remarriage after divorce, Jesus simultaneously forbade polygamy. The Old Testament is therefore not inconsistent in both allowing divorce and holding that a bond still subsists between the original partners. If a polygamous man could have relations with more than one wife, so could a remarried divorcee.

CHAPTER SIX

A Critique of the Erasmian View: New Testament Considerations

In the previous chapter we examined the biblical kinship understanding of the marriage relationship. We found that a binding, perhaps even metaphysical relationship results when a man and woman leave their respective families, cleave to one another and consummate their marriage. Husband and wife have become as closely related to one another as they will be to their own children. We observed that two other pieces of Old Testament legislation have their roots in the Genesis 2: 24 principle that man and wife are 'one flesh', that is, kin or blood relations. First, the Leviticus 18 laws concerning forbidden unions are not only predicated on literal blood lines but also on 'blood' relationships created through marriage. The relationships that come into being through marital relations with one's partner are not dissolved by his divorcing her or by her death. Though Leviticus 18 makes it clear that legal divorce does not dissolve the marital union and the relationships established through that marriage, it does not make it perfectly clear whether or not extramarital relations so defile the original union that it is annulled. The second piece of Old Testament legislation, Deuteronomy 24: 1–4, gave us some help here. We found that this passage understands the 'one flesh' principle to survive legal divorce as well as sexual relations with a third party. That some kind of relationship still exists between the original couple is the very basis for the legislation found in Deuteronomy 24: 4. Finally, we should remember that every marriage is witnessed by God (Mal. 2: 14: Matt. 19: 6).

This means that the first of the two main Erasmian pillars – the idea of a Mosaic 'dissolution divorce' which is carried into the New Testament – is simply without foundation. If our interpretation of the Old Testament data is correct we could almost conclude our study here, for Jesus derived His teaching from the concepts found in Genesis 2: 24. But we must now consider the second pillar of the Erasmian superstructure. This, in turn, will be followed by an analysis of the other lines of defence put forward in the fourth chapter. In what follows we only wish to show that a modified form of the early church's interpretation has a far better probability of fitting the New Testament evidence than does the Erasmian interpretation.

The Synoptic Gospels

The Syntax of the Protasis of Matthew 19: 9

The other main pillar of the Erasmian view is the belief that the exception clause in Matthew 19: 9 qualifies the entire compound conditional relative clause (put away *and* remarry = the protasis), thus permitting divorce *and* remarriage to the innocent party in the case of unchastity. Matthew 19: 9 reads:

> And I say to you, whoever divorces his wife, except for immorality, and marries another [protasis], commits adultery [apodosis]. (*legō de hymin hoti hos an apolysē tēn gynaika autou, mē epi porneia, kai gamēsē allēn [protasis], moichatai [apodosis].*)[1]

We have already seen that the early Christian Fathers did not understand the 'divorce' which Jesus permitted for unchastity to include the right of remarriage. The Fathers' understanding may be intrinsically associated with the position of the exception clause, 'except for immorality', in relation to the verb that precedes the clause ('to put away') and the one that follows it ('to [re]marry'). It should be remembered that syntactical relations and the groupings of words are 'factors just as important for the bearing of significance as the more purely lexicographical aspect of the single word'.[2] In other words, even though 'divorce' in the first-century setting automatically included the right of remarriage for Jesus' audience, how Jesus used this term in relation to other words and concepts in His statements about divorce and remarriage may clearly indicate that He did not employ this term in the same way His listeners did. This is why an examination of the word order which Matthew chose in the protasis of Matthew

19: 9 is an important consideration in the proper interpretation of this passage.

Though Greek word order is far less significant to the meaning of a sentence than the order of words in an English sentence, the following comment in Blass-Debrunner should be kept in mind: 'Word order in Greek and so in the NT is freer by far than in modern languages. There are, nevertheless, certain tendencies and habits (in the NT especially in narrative) which have created something like a normal word order.'[3] In fact, certain tendencies and habits of the New Testament authors may only be revealed through tedious analysis of certain words or grammatical units in combination with other words and their syntactical relation to other parts of speech in a sentence.

In considering this matter of Greek word order, it would perhaps be helpful to quote K.J. Dover's caution found in the Preface of his analysis of classical Greek structure.

> I believe students of any language should be receptive to ideas which come from the students of any other language; but I believe at the same time that no language should be described and analyzed except in the terms which are positively suggested by its own peculiar nature and the nature of our knowledge of it.[4]

Unfortunately evangelicals move too hastily in analysing the syntax of Matthew 19: 9, even attempting to base analysis on their conception of English word order. G. Duty, for example, approaches the syntactical possibilities of this verse by saying rather unscientifically:

> In the Greek sentence, as in the English, it does not matter which position in the sentence the exception takes. It can be at the beginning, middle, or end [by which he means after 'commit adultery'!], and the meaning of the law remains the same. But the exception *sounds better* [italics ours] in the middle of the Greek sentence and it is the proper place for it to be.[5]

Duty and others, of course, do not discuss the fact that this is one of the few (the only?) if/then constructions in the New Testament in which the 'if' portion contains a compound conditional clause consisting of two verbs connected by 'and' (*kai*), the first of which is closely related to and qualified by a negated prepositional phrase ('except for immorality') that is placed *before* the

co-ordinating 'and'.[6] Prepositional phrases are adverbial and normally qualify the verb which they *follow*.[7] Yet before Erasmians
can make confident assertions about what the exception clause
qualifies they must demonstrate from New Testament word
order in general and Matthean style in particular that what they
are saying is supported by other considerations. This we hope to
do in defence of the early church's understanding that the
exception clause does not sanction remarriage if divorce for
immorality is allowed.

A.C. Thiselton, in his excellent essay on 'Semantics and New
Testament Interpretation', informs us that 'meaning implies
choice'.[8] This means that through word choice and word order an
author has a number of different ways in which he can convey to
his readers the message he wants them to understand. In the
word order of the compound conditional clause in Matthew 19:9
there are clearly three possible positions Matthew could have
placed 'except for immorality' in order to express Jesus' saying on
divorce and remarriage. First, Matthew could have placed the
exception clause before 'divorces' and after 'whoever', in which
case Jesus' statement would have meant something like this:
'Whoever does not put away his wife for unchastity and does not
marry another, commits adultery.' This makes divorce and remarriage mandatory in unchastity cases.[9] Second, Matthew
could have placed 'except for immorality' where he did place it in
the Greek text. To bring out the syntactical function of this
construction, it can be expanded as follows: 'Whoever puts away
his wife, if it is not for unchastity that he puts her away, and
marries another, commits adultery.' Third, Matthew could have
placed the exception clause after the second verbal action, 'marries another', and before 'commits adultery'. The co-ordinating
'and' would then connect the two sequential actions ('put away
and marry another'), and Matthew would have meant something
like this: 'Whoever puts away his wife *and* marries another, if it is
not for unchastity that he puts her away and marries another,
commits adultery.' This last construction comes close to *requiring*
the interpretation of Matthew 19:9 Erasmians now give to it.
Thus although the present position of the exception clause does
not eliminate all ambiguity, another word order would have
served Matthew even less well, assuming that he wished to
express the early church view. Had the clause come after 'marries
another', it would have expressly sanctioned remarriage; while

placed before 'puts away' it would have made separation mandatory for unchastity.

Murray's Understanding of Matthew 19:9

What remains to be evaluated here is Murray's understanding of
the nature of exceptions to general statements in Greek syntax
and the need he feels to maintain the co-ordination of divorce *and*
remarriage if Matthew 19:9 is to make sense as a whole.

It is our contention that if anyone may speak of an understanding of Matthew 19:9 that is grammatically 'harsh', it is the
Erasmian and not the early church view that fits this description.
Confusion arises when the interpreter attempts to explain the
double conditional clause from a potentially ambiguous English
translation instead of allowing the Greek construction to speak
for itself. Matthew 19:9 is admittedly difficult, but we believe a
clear explanation is possible if the sentence is approached from
the Greek standpoint.

In referring to certain uses of *ei mē* ('except, unless'),[10] Murray
said that usually the statement of that to which a more general
exception is appended is given first in its completeness, and then
the exception in its completeness follows. This is true in numerous uses of *ei mē* in Matthew's Gospel. Yet each of these instances
makes an exception or qualification or refinement to a verbal
statement that *precedes* it,[11] and does not pick up a subsequent
verbal statement which follows. Now, when Murray notes the
peculiar syntax of Matthew 19:9 – that the exception clause is
inserted *before* the statement as a whole is completed, by which he
means the entire conditional sentence, both the 'if' and the 'then'
portion – we perceive that he is trying to relate the exception
clause to the *whole* sentence. Since this does not fit the analogy of
other general exceptions appended to specific statements he has
observed, he concludes that the example of Matthew 19:9 does
not belong to this category.

The more accurate approach, however, is not to attempt to
relate the exception clause to the entire statement; rather by
recognising the relative independence between 'if' (protasis) and
'then' (apodosis) expressions,[12] Murray should have sought to
understand the function of the negated prepositional phrase in
the protasis alone ('Whoever divorces his wife, *except for immorality*, and marries another'). Does it qualify only the verbal action

which precedes it (as our following word order survey will suggest), or does it qualify both what precedes and what follows ('Whoever divorces . . . and marries another')?

What Murray and most other exegetes do not realise is that the 'not' (*mē*) in 'not on the grounds of immorality' (*mē epi porneia*) is not merely the simple negative particle nullifying 'on the grounds of' (often compared with the construction in Matt. 26: 5); 'not' in Matthew 19: 9 is governed by the introductory conditional formula 'whoever' (*hos an = ean*), and thus it is no different from 'if not, unless, except' (*ean mē*).[13] As we have already noted in chapter 2, the elliptical phrase 'except for immorality' does not contain a verb, and the one to be supplied is the one immediately *preceding* it – 'put away' – the one Matthew's readers just passed over. It would indeed be grammatically harsh to force another verb – 'marries another' – into this elliptical clause that is clearly, by the nature of its position in the protasis, linked only with 'put away'. The construction of Matthew 19: 9 basically indicates that we are dealing with two conditional statements, one that is qualified and one that is unqualified or absolute:

1 A man may not put away his wife *unless* she is guilty of adultery

2 Whoever marries another after putting away his wife commits adultery

Or, to paraphrase the idea in another way: 'Putting away for reasons other than unchastity is forbidden; and remarriage after every divorce is adulterous.'[14] But what Matthew 19: 9 may well mean in the context of Jewish marriage laws as yet remains to be specified.

We believe Greek word order in general adds further support to the above analysis. In a study of the function of all the negated prepositional phrases in the New Testament (about forty with *mē* preceding), the following norm emerged: it appears that every time a prepositional phrase immediately follows the negative particle *mē* (unless a postpositive particle intervenes), the negative particle negates the verb which the prepositional phrase *follows* unless the qualification is emphatic, in which case it precedes the verb it qualifies.[15] Similarly, in an examination of over 250 prepositional phrases in the first seven chapters of Matthew's Gospel, it is clear that Matthew usually has a qualifying prepositional phrase *follow* its intended object (ratio 4:1). Those which precede the unit to which they add precision are usually emphatic phrases moved forward, quotes from the Septuagint or phrases beginning new sections or movements in Matthew's Gospel.

All of this seems to mean that on the grounds of New Testament word order in general and Matthean style in particular, the elliptical negated prepositional phrase, 'except for immorality', is intended as a simple limitation of the verbal action that immediately precedes it: 'put away'. Matthew did not intend the phrase also to qualify the action which follows: 'marries another'. This is further supported by recent studies on the function of the eunuch-saying in its context of Matthew 19: 3–12. Is it not probable that the syntactical grid which we have laboured to understand in the context of the Greek language was intuitive for the early Fathers who thought, spoke and wrote in their mother tongue, and this is why the early church did not permit remarriage after divorce for whatever cause?

Therefore, when Murray insists that the co-ordination of putting away and remarriage must not be broken, and that this co-ordination must not be disturbed in any way, it is evident that he is assuming what he wants to prove. This is not the proper approach to exegesis. To insist that the exception clause *must* qualify both to put away *and* remarry, is to impose one's interpretation on the text. It is not denied that this dual qualification is somewhat *possible* – which may even be allowing too much – but considering the actual position of the negated prepositional phrase in the protasis of Matthew 19: 9, the burden of proof is certainly on the Erasmian, not the Fathers' interpretation.

Unfortunately P.H. Wiebe has made the same assumption as Murray in presuming the elliptical exception phrase *must* be linked to both the divorce and the remarriage conditions of the protasis. Wiebe correctly understands that Matthew 19: 9 is a conditional statement, but he does not understand the compound conditional nature of the protasis. The example on which he builds his entire article is inadequate as a starting point for his 'logical' discussion of the implications of Matthew 19: 9: 'All major political parties in Canada, except the Parti Québecois, support the continuation of a united Canada.'[16] This English example, and a defective one at that, is hardly parallel to the Matthean sentence. Whereas Wiebe's example contains only one actual simple condition, the protasis of Matthew 19: 9 contains a compound or double condition: 'to put away . . . and to remarry'.

When *both* of these conditions are fulfilled, then the sin stated in the apodosis is realised: 'he commits adultery'. Now while Wiebe wants to believe that Jesus teaches, '*If* a man *divorces* his wife, and the ground for the divorce is his wife's unchastity, *and* the man *marries* another, *then* he does not commit adultery' [italics ours], he would have been correct had he said '. . . and the man *does not* marry another, *then* he *does not* commit adultery'. The protasis of Matthew 19:9 consists of divorce *and* marriage. The occurrence of these two sequential events *always* amounts to adultery.

Wiebe's unconscious assumption that the thrust of Jesus' teaching was against the wrong of divorce and not the wrong of remarriage leads to his 'logical' error in confusing Jesus' teaching on this subject. Both Murray and Wiebe would have had some basis for their assertions had the exception clause been placed after the two verbs in co-ordination ('put away and remarry') and just before 'commits adultery', but Matthew 19:9 is not constructed this way. That Murray did not consider other syntactical options possible for Jesus' divorce saying in Matthew is evident from the comment at the close of his discussion of the syntax of the passage: 'Where else could the exceptive clause be placed if it applies to all three elements [to put away, marry another and commit adultery] of the situation expressed?'[17]

In the light of these considerations it appears that Murray was basically misinformed when he attempted to sort out the syntactical and grammatical implications of verse 9. Subsequent writers who have referred to Murray's understanding of this double conditional sentence – one which to them appeared to be the definitive treatment in support of the Erasmian view – should have studied the nature of conditional sentences and Greek word order for themselves. That Matthew 19:9 is, in all probability, an abridgement of 5:32 that was never intended to permit remarriage should also have been considered. We conclude that Murray's understanding of exceptions to general statements in Greek syntax and his insistence that the co-ordination of divorce *and* remarriage not be broken is hardly defensible. This insistence is a logical one which he imposes on the text. Divorces *do* take place without remarriage following. These are sequential actions that do not have to follow one another, indeed, must not follow one another if it is understood that Jesus taught that all remarriage during the lifetime of one's original partner amounts to adultery.[18]

To sum up our understanding of the divorce and remarriage sayings in Matthew, we feel that Matthew intends his readers to understand 19:9 in light of 5:32 and that 19:9 is likely to be an abridgement of 5:32. From 5:27–32 three propositions about divorce addressed to the man were deduced:

1 To divorce one's wife is tantamount to committing adultery (vv. 27–32a)
2 To divorce one's wife for unchastity is not tantamount to committing adultery (v. 32a)
3 To marry a divorced woman is to commit adultery (v. 32b)

We have seen that to say 'divorce, except for unchastity, is tantamount to committing adultery' is an idea peculiar to Matthew's Gospel. Mark and Luke always state that divorce followed by remarriage is adulterous. Matthew does too, but in a more roundabout way. What we appear to have in Matthew 19:9, then, is a combination of the common synoptic principle with Matthew's special emphasis[19] rolled together in a potentially ambiguous sentence. When 19:9 is analysed into its constituent parts, the ambiguity disappears and it makes a fitting retort to the catch question of the Pharisees. They asked in verse 3: 'Is it lawful for a man to divorce his wife *for any cause at all*?' Jesus replied: 'It is always wrong to divorce what God has joined together: what is more, divorce, *except for unchastity*, is tantamount to committing adultery; and remarriage after divorce is always so.'[20]

Harmonisation with Mark and Luke

Another serious problem confronting proponents of the Erasmian interpretation concerns the nature of biblical authority. G. Bromiley has recently observed

> . . . no plain mandate for remarriage occurs in any of the sayings – Matthew 19:9 comes closest – so that even if many circumstances can arise which make separation wise or necessary, divorce in the full sense, with the freedom to remarry during the lifetime of the original partner, does not seem to come unequivocally into the picture.[21]

It must be admitted, with Bromiley, that what is clearly present in all the divorce sayings is Jesus' statement that divorce followed by remarriage always amounts to adultery (Matt. 5:32; 19:9; Mark 10:11–12; Luke 16:18; cf. 1 Cor. 7:10–11). That Jesus in Mark's account permitted *no* exception which would allow divorce *and* remarriage is practically unassailable. Mark is writing his gospel with a particular group of people in mind who, in all probability (even if Marcan priority is denied), did not have Matthew's account before them. If Marcan priority is assumed, along with the majority of New Testament scholars, there can hardly be any doubt that Jesus teaches that all divorce followed by remarriage is adulterous. We cannot presume that Mark's or Luke's (or even Paul's) readers had access to the tradition preserved in Matthew's Gospel in the early stages of the transmission of Jesus' teaching.[22] We can only assume that these writers intended to convey to their readers precisely what they have written. That the other gospel writers assumed the implicit operation of Matthew's exception clause – and an interpretation of the exception that permitted remarriage – in addition to what they have clearly stated in their accounts is hardly the proper approach to the synoptic differences in the divorce sayings. What the texts in Mark and Luke do not make clear is whether or not Jesus would have allowed a divorce that was not followed by remarriage. This interpretation is left open as a possibility.[23]

Once again Murray's solution to the problem of harmonisation within the synoptic divorce accounts involves beginning with a premise of his own which he then uses to reason his way through the texts. He assumes that the burden of emphasis in Mark 10: 2–12 and Matthew 19: 3–9 is upon the abrogation of the Mosaic permission of Deuteronomy 24. In beginning with this premise he is following the reasoning of the Reformers and, in particular, the work of R.H. Charles in 1921: Jesus revokes all other reasons for divorce envisaged in Deuteronomy except divorce for adultery which was not provided for in the Mosaic law. Murray then notes that even Luke 16: 18 agrees with his premise: there is no exception to the abrogation of the permission implied in Deuteronomy 24: 1–4. By establishing a point of potential agreement within each of the synoptic accounts Murray is attempting to mitigate what amounts, in the end, to a blatant contradiction within the synoptic tradition.

Murray's next step is again deficient from an exegetical standpoint because he assumes what he wants to prove. He notes the remarkable omission in Mark and Luke of the right of a man to put away his wife and remarry for adultery. He then says that there is nevertheless no question about the propriety of such a dismissal which Matthew 5: 32 and 19: 9 clearly establish. Therefore, Mark and Luke's silence concerning this right does not in any way prejudice the right itself. What Murray has said so far is already suspect because he is building upon his own peculiar interpretation of Matthew's exception clauses. It is the next point of his argument that will not bear the weight of the burden he places upon it.

Murray then quite frankly concludes that since Mark and Luke do not refer to *divorce for adultery* they would not therefore have had to refer to the *right of remarriage* in the event of such a case. Thus Mark and Luke are not envisaging the situation created in the event of adultery and are not reflecting on the rights of the innocent partner! But it is impossible to determine what Mark and Luke mean by what they do not say. Not only is Murray assuming what he wants to prove, but he also passes over the clear teaching of all the synoptics: remarriage after divorce amounts to adultery. Murray himself remarked in his discussion of the syntax of Matthew 19: 9: 'it is the thought of committing adultery by remarriage that is the ruling thought of this passage . . .'[24] In this connection we may note that in legal sayings in the Bible the most important element tends to come at the end. The second commandment, for instance, is not concerned about banning all sculpture and artwork (Exod. 20: 4) but with prohibiting idolatry (worshipping them, v. 5). Similarly, Deuteronomy 24: 1–4 is not concerned with regulating divorce (vv. 1–3) but with outlawing the remarriage of the original couple (v. 4). If we assume that Jesus constructed His divorce sayings in the same fashion, it is clear that His primary emphasis falls on remarriage after divorce.

Finally, we find it hard to swallow the Erasmians' attempt to reconcile their interpretation of Matthew's exception with the absolute prohibition of divorce *and* remarriage in Mark and Luke. We are told that Mark and Luke give the general law of marriage and Matthew's fuller account gives the exception to it. Though this general principle/specific instance type of hermeneutic may have application elsewhere, it is out of place here. The Erasmian view of the Matthean clauses is diametrically opposed to the clear teaching of Mark, Luke and Paul. Chapter 1, Section 9 of the Westminster Confession states:

> The infallible rule of interpretation of Scripture is the Scripture itself; and therefore, when there is a question about the true and full sense of any Scripture (which is not manifold [Matt. 19: 4–8; Mark 10: 2–12;

Luke 16: 18; Rom. 7: 2–3; 1 Cor. 7: 10–11, 39], but one [Matt. 5: 32 –19: 9]), it must be searched and known by other places that speak more clearly.[25]

In response to those few interpreters who believe that Matthew may contain the clearer teaching, and that Mark and Luke condensed his account, we are not overly troubled by a condensed report, but a contradictory one no matter how full or condensed is a problem. Again, we believe that the problem does not arise with the clear teaching of Mark, Luke or Paul, but with the interpreter who imposes his view of the exception clause on the rest of the New Testament teaching.

Harmonisation and Historical-Cultural Concerns

When the twentieth-century interpreter approaches Jesus' divorce sayings to understand them, he lacks a significant variable readily available to the disciples of the first century: a cultural matrix very different from ours within which Jesus spoke His words and through which His listeners perceived them. Murray is correct when he states that the propriety of divorce for adultery was not in question among the Jews, Greeks, and Romans at the time of Christ. Of particular interest for Mark's Gospel is the legal enactment which F. Hauck records:

> In Roman law up to the time of the Republic the husband has, in a case of *adulterium*, the one-sided right of private revenge against the guilty wife even to putting to death . . . The punishment of adultery is thus a family affair (*iudicium domesticum*). Only the increasing moral disintegration of the imperial period led to legal measures by the state. Augustus passed the Lex Julia de Adulteriis [18 BC]. This declares adultery a penal offence, punishes offenders by banishment and forbids the husband to pardon or to quash the matter. He may be punished himself if he continues the marriage.[26]

It is clear in Mark's Gospel that it is divorce *and* remarriage that amount to adultery and not divorce alone. Mark's Gospel therefore leaves open the possibility of the cultural-legal influence of the day: divorce for adultery may be conceded if demanded by the legal enactments or social mores of one's culture; but remarriage, though permitted by the culture, is forbidden to the disciple by the teaching of his Master.[27] Here we find our observations supported by Evald Lövestam's insightful remarks on Mark 10: 11–12.

> The fact that this passage is formulated with the Graeco-Roman situation in mind does not imply that it accepts Graeco-Roman marital laws as such. It merely presupposes the legal circumstances in the area in which the readers live and addresses them in their actual situation. However, within this framework their behaviour is related to the commandment of God and seen in the perspective of responsibility and guilt before God. Man and woman are then expressly mentioned separately. In the one case it is the man who bears the burden of guilt according to the commandment, in the other it is the woman.[28]

Why, then, is the exception clause in Matthew's Gospel and not in Mark's? It is obvious to students of Matthew's Gospel that he is greatly concerned with issues important to the Jewish conscience. Adultery was for the Jews, as for the Romans, a crime against the husband. But far more than that, and unlike Roman law in which adultery was historically a matter of private family law, adultery in Jewish law was first and foremost a sin against God (cf. Exod. 20: 14; Prov. 2: 16–17).[29] This sin demanded punishment by the Jewish community as a whole, and the husband of an adulterous wife would not be allowed to pardon her.[30] David Hill, in his commentary on Matthew, is correct when he says that 'A man was not allowed, he was *compelled*, by Jewish law (in New Testament times) to divorce his wife when fornication before marriage was discovered (cf. Mt. 1. 19; Dt. 22. 13ff.) or adultery detected . . .''[31] The Jewish husband's moral duty was to divorce his wife in such cases. Thus Matthew writes of Joseph when he learned of his potentially unfaithful espoused wife: 'And Joseph her husband, being a righteous man, and not wanting to disgrace her, desired to put her away secretly' (Matt. 1: 19). As an observer of the law, Joseph must either expose his betrothed to the shameful trial of the suspected adulteress, or take upon himself the responsibility of the act of divorce without public trial. He had decided upon the latter course of action, but when the angel removed the suspicion of adultery (Matt. 1: 20), Mary became acceptable to Joseph again, and he took her as his wife.[32] These are the Jewish marriage customs with which Matthew's readers were familiar.

Few evangelicals take these cultural/Jewish legal considerations into account when examining the 'exception' clause in Matthew. This is the reason the 'plain' or 'natural' meaning idea, which Erasmians so often urge in support of their view of Matthew's teaching, does so little to clarify the real issues involved. When Jesus spoke these words, and when Matthew's largely Jewish audience read them, they were understood within a cultural context that is unlike that of the modern reader. On this understanding, the exception clauses in Matthew's Gospel were never intended to give 'grounds' for divorce as is commonly believed today; but rather, as F. Hauck and S. Schulz understand:

> The drift of the clauses, then, is not that the Christian husband, should his wife be unfaithful, is permitted to divorce her, but that if he is legally forced to do this he should not be open to criticism if by her conduct his wife has made the continuation of the marriage quite impossible.[33]

Lövestam writes along these same lines. His understanding of the Matthean exceptions is one that neither sanctions divorce for immorality nor permits remarriage should this kind of separation occur.

> According to Jewish marital laws the wife could cause the break-up of a marriage by being unfaithful and the man had no say in the matter. If the wife was unfaithful, it was thus she and not the man who was responsible for the divorce. When the teachings in question are intended for people with this background, they relieve the man in this case of the responsibility for the divorce and its consequences. The wife bears it. That is what the exceptive clause means.[34]

Should we not expect that Jesus, the Son of God, would desire His disciples to reflect the loyal love of covenant faithfulness that God required of Hosea when his unfaithful Gomer persisted in her immorality?[35] If Genesis 2:24 presents God's ideal for marriage, then Hosea illustrates God's ideal in the case of a broken marriage. Furthermore, it is almost impossible to interpret Jesus' teaching in Matthew 19:4-8 as anything but an absolute prohibition of divorce.

These considerations make it very likely that Jesus, by means of the legally precise exception clause,[36] is not adopting His culture's mores respecting the need to put away an unfaithful wife; nor is He sanctioning 'grounds' for divorce in this situation as though they were available to the believer today. He, in all probability, is saying that He does not hold His disciples guilty for violating His absolute prohibition of divorce (Matt. 19:4-8) should they be forced by the mores of the community around them to put away a wilfully adulterous spouse. Like Paul who did not confront head-on the problem of slavery in his day but encouraged believers to find their freedom in the Lord, Jesus exempts His disciples from the responsibility for the divorce which an unfaithful Jewish wife brings about.[37] The exception clause does not consider the 'ground' on which a Jewish husband may claim his right to divorce and remarry. Jesus, instead, seems to be reflecting on a situation his disciples would face in a legal and sociological environment in which certain sexual sins were looked upon as making the continuation of a marriage impossible.

Furthermore, in the event of marital unfaithfulness we believe that Jesus would surely require the forgiveness of seventy times seven (Matt. 18: 21–35) and the goal of restoration exhibited by Hosea. That Jesus would give 'grounds' for divorce in such cases, as if He were substituting divorce for unfaithfulness in place of the Old Covenant maximum penalty of death, seems to be a return to the *letter* of the law, not the *spirit* of the law with its much higher standards as explained in Matthew 5: 21–48.[38] Should reconciliation be impossible, Jesus makes it clear that His disciples have been given divine resources to remain single after divorce lest they, like the unbelieving outsiders, should marry another and commit adultery.

The Erasmian attempt to harmonise the teaching of Jesus in Matthew with the absolute prohibition of divorce and remarriage in Mark and Luke is flawed by modern assumptions that Jesus taught against the wrong of unwarranted divorce (a 'breaking' of the conjugal life) and not the wrong of remarriage (an attempt to break the union completely, reversing what God has done). Jesus was against both; but if a divorce today should take place against the Master's will, the faithful disciple must not compound the problem by remarrying. The disciple must above all have that faith which counts His Lord's word as good and perfect. And remarriage, which Jesus calls adultery, cannot be God's best for His children.

The Contextual Congruence Problem

Still another problem with the Erasmian interpretation of the Matthean account of Jesus' controversy with the Pharisees is the contextual incongruency that arises at two points. First, Matthew 19: 3–12 begins with the Pharisees asking Jesus about possible grounds for divorce (v. 3). They assume the then dominant Hillelite position.[39] Jesus responds with an absolute prohibition of divorce based on His exegesis of Genesis 1: 27; 2: 24 (vv. 4–6).[40] The Pharisees recognise that this is exactly what Jesus has done because they appeal to Deuteronomy 24: 1 in hopes of refuting the prohibition of divorce which Jesus had derived from Genesis (v. 7). Jesus resumes the controversy by interpreting the Mosaic writing as a mere concession to the Israelites' well-known track record: wilful disobedience to God's revealed will. Then He adds verse 9: a precept that supposedly prohibits divorce and remarriage except where immorality has occurred. In a discussion of the Hillelite view, Jesus ultimately appears to side with the Shammaites! Shammai allowed or demanded divorce in the case of unchastity, basing his view on Deuteronomy 24: 1. Yet Jesus has just unambiguously said that that text has no bearing whatsoever on His teaching on divorce and remarriage.[41]. In the Erasmian view verse 9 does not belong naturally with what precedes, because verses 4–8 do not discuss grounds for divorce at all. If the Erasmian view is accepted then it is almost impossible to escape the fact that Jesus is contradicting Himself. David Catchpole brings out the flavour of the debate much more precisely:

> What Moses commanded, the historical Jesus rejects. In Mark x. 2–9 Jesus makes a decision about divorce, in effect, a decision about Moses. Nothing should blunt the sharp edge of his words. He diverges from all tradition, whether of Hillelite liberals or of Shammaïte conservatives. Paradoxically, by taking a position more conservative than that of the conservative Shammaïtes, he takes a position more radical than all. For this is an abrogation of a law, 'an openly declared criticism of the law of Moses', 'not an accentuation of the Torah but an annulling of it'.[42]

As we have already seen, Jesus did not really 'annul' the Mosaic divorce law, for there is no legislation laying grounds for divorce anywhere in the Old Testament, only a concession to man's sinfulness similar to the concession of polygamy. But this does not detract from Catchpole's observation concerning Jesus' great distance from both rabbinical schools of thought.

We may also compare this with the Erasmian understanding of Matthew 5: 32 in the context of the Sermon on the Mount whose controlling thought is found in verse 48: 'Therefore you are to be perfect (*teleioi*), as your heavenly Father is perfect.' Bruce Metzger makes the point that if the Erasmian interpretation of verse 32 is accepted, Jesus is *not* substituting the perfect standard of God for the standard recognised by the Jews of His day, but rather is giving a teaching 'no higher than Shammai's.'[43] Jesus would not be upholding the ideal but would be teaching an ideal with one exception.

Yet modern-day defenders of the Erasmian view believe that Jesus' grounds for divorce and remarriage in Matthew 19: 9 were more restricted than Shammai's and thus far more difficult to accept.[44] If this is correct then the above argument would have to be modified to say that Jesus did eventually go beyond both rabbinical schools of thought. But Matthew's exception, on the Erasmian understanding, is still contextually incongruent with Jesus' absolute prohibition of divorce and remarriage found in verses 4–8.

The problem in this discussion is whether or not Shammai allowed full divorce only for unchastity or, as some later rabbis interpreted him, for acts of social immodesty as well: going outside with hair unfastened, spinning cloth in the streets with armpits uncovered, and bathing with the men (*b. Giṭ.* 90a–b).[45] A number of reputable scholars adopt the view that Shammai permitted divorce and remarriage only on the grounds of unchastity.[46] We should not be concerned, therefore, with later Talmudic extensions that may or may not have been in keeping with the spirit of Shammai's regulation. We should rather try to determine (if possible) the view of the school of Shammai at the time of Jesus. Though we do not believe Jesus adopts the view of Shammai on divorce and remarriage, it seems almost certain that the *logou porneias* (thing/matter of unchastity) of Matthew 5: 32 is a cryptic reference to the school of Shammai's reading of the 'some indecency' of Deuteronomy 24: 1.[47] *Porneia* (immorality) in 19: 9 is most likely an abbreviated form intended to be understood like the earlier statement. All of this is to say that Christ's absolute prohibition of divorce and remarriage and the exceptions recorded by Matthew point to the obvious context of Jewish marriage customs in which Jesus' debate with the Pharisees transpired. If there could not be a community consensus strong enough to compel divorce for all of Hillel's causes, there could be for transgressions of Shammai's. The exceptions in Matthew exempt Jesus' disciples from the responsibility for the divorce which an unfaithful Jewish wife brings about.

Further evidence that Jesus was not promulgating the strictest view among the Jews of His day nor the Erasmian view of our day is the astonishment manifest in the disciples' response to Jesus' final saying: 'If the relationship of the man with his wife is like this, it is better not to marry' (v. 10). This reaction is incomprehensible if the Erasmian interpretation is followed.

> The remark of the disciples (10) confirms the view that Christ forbade divorce, even in the case of the wife's unchastity. If that was His decision, their remark is intelligible. It would then mean that marriage is a dangerous condition, if a man cannot free himself from an adulterous wife. But, if He taught that the divorce of an adulterous wife was allowable, then their remark would mean that marriage is a hard lot, if a man may not get rid of a wife whom he dislikes; and it is hardly likely that they can have meant this. After being Christ's disciples so long, they would not hold that what even Jews of the stricter school of Shammai maintained respecting the marriage-tie was an intolerable obligation.[48]

The amazed and perhaps frightened reaction of the disciples in combination with Jesus' further remarks in verses 11–12 can only be explained if (1) Jesus had prohibited separation or divorce absolutely; (2) prohibited remarriage after divorce for whatever reason; (3) given an 'exception' that was either an annulment of a promise of marriage or a forbidden relationship; or (4) the suggestion we prefer would also explain the disciples' surprise: the 'exception' clause does not establish 'grounds' for divorce at all, but would have been culturally understood by Matthew's readers in the context of Jesus' absolute prohibition of divorce. And no matter how 'immorality' (*porneia*) is to be interpreted or the syntax understood, our exegesis of the function of verses 10–12 in Matthew 19: 3–12 makes it most probable that Jesus exhorts His disciples either to remain single or to be reconciled after divorce for whatever cause. This is also what Paul wanted his readers in Corinth to understand about the Lord's teaching (1 Cor. 7: 10–11).

The Meaning of 'Divorce' in Matthew 19: 9

The early church understood the word 'divorce' (*apolyō*) in Matthew 19: 9 to permit separation for the reason of immorality but not remarriage. This has been severely criticised in the past, however, in the light of the obvious way in which the Pharisees use the word in the same context. R.A. Dyson and B. Leeming note that the early church view

> . . . must take the word *apoluein*, to put away, in two different senses: first of a complete divorce and then of a mere separation from bed and board. In verse 3 of chapter 19 the Jews ask Christ: 'Is it lawful for a man to put away his wife for any cause?' and in verse 8, Christ says, 'Moses by reason of the hardness of your hearts permitted you to put away your wives'; in both instances the word *apoluein*, to put away, is taken in the meaning of complete severance of the bond, with freedom to marry again. Why then in verse 9, 'whosoever shall put away his wife,' should the same word be given a different meaning? And a meaning which would have been scarcely intelligible to the Jews, among whom a legal separation, with the bond remaining, was unknown.[49]

This is also one of the chief arguments in favour of the Erasmian view. David Field, in a helpful survey of the voices involved in the contemporary divorce debate, argues that

> . . . the context of Matthew 19 is the rabbinic dispute about the meaning of Deuteronomy 24. In that debate the divorcee's right to remarry was assumed. As the Mishnah makes plain, an essential part of a bill of divorce was the clause, 'You are free to marry again'. The modern distinction between divorce proper (*a vinculo*) and legal separation (*a mensa et thoro*) was not something a Jew would have easily grasped. So if Jesus had used the word 'divorce' in a sense that barred remarriage – without making it crystal clear that he was doing so – he would certainly have been misunderstood.[50]

To this we could add that the Jews, Greeks and Romans of Jesus' day knew of no such separation without the right to remarry. The Pharisees' question in verse 3 did not concern whether or not remarriage after divorce was allowed, but rather on what grounds was such a complete divorce allowed. Both Hillel and Shammai assumed remarriage, so the natural assumption is that Jesus was speaking on their terms. Is it not logical to assume that if the Matthean texts permit an exception to Jesus' 'no divorce' teaching, that in the case of the genuine exception Matthew intends us to understand that Jesus also permitted the 'innocent' party to remarry? Since Jesus does not appear to be using this standard term for complete divorce any differently from the Jews, how is it possible for someone to claim that Matthew's account permits only separation in the case of the exception and not also remarriage?

Let us slow down this discussion and move a bit more cautiously and see if the criticisms of a 'no remarriage' understanding of the Matthean exception texts are as weighty as they first appear. In Matthew's account does Jesus use the Jewish divorce term in the same way as the Pharisees, or does He invest it with new significance? Does the flow of the argument in verses 3–9 make it clear that Jesus employs the Jewish divorce terminology with a different meaning?

In responding to these criticisms we must first ask a methodological question. Is it accurate to make the assumption that Jesus must have taught the same kind of divorce prevalent among the Jews of His day? Or did He break with the Jews of His day and teach a new standard? If the evidence leads the interpreter to the latter, then he should not force the assumption of the former. Almost everyone agrees that the Jesus of Matthew's account in some way restricts the wider Jewish grounds for divorce to one, namely, unchastity. But is the idea of separation without remarriage introduced here? Interestingly, if Jesus did not introduce the idea of separation without remarriage, then someone else must have. The notion is clear in the Fathers from Hermas (c. 100–40) onwards. Though we may be able to attribute certain extremes in the Fathers' teaching on marriage and divorce to the sexual asceticism prevalent in that day, it would be rash simply to dismiss their near-unanimous testimony on this subject throughout the first five centuries. This is especially true when we remember that the socio-cultural environment maintained that every divorce automatically included the right of remarriage. Consider also the argument of tradition critics who accuse Matthew of introducing the exception clause in order to justify the practice of the early church in which Jesus' absolute prohibition of divorce proved too difficult to uphold. How does this jibe with the assertion by others that ascetic practices account for the no-remarriage position of the early Christian writers? At any rate, the testimony of the Fathers can only be secondary support for the teaching found in the New Testament.

Perhaps we may elucidate this first point – that it is improper to make the assumption that the Jesus of Matthew's Gospel, like the Jews, knew only of a divorce that automatically included remarriage – by reference to another comparable problem of interpretation. Scholars have observed that J. Jeremias adopts as his main presupposition when interpreting the parables of Jesus that their original meaning can be recovered only in terms of what they must have meant to Jesus' Jewish hearers. To this George Ladd replies in a manner appropriate to our discussion:

> This assumes that the proper *Sitz im Leben* of the parables is Judaism, not the teaching of Jesus. This tends to limit the originality of Jesus. We must make allowance for the possibility that his teachings transcended Jewish ideas. Therefore the proper *Sitz im Leben* of the parables in [sic] Jesus' teaching, not Judaism.[51]

Jesus obviously introduced a new standard of forgiveness that differed from the 'up to the seven times' limit suggested by Peter (Matt. 18: 21). Jesus firmly said, 'I do not say to you, up to seven times, but up to seventy times seven' (v. 22). He gave the Jewish concept of 'forgiveness' an entirely new significance. Consider also Jesus' revolutionary attitude toward women. Certainly the assumption that Jesus had to be thinking of the complete divorce allowed by the Jews of His time is an improper one to begin with. But is there anything in the argument of Matthew 19: 3–9 that makes it crystal clear how Jesus uses the term 'divorce'?

Before examining the different nuances of 'divorce' in Matthew 19: 3–9, there are some basic matters in the study of semantics that we ought to recall in the light of the prevalent opinion that 'divorce' is somehow a technical term that must have the same meaning in every place it pops up. James Barr, in his epoch-making book *The Semantics of Biblical Language*, states: 'a term may be technical and still . . . require definition in respect of particular occasions'.[52] Words alone are not the basic carriers of meaning. 'The primary units of speaking and understanding are larger, sentence-like groupings of words.'[53] 'Words or other linguistic signs have no "force", validity, or meaning, independently of the relations of equivalence and contrast which hold between them.'[54] Now it is true that in each word there is usually a hard core of meaning (shared traits), relatively stable, that is only malleable to a certain extent. Yet meaning does not originate with language symbols but with those who use them, and within certain limits the users determine the meaning as precise or general, specific or vague. Those who seek to atomise language and still think that 'sentences convey the exact sum of the semantic values of their verbal components', should keep in mind for our present discussion that

> . . . the meaning of a word depends not on what it is in itself, but on its relation to other words and to other sentences which form its context. Dictionary-entries about words are rule-of-thumb generalizations based on assumptions about characteristic contexts.[55]

In other words, we assume that the reader will agree that it is the context in which a word appears, where it is used on the lips of a particular individual, with a given meaning that he intends to convey – all of this indicates to us the semantic value of a particular language symbol. We are all aware of the mistake made too often in the exegetical practices of the past where a single word virtually becomes autonomous and carries a perceived meaning wherever it occurs. In contrast to this, we shall see that 'divorce' in Matthew 19: 3–9 is used by different individuals with reference to different concepts in the Old Testament and thus with different nuances.

In returning to the argument that it is unlikely that Jesus used the word 'divorce' with the meaning of separation without the right to remarry, it is usually pointed out that the Pharisees use 'divorce' in Matthew 19: 3, 7 with the sense of complete divorce. Then Jesus uses it when he refers to the Mosaic concession which allowed remarriage (v. 8), and so He apparently is using the term with the same meaning-content as the Pharisees do. So how can anyone argue that the word 'divorce', in the light of the exception in verse 9, carries the meaning of simple separation?

At first glance these arguments appear attractive. How can 'divorce' (*apolyō*) mean complete divorce with the right to remarry in one place and simple separation in another and that in the same context? This is highly unorthodox from an exegetical standpoint.

But first notice *who* is using the word 'divorce' and *what* is being stated. 'Divorce' *is* being used for complete divorce with the right to remarry on the lips of the Pharisees in Matthew 19: 3, 7. It also has this meaning on Jesus' lips in verse 8. It is clear, however, that in verse 8 Jesus is referring to the Mosaic concession which did not legislate against marrying a second time after a man had divorced his wife.[56] Yet as we have learned in our interpretation of Deuteronomy 24: 1–4, the circumstantial divorce did *not* dissolve the 'one flesh' relationship. Divorce in the Old Testament, like polygamy, was a concession to Israel's obdurate sinfulness. Why, then, in Matthew 19, would Jesus have used 'divorce' in verse 9 in the sense of the Mosaic 'dissolution divorce', as so many interpreters believe, when Jesus Himself brushes aside Deuteronomy's concession in favour of Genesis 2: 24? The enduring nature of the 'one flesh' kinship/covenant bond established in marriage is the very basis for the legislation found in Deuteronomy 24: 4. Hence it is illegitimate to assume, as many do, that because Jesus refers to the Deuteronomy 24: 1 divorce in verse 8, he must be talking of the same 'dissolution divorce' in verse 9.

On the contrary, as we noted briefly in chapter 2, those who believe that Jesus actually allows remarriage after divorce for unchastity are faced with an even greater problem of changing meanings. 'Divorce' is given two different senses, and this in one verse! Notice:

1 Putting away for unchastity plus remarriage does not equal adultery

2 Putting away for other reasons plus remarriage equals adultery.

In the first case, since remarriage does not constitute adultery, putting away obviously dissolves the marriage completely as traditional Jewish divorce was believed to do. This means that in statement (1) 'divorce' means complete divorce with the right to remarry. In the second case, 'divorce' cannot have this significance because remarriage involves adultery. This means that in statement (2) 'divorce' means only simple separation. Thus two different senses have been given to 'divorce' on the lips of Jesus. The Erasmian view results in semantic confusion in a legal context where we would expect Jesus to be very precise considering the importance of the subject.

Now if it is allegedly unorthodox to use a single word in two different senses employed by two different individuals (Pharisees and Jesus) who refer to two different Old Testament contexts for their concept of 'divorce' (Deut. 24: 1 and Gen. 1: 27; 2: 24), then it is certainly suspect to give two senses to a single word used by Jesus alone in a single context (v. 9)! No such confusion arises in the early church view, for 'divorce' means 'separate' without the right of remarriage in both instances considered by Jesus. We may further conjecture that if there was any doubt left about the nature of the 'divorce' Jesus was teaching, His addition of the unqualified conditional statement, 'And whoever marries a divorced woman commits adultery' (Matt. 5: 32b; longer reading of 19: 9; cf. Luke 16: 18b), should have made clear to His listeners that legal divorce, even for immorality, does not dissolve a previously existing marriage.

When it comes to Jesus' use of the word 'divorce', we can safely say, using the Erasmian criteria, that is *not* the early church's interpretation that results in confused semantics, but the Erasmian.

The Meaning of 'Immorality' in the Exception Clauses

Before making the transition to Paul's witness to the New Testament teaching on divorce and remarriage, we shall briefly consider the Erasmian interpretation of 'immorality' (*porneia*)[57] in the Matthean exception clauses. Erasmians who understand 'immorality' as denoting the unfaithfulness of a married woman, namely, adultery, often criticise others who defend the meaning of 'immorality' (*porneia*) in the Matthean clauses in what they feel is a 'restricted' use of the word. Sexual unfaithfulness during the betrothal period (= legal marriage in biblical and Talmudic law) and 'marriages' within the forbidden degrees (Lev. 18: 6–18) are two possible interpretations usually so criticised. What is often overlooked in such criticism is the fact that giving 'immorality' the specific meaning of 'adultery' (*moicheia*) is just as restricted as the meanings they criticise! Whereas other meanings can be supported from uses of 'immorality' in the Septuagint, pre-Christian Jewish literature, the New Testament, Qumran literature and patristic material, there is no unequivocal reference in the Septuagint, pre-Christian Jewish literature, or in the New Testament that would intimate the equation of 'immorality' (*porneia*) with 'adultery' (*moicheia*) in the way Murray and others want to restrict it in the Erasmian view.

Typical of the support offered by Erasmians for their interpretation of 'immorality', over and above other possibilities, is the following:

Many identifications have been proposed for the *porneia* (here listed in descending order of probability): (i) adultery (cf. Sir. 23: 23); (ii) marriage (entered in good faith) within the prohibited degrees of consanguinity (Lev. 18: 6–18; cf. Acts 15: 20, 29; 1 Cor. 5: 1 where incest = *porneia*) where *porneia* = Heb. $z^e nût$; (iii) pre-marital unchastity discovered after marriage (cf. Deut. 22: 13–21); (iv) moral or spiritual adultery (since figuratively $z^e nût$ can denote apostasy or violation of the covenant, e.g., Num. 14: 33); (v) *logos porneias* (Matt. 5: 32) = Heb. *'erwat dābār* (Deut. 24: 1, LXX *aschēmon pragma*), 'some indecency'; (vi) a mixed marriage between a Jew or Christian and a pagan; (vii) prostitution.[58]

What is amazing in this listing is the placement of 'adultery' first on the sole basis of the reference in Sirach 23: 23, which, in the words of B. Vawter, is 'a very difficult thing to prove, if it is to be taken in the sense of marital infidelity.'[59]

A. Isaksson and others have demonstrated that there is a distinction between what is regarded as 'adultery' and what is regarded as 'immorality' throughout the New Testament (Matt. 5: 27–32; 15: 19; 19: 9; Mark 7: 21; 1 Cor. 6: 9; Heb. 13: 4). It seems improbable that Matthew would use 'immorality' (*porneia*) for what 'adultery' (*moicheia*) explicitly requires. The oft-quoted reference in Sirach 23: 23 as a sure example of where 'immorality' is semantically equivalent to 'adultery' is far from certain. J. Jensen, author of probably the best article examining the uses of 'immorality' in the relevant literature, translates Sirach 23: 23, 'she has wantonly committed adultery' (*en porneia emoicheusthē*).[60] Isaksson noted back in 1965 that 'immorality' in this verse most likely refers to the 'sexual desire' that led the wife to commit the adultery.[61] The same is probably true of 'immorality' in *The Shepherd of Hermas* Mandate 4.1.5 and Tobit 8: 7.

Some Erasmians have concluded from passages like Jeremiah 3: 8, Isaiah 50: 1 and Hosea 1: 9 and 2: 2 (LXX), that 'immorality' is the equivalent of 'adultery', that God Himself is a divorcee, and so we should not consider divorce and remarriage strange in Jesus' teaching. By using this type of allegorical hermeneutic, polygamy might also be permitted to the Christian because Jeremiah 3: 8 states that God married both Israel and her sister Judah! Nor should the interpreter press such poetical and metaphorical language into the service of determining the exact meaning of 'immorality' in legal passages in Matthew's Gospel. F.I. Andersen and D.N. Freedman's extensive discussion of the Hebrew root *znh* (to commit fornication, be a harlot) and related nouns in the Old Testament demonstrates further that passages like Hosea 1– 3 and Ezekiel 16 cannot be invoked to support the view that 'immorality' and 'adultery' are ever used as synonymous terms.[62]

If 'immorality' (*porneia*) is not to be understood in one of the restricted senses, nor the preteritive 'undefined' sense, then it most likely refers to those sexual sins punishable by death in Leviticus 18 and 20: adultery, incest, homosexuality and bestiality. Sexual aberrations which involved flagrant, unthinkable violations of the law, something abhorrent to the Jewish conscience, would be described by the term 'immorality' and its related Greek and Hebrew forms. On this point we are basically in agreement with modern-day defenders of the Erasmian view.

Paul's Teaching in 1 Corinthians

Many errors can be avoided in the interpretation of 1 Corinthians 7 once we identify the overall structure and the various groups of individuals that Paul is addressing. He uses the structural marker, 'Now concerning' (*Peri de:* 7: 1, 25; 8: 1; 12: 1; 16: 1, 12), to indicate his answers to the various questions which the Corinthians addressed to him.[63] It is clear that chapter 7 has two main divisions, a brief outline of which here follows:[64]

A (7: 1b–24) Paul gives directions to married couples and those formerly married

  1 (7: 1b–7) Directions to married believers who thought it was best to abstain from sexual relations[65]

  2 (7: 8–9) Directions to widowers[66] and widows who cannot control their desires (they may marry again)

  3 (7: 10–11) Both Paul and the Lord command believing partners not to seek a divorce, but should divorce occur they must stay single or be reconciled

  4 (7: 12–16) Believers should live harmoniously with their unbelieving partners in both marriage and separation because their influence may bring the unbeliever to faith

  5 (7: 17–24) Principle: Believers should remain in the same situation in life which they were in when saved because what Christ demands of His 'slaves' is obedience to Him rather than other masters

B (7: 25–38) Paul gives directions to the previously unmarried
   (i.e., engaged couples)[67]
C (7: 39–40) Concluding exhortation: A widow is free to marry
   whomever she desires as long as he is a believer, though
   Paul believes she would be happier if single

1 Corinthians 7: 10–11

Following in the footsteps of the Reformers, modern-day Erasmians harmonise their understanding of Matthew's exceptions
with 1 Corinthians 7: 10–11 by declaring that Paul is not here
considering the matter of divorce for adultery: separation on
grounds short of immorality is in the back of Paul's mind. This is a
problematic analysis for, despite the fact that whatever the reason
for divorce in 1 Corinthians 7: 10–11, Paul's understanding of the
Lord's teaching permitted only two courses of action after any
divorce: remain single/unmarried or be reconciled.[68] The fact that
Paul adds 'remain unmarried' indicates that we are in the realm of
legal divorce procedure that permitted remarriage. Both of the
terms Paul employs here – 'to separate' (*chōrizō*) and 'to divorce'
(*aphiēmi*) – are found in legal papyri with the meaning of full
divorce and would have been understood that way by Paul's
readers. Though Paul uses the secular divorce terminology, he
plainly intends these words to be understood as divorce *without*
the right to remarry. He does this by the addition of a qualification
should divorce and/or separation occur: 'let [them] remain unmarried, or else be reconciled' (v. 11a).

Paul's qualifying exhortation stands in the way of R.H.
Charles's understanding of the New Testament teaching on
divorce. In his own words, 1 Corinthians 7: 11a *'contains the only
words in the New Testament which forbid remarriage after divorce'.*[69]
Though we do not agree that these are the 'only' words in the
New Testament forbidding remarriage after divorce, this passage
poses quite a problem to Charles's particular understanding of
the Matthean exceptions. He is forced to deal with this difficulty
by viewing verse 11a as an interpolation: 'This clause appears to
have been a marginal and misleading gloss, which was subsequently incorporated into the text.'[70] We can hardly sanction the
Erasmians' use of the intentional fallacy – the error of supposing
that Paul assumes permission to divorce and remarry in the event
of Matthew's exception even though he gives no indication of this

and hints elsewhere that only the death of a spouse permits remarriage (1 Cor. 7: 39; Rom. 7: 1–3) – and Charles's appeal to the tampered text, as roadways for pressing a particular understanding of Matthew's exception upon Paul. This is not exegesis, it is eisegesis: reading into the text the interpreter's meaning and not Paul's.[71]

There is a possibility that Paul's qualification of the secular divorce terminology has its parallel in Jesus' unqualified statement, 'And whoever marries a divorced [person] commits adultery.' The Christian, now under a new Master (not just the Roman authority), does not have the right to remarry after divorce, whatever the cause, because that is adultery in the light of the command of the Lord (Mark 10: 11–12//Matt. 19: 9) despite what the legal authorities permit.

David Dungan, in *The Sayings of Jesus in the Churches of Paul* (1971), argued that Paul's statement in 1 Corinthians 7: 11a represents a concession and indicates that Jesus could not have taught a strict prohibition of divorce. He believes verses 10–11 do allow divorce but prohibit remarriage.[72] But this is extremely unlikely. Dungan's 'concession' interpretation has precipitated the correctives of at least three writers; Catchpole is one of them:

> Firstly, such a flat contradiction requires us to regard Paul as intellectually confused and pastorally confusing, which is hard to credit. Secondly, the form of the section, i.e. a statement of basic principle in two parts, surrounding advice about a real situation, is paralleled in the relationship between verses 1b, 7 and 2–6, and between verses 12–14, 16 and 15. Therefore verse 11a is to be taken as a situational parenthesis in which a less than ideal situation has posed a problem and receives a solution.[73]

Finally, we should mention that some commentators feel that Paul's use of two different words for divorce in verses 10–15 – 'to separate' (*chōrizō*, vv. 10, 11, 15) and 'to divorce' (*aphiēmi*, vv. 11, 12, 13) – may reflect the fact that in the Jewish law of divorce only the husband had the right to divorce. But Paul is no doubt using the terms interchangeably to mean divorce under whatever technicalities of law existed.[74] Though in Jewish law a woman did not have the right to divorce her husband,[75] in Greek and Roman law she did. The practice in Corinth would have been in line with Greek and Roman customs. The clue that Paul is not using one term to refer to the wife's act of separating and the other to refer to the husband's act of divorcing is Paul's use of 'to separate' (*chōrizō*) of *both* the husband or wife who divorces in verse 15.

1 Corinthians 7:15

In verses 12–16 Paul turns his attention to Christians who are married to unbelievers.[76] Erasmians believe that Paul allows the believer to remarry after the divorce which he permits in verse 15: 'Yet if the unbelieving one leaves, let him leave; the brother or sister is not under bondage in such cases, but God has called us to peace.' We saw that many of the Reformers felt that this was in line with Jesus' saying that adultery was the *only* reason for divorce and remarriage because they could not envisage an unbeliever deserting without also attaching himself to another woman (which amounts to adultery). Some modern-day defenders of the Erasmian view also take this approach. The Westminster Confession makes it clear that the adulterer is viewed *as if he were dead*. Apparently this legal fiction enabled the Reformers to justify the remarriage of only the innocent deserted party in view of Paul's other statements that death dissolves the marriage union (Rom. 7:2–3; 1 Cor. 7:39). Modern Erasmians do not defend the so-called 'Pauline privilege' with this last argument, but instead appeal to individual meanings of words and various psychological and humanistic reasons for allowing remarriage. But we find at least seven reasons why verse 15 cannot be construed to permit remarriage to the deserted Christian.

The first and most important consideration is the nature of marriage itself: it is a creation ordinance and binding on all irrespective of one's faith or the lack thereof.[77] Whether a spouse is a Christian or a non-Christian appears to have little to do with Christ's teaching on the indissolubility of marriage which he derives from Genesis 1:27; 2:24.[78]

Secondly, the entire context of verses 10–16 revolves around and does not depart from Paul's and the Lord's command that a believer must not divorce. The question we should ask is what does Paul's statement in verse 15b – 'the brother or the sister is not under bondage (*ou dedoulōtai*) in such cases' – mean in the context of vv. 10–16? When D. Atkinson tries to belittle the early church view by saying '"Free to be deserted" makes nonsense of the paragraph',[79] he is *not* interpreting contextually. A. Robertson and A. Plummer *have* interpreted contextually when they state: 'All that *ou dedoulōtai* clearly means is that he or she need not feel so bound by Christ's prohibition of divorce as to be afraid to depart when the heathen partner insists on separation.'[80] Paul cannot be saying that the believer is no longer 'bound in marriage' to his unbelieving spouse because this introduces an idea foreign to the whole context and contrary to the nature of marriage as a creation ordinance. Paul knows the binding nature of creation directives because he appeals to them in support of his teaching elsewhere (1 Cor. 11: 2–16; Eph. 5: 22–33; 1 Tim. 2: 12–15).

Thirdly, Paul uses in verse 15 the same word for 'divorce' (*chōrizō*) that he does in verse 11 where he clearly states the content of his use of it: it does not include the right to remarry. J.A. Bengel speaks of the believer's freedom from feeling they somehow had to change the desire of their mate to be divorced, yet adds 'but with that exception, *let her remain unmarried*, ver. 11'.[81]

Fourthly, Dungan notes the 'similarity between "let her remain unmarried *or be reconciled*" (v. 11a) with the general hopeful outlook in v. 16 that not divorce but conversion occur'.[82] It is interesting that the early church Fathers connected verse 16 with the distant verse 13, whereas modern commentators from the thirteenth-century onwards hold that verse 16 is the explanation of verse 15.[83] These two options depend upon how verse 16 is to be translated. The *NASB* reads: 'For how do you know, O wife, whether you will save your husband? Or how do you know, O husband, whether you will save your wife?' This translation implies that the hope of conversion is remote. This means verse 16 would most naturally refer to verse 15. In contrast, the *NEB* reads: 'Think of it: as a wife you may be your husband's salvation; as a husband you may be your wife's salvation.' This translation implies that the hope of conversion is good. This means verse 16 looks back to verses 12–13, both of which conclude with a prohibition of divorce. We believe the *NEB* translation is correct because lexical usage (of interrogative *ei*) allows for it and contextual congruency favours it. Thus we believe verse 16 provides a reason for Paul's remarks in verses 12–15 as a whole. Why should believers live harmoniously with their unbelieving mates either in marriage or separation? Because they may very well be the channel through whom God brings their unbelieving partner to faith.

Fifthly, the lexical argument which R.H. Charles offers is

tortuous. His point is that 'is not under bondage' (*ou dedoulōtai*) in verse 15 supposedly has the same meaning as 'free' (*eleuthera*) in 1 Corinthians 7: 39 and Romans 7: 3. A comparison of these passages, however, will reveal that whenever Paul is speaking about the legal aspects of being 'bound' to one's partner (or bound by a promise of marriage to one's betrothed, 1 Cor. 7: 27), he uses the verb *deō* (Rom. 7: 2; 1 Cor. 7: 39), not *douloō* ('enslave, subject') as he does in 1 Corinthians 7: 15. The burden of proof is on the interpreter who attempts to show that something other than the actual, literal death of one's partner provides a basis for remarriage. The only clear precept about remarriage in Paul's theology and explicitly stated in Scripture is that remarriage is permitted to an individual after the partner has died. To introduce the consideration that some kind of divorce or desertion 'breaks' the marriage bond and permits the 'innocent' party to remarry is an attempt at eisegesis of the writings of Paul.

Some Erasmians have further argued that *douloō* (v. 15) and *deō* (vv. 27, 39; Rom. 7: 2) have a common root and are therefore etymologically related. This is supposed to hint that the two words may be used interchangeably, whatever their context, and Paul implies that desertion is like death when it comes to breaking the 'law of marriage.' This type of argument exemplifies what Barr calls 'the root fallacy': the belief that the meaning of the root of a word can confidently be taken to be part of the semantic value of any word in which it occurs.[84] A similar error is 'etymologising,' or giving excessive weight to the origin of a word over and against its actual semantic value in a given context.

Even if these two words do have a similar root, which is highly suspect, 'the test of explanations of words is by their contexts',[85] not their root. A simple concordance study will show where Paul employs *deō* and where he employs *douloō*. Never does Paul use *douloō* (1 Cor. 7: 15) in reference to that *legal* aspect of marriage which, in Paul's theology, can only be broken by the death of one of the partners. And even if Paul had used *deō* in verse 15, the word's occurrence in its immediate context of Christ's command not to divorce, and not its usage in a different context, determines its semantic value. The arguments for no remarriage after desertion would still apply even if Paul had used *deō* in verse 15 instead of *douloō*. What Paul is saying to the deserted Christian is in principle in line with what we have said about the exception clauses in Matthew: Paul exempts the Christian from the responsibility for the divorce which an unbelieving partner brings about.[86]

The sixth reason that 1 Corinthians 7:15 should not be understood as giving grounds for the deserted Christian to remarry concerns the testimony of the Fathers in the first centuries. We have already noted the testimony of Tertullian on this issue in chapter one. He speaks quite firmly about the permanence of marriage even with non-Christian spouses: complete divorce with the right to remarry appears to be ruled out.[87] H. Crouzel's study likewise concluded that the only Father in the first five centuries who permits the deserted Christian to remarry is the Latin Father Ambrosiaster (who wrote between 366 and 383). This is a fact of which many present-day canonists are unaware.

Finally, the principle which Paul teaches in verses 17–24 immediately following this question of desertion is further evidence that Paul did not permit the deserted believer to change his status. J.A. Fischer, in his interesting 'word distribution' study of 1 Corinthians 7: 8–24, notes there is a difference between vv. 8–16 and the section which follows in verses 17–24.

> Nevertheless a connection occurs in the use of *kaleō* [to call] in 7: 15 and the multiple uses of 'call' in 7: 17–24; a lesser ligature occurs between *douloō* [to enslave, bring into bondage] in 7: 15 and the multiple use of 'slave' in 7: 17–24. In conclusion, the analysis indicates that the passage extends from v 8 to v 24 (not to v 16 as in my original supposition and as is generally printed in translations) and that within this pericope 1 Cor. 7: 8–16 is a specific application of a more generic teaching in 1 Cor 7: 17–24.[88]

At least three times in verses 17–24 Paul states the equivalent of, 'Let each man remain in that condition in which he was called.' The principle is this: Believers should remain in the same situation in life in which they were when they became Christian because Christ demands of His 'slaves' sole obedience to Him not a shared allegiance to other masters. We believe that here also is the answer to the question: 'What if I was divorced before becoming a Christian? May I remarry as a believer?'[89] We believe the answer to this question is a difficult 'No'. Some Erasmians cite 2 Corinthians 5: 17, 'the old things passed away; behold, new things have come', in support of the contention that pre-Christian divorce is somehow different, and all of that is changed once a person becomes a believer. But this verse really does not support such a consideration,[90] and it actually teaches that a believer, as a new creation in Christ, now has the resources to obey Christ's commands which bring true happiness and fulfilment, including the realm of marriage as a creation ordinance.

In the light of these seven points we feel the burden of proof is really upon defenders of the Erasmian view and Roman Catholics who propose that Paul here permits the deserted Christian to remarry. The evidence which they cite does not establish their case. In saying 'the believer is not bound', Paul is simply allowing the believer to agree to an unbeliever's insistent demand for divorce. The responsibility for this divorce lies on the unbeliever's head. Paul is not thereby suggesting that the Christian divorcee may then remarry. This would be a contradiction of our understanding of the meaning of 'one flesh' in Genesis 2: 24: the basis for Jesus' teaching that all remarriage after divorce amounts to adultery.

1 Corinthians 7: 27–8

The most recent Erasmian argument to support the claim that Paul did not consider remarriage after divorce a sin concerns the interpretation of 1 Corinthians 7: 27–8. The mistake Erasmians make here provides a good lesson in careful contextual interpretation where a single word used in different contexts has different nuances, although each nuance falls within the semantic range of the word.

The word 'unmarried' (*agamos*) is used four times in the New Testament, and all of these occur in 1 Corinthians 7 (vv. 8, 11, 32, 34). In verse 8 it is masculine and is used in parallelism with 'widow' (*chēra*) where Paul says: 'But I say to the *unmarried* and to widows that it is good for them if they remain even as I.' There is a word for 'widower' in Greek (*chēros*), but it is not used in the New Testament or in the Septuagint. A glance at Liddell and Scott's *Greek–English Lexicon* will reveal that 'unmarried' is used to denote both 'bachelors' and 'widowers'. The parallelism thus suggests that in 1 Corinthians 7: 8 'unmarried' refers *only* to 'widowers',[91] and not to any bachelor or single person. Furthermore, Paul, in this context, specifically points to himself as an example of one of these 'unmarried' who has decided to remain single. In the context of verses 8–9 this may well confirm what many believe: Paul himself was a widower.[92] Unmarried rabbis were few and marriage appears to have been obligatory for all Jewish men (*m. Yebam.* 6: 6).

The reason that some interpreters still contend that 'unmarried' in verse 8 may also denote bachelors and single people in general is probably due to their misinterpretation of 1 Corinthians 7: 1–7. Gordon Fee, in our opinion, has pointed the way to an accurate and contextually congruent interpretation of these verses.[93] Fee points out that the usual approach to this passage is to say that Paul is advising marriage for those who are not able to avoid sexual immorality. Note the way the *NIV* translates verses 1–2:

> Now for the matters you wrote about: It is good for a man not to marry.
> 2 But since there is so much immorality, each man should have his own wife, and each woman her own husband.

The whole chapter is then seen as addressing the question of 'to marry or not to marry', and verses 1–7 are understood as an introduction to the whole.

> Thus it is suggested that on this question Paul prefers celibacy (v 1) but that because of sexual passions (v 2 interpreted in light of vv 9, 36) he concedes marriage (vv 2, 6). If there is a marriage, then there should be full sexual relations (vv 3–4) except for occasional periods of abstinence for prayer (v 5). In v 7, however, Paul reverts to his initial preferences expressed in v 1. Since Paul so clearly affirms sexual relations in vv 3–5 it is hard for these interpreters to believe that he would deny them in v 1, and hence the idiom – with no philological support – is expanded into 'to marry.'[94]

This makes it easy to see why 'unmarried' in verse 8 may denote single people in general. The above approach to these verses finds Paul resuming his preference for singleness in verse 7.

This interpretation, however, is faced with insuperable difficulties. The word which the *NIV* translates as 'to marry' is better left in its figurative form of 'to touch' (*NASB*). As Fee has shown, this word universally appears in classical Greek and in the Greek Old Testament as a figurative expression for sexual intercourse (cf. Gen. 20: 6). 1 Corinthians 7: 1b is a slogan of the ascetics at Corinth, and they have written to Paul that 'it is good for a man to abstain from sexual relations with a woman'. As Paul does elsewhere (1 Cor. 6: 12b, 12d, 13b, 18c) he counters the Corinthian

slogan in verse 2. Here arises the second lexical mistake of the
common interpretation. Paul's statement, 'let each man *have* his
own wife . . .' does not mean 'let each man get married'; but as
Fee demonstrates, it has here its normal usage (even in Paul, cf.
5: 1) with sexual overtones. Paul is saying to the *married* Corinthian Christians who were advocating abstention from marital
relations, 'Continue in marital relations with your own wife,
and you wives likewise with your own husbands!' Paul's remarks to both the husband and the wife in verses 3–5 – far from
being a digression as in the traditional approach to these verses – then make perfect sense. As Fee suggests, the 'because
of immoralities' in verse 2 is probably a direct reference back to
6: 12–20 where men, in all probability married, were going to the
prostitutes (and possibly even at the suggestion of their ascetic
wives!).[95]

To complete Fee's analysis, verse 5 makes it clear that sexual
abstinence is *not* the norm. It may be allowed, but it must only be
temporary. Verse 6 is not to be taken with what follows, but
makes the point that abstinence is not something to be desired. It
is only a concession to the ascetic Christians at Corinth. In verse 7
Paul agrees in principle that 'it is good for a man not to have
relations with a woman', but that this is true only for the single
gifted person who is completely free from the need of sexual
fulfilment. Celibacy of this kind is good, but not for the married.[96]

We have obviously belaboured this point but we have done so
for a reason. We have attempted to show that beginning with 1
Corinthians 7: 1b Paul begins giving directions to those who are
married or were at one time married (see outline above). Verses
8–9 concern directions to the 'unmarried' who were at one time
married and therefore can *only* be widowers. Paul does not even
start to discuss the situation of the previously unmarried until
verse 25. The disregard for the context in which 'unmarried'
occurs is what results in the latest Erasmian argument that
divorcees may remarry according to verses 27–8. Here is how the
argument goes.

In verse 11, 'unmarried' clearly means living in a state of
separation from one's husband or wife. From this use of 'unmarried' in verse 11, Colin Brown concludes that Paul uses this word
to refer to 'the divorced'. In a show of poor exegesis he then
almost dogmatically states that verses 27–8 not only apply to
'the single, widowers and widows,' but also to the divorced. He

translates 'virgins' (*tōn parthenōn*) in verse 25 as 'unmarried' so his readers will 'understand' that it includes the 'unmarried' (*agamos*) of verse 11: the divorced![97] Not only does this make Paul contradict himself in the space of a few verses, for he has just told the divorced they must remain single or be reconciled (v. 11a); but it passes right over Paul's structural marker ('Now concerning') which he uses to denote a change of subject in verse 25. Paul has already spoken of the problems of the married and formerly married (widowed and divorced) in verses 1–24. Now in verses 25–38 he addresses the 'virgins.'

But who are these 'virgins'? This question is usually focused on the interpretation of verses 36–8. Some feel that Paul is giving advice to the father of a girl who is beyond marriageable age (cf. *NASB*).[98] Others believe that Paul is describing a kind of spiritual marriage in which couples live together without having sexual relations (cf. Moffatt's trans.).[99] Still another view is that Paul is speaking about a widowed sister-in-law and the Corinthians want to know if they are bound by the Jewish custom of Levirate marriage.[100] But by far the best interpretation, in our view, is the one convincingly argued by J.K. Elliott.[101] He demonstrates that these 'virgins' (*tōn parthenōn*, only gen. pl. in NT) are engaged couples (cf. *RSV*, *NIV*). In the rest of the New Testament 'virgin' is commonly used of a betrothed girl (Luke 1: 27; Matt. 1: 18, 23; 25: 1–13; 2 Cor. 11: 2), and throughout verses 25–38 Paul addresses the men and his special notations are to the women (cf. vv. 28b, 34). The question these engaged couples ask Paul is whether or not to fulfil their promises of marriage in view of the present distress. So when Paul says in verse 28, 'But if you should marry, you have not sinned', he is not speaking to divorced individuals as a good number of Erasmians suppose. He is speaking to those who are bound by a promise of marriage (= engaged) in verse 27. It is to this group that Paul says, 'But if you should marry, you have not sinned' (v. 28a).

It is interesting that when Paul says in verse 27, 'Are you bound to a woman? Do not seek *to be released* (*lysin*)',[102] he uses the verb *lyō* (set free, release). But when Paul speaks of divorce in 1 Corinthians 7, the verb he uses is not *lyō* (or *apolyō*, Matt. 1: 19; 5: 32; 19: 9, etc.), but *chōrizō* (vv. 10, 11, 15; cf. Matt. 19: 6//Mark 10: 9) or *aphiēmi* (vv. 11, 12, 13).

The last two cases of 'unmarried' occur in this section (vv. 25–38) that gives advice to engaged couples. In verse 32 the gender of 'unmarried' is masculine and refers to the man who is still single, though engaged; and in verse 34, it refers to the unmarried betrothed girl (or virgin).[103] What characterises the life of the single individual and the engaged person is the fact that they are still free to serve the Lord with full devotion.

In summary, it appears that there is no evidence in 1 Corinthians 7 that lends support to the Erasmian view of divorce and remarriage in the two cases of desertion by an unbeliever and divorce because of a serious sexual sin. One final passage in 1 Corinthians will be considered.

1 Corinthians 6: 12–20

The subject of this passage is that a believer should not give himself or herself to immorality. It is G.R. Dunstan's contention that 'the assumptions brought to the interpretation of this text in the last two or three decades are erroneous in themselves, and so have confused our understanding of it.'[104] Much too much has been read into verse 16 by evangelicals eager to support the idea that a serious sexual sin outside of one's marriage dissolves the marriage bond. That this notion is still influential is evident by the continued acceptance of a translation of verse 18 that is undoubtedly affected by a reactionary view of sexual sin: 'Every *other* sin that a man commits is outside the body, but the immoral man sins against his own body.' By inserting 'other' after 'every' (*pan* with an anarthrous noun), the *NASB* and other modern translations commit a lexical aberration, for 'every' (*pas*) in this type of construction means every kind of sin or all sorts of sin.[105] The word 'other' cannot legitimately stand in this verse. This translation has caused commentators to perform all sorts of exegetical gymnastics to show that the sin of 'immorality' (*porneia*) is somehow different from all other sins. The sin of immorality *is* bad, but by the insertion of 'other' it is made even worse! Indeed, one might even consider it so bad that it 'dissolves' the marriage bond! Yet this can hardly be maintained.

It is well known that in 1 Corinthians Paul often introduces his response to a Corinthian problem with a popular Corinthian slogan, a statement that sums up his readers' attitudes or beliefs about an issue of Christian living. 'All things are lawful for me' (6: 12); 'Food is for the stomach, and the stomach is for food' (6: 13); and 'it is good for a man not to touch [= have sexual relations with] a woman' (7: 1b), are a few of these Corinthian slogans. We believe that there may possibly be another Corinthian slogan in verses 12–20 of chapter 6, and this would solve the problems which commentators encounter when they try to explain the meaning of 'other' in verse 18.

Most interpreters think that verse 18 is a statement made by Paul in support of his argument against the immoral practices of the Corinthians. But C.F.D. Moule[106] has made the suggestion that a proper translation of verse 18b, 'Every sin that a man commits is outside the body', indicates that we are facing another Corinthian slogan in support of their opinion that such immoral practices were not harmful. This would solve the basic difficulties commentators always wrestle with in this passage. On this understanding, a parallelism in the structure of Paul's argument emerges in verses 12–20. In verses 12–13 Paul presents the popular Corinthian slogans which they used to justify their God-dishonouring life styles. These are immediately qualified by Paul's understanding. (He uses *alla* and adversative *de*. The slogans are introduced asyndetically.) He follows his qualification with a refutation of their justification for immorality and finishes with a corresponding command: 'Flee immorality' (v. 18a). In verse 18b Paul quotes one of their other justifications for immorality, qualifies and refutes it, and again culminates with a resultant command: 'therefore glorify God in your body' (v. 20b). The introduction of the Corinthian's justifications by 'all' (*panta*) in verse 12 and by 'every' (*pan*) in verse 18b further suggests this may be the correct analysis of the passage. Thus we are not facing a sin that is different from other sins against the body, and we do not have to explain the presence of the word 'other' in verse 18 because it does not belong there anyway. Verse 18b is perhaps another Corinthian slogan presented as a justification for their immoral practices.

Paul is teaching in 1 Corinthians 6: 12–20 that there is a grave contradiction involved when a man who belongs to Christ (holy and pure) is having relations with a prostitute (defiled and impure). Not only is the thought of the sinfulness of intercourse with a prostitute present, but even more importantly such activity is performed for or in deference to the god whom the prostitute represents (= is in covenant with). Paul seems to be saying that when an individual becomes one body with a prostitute at the point of physical union, though this does not sever one from

Christ (nor from one's spouse if married), the union is an unthinkable, monstrous union by virtue of the fact that the Christian has been redeemed. R.H. Gundry writes:

> Paul opposes the disparity between carnal union with a harlot and spiritual union with the Lord because although body and spirit differ, they belong together in the service of Christ. Redemption includes the whole man, of which the body forms as proper and essential a part as does the spirit.[107]

M. Barth has observed in his commentary on Ephesians that the concept of 'one flesh' is related to similar concepts in Paul:

> Just as the vss. 2:25, 16, 18 [in Ephesians] speak of two groups of persons that become 'a single new man' in 'one single body' through 'one single Spirit,' so the OT and Pauline formula 'one flesh' describes the amazing result of the union of 'two,' even of a man and a woman, in 'one.' Certainly their sexual relationship is in mind, but not only this expression and means of union. Their physical intercourse and their life together is to be determined by their spiritual communion, according to 1 Cor 7:3–5, 10–16; cf. 26–39. A bond which is no more than sexual, or 'carnal,' constitutes 'one body' – but in a sense that is irreconcilable with 'belonging to Christ' (1 Cor 6:16–17).[108]

We find it difficult to perceive whether Paul is using 'one flesh' in 1 Corinthians 6:16 in the specific Genesis 2:24 sense of a kinship unit, or if he is thinking merely of the act of intercourse which establishes that union in a very real way. Perhaps the latter is in view in the light of the fact that no intent of marriage, hence no covenant commitment, is in view between the Christian and the prostitute here in 1 Corinthians 6.

Doubtless 1 Corinthians 6:16 is a somewhat ambiguous passage, but it cannot be cited in order to promulgate a view of divorce and remarriage which has no support elsewhere in the New Testament. One thing appears certain, that Paul is not using the partial quote from Genesis 2:24 in the development of a positive understanding of marriage.

Conclusion

This completes our critique of the Erasmian view as it is expounded by many evangelical writers. A desire to be fair and thorough has made this chapter longer than we should have wished. Erasmians generally affirm that their reading of the texts is both simpler and more natural than the alternatives. We have attempted to show that the early church view is both clearer and more coherent than the Erasmian. The early church view does not assume incoherence or inconsistency in the recorded teaching of Jesus in Matthew 19, contradictions between Jesus and the evangelists, between Paul and the evangelists, or between the teaching of the New Testament and the early church. According to the early church view Jesus rejected the Jewish notions of divorce, and his teaching was followed by the gospel writers, St Paul and the early church. On the Erasmian view Jesus is made to agree with Shammaite Jews against the more liberal Hillelites by permitting remarriage after divorce in certain instances. In order to prove that the evangelists and Paul followed Jesus in this respect, Erasmians then reinterpret all the passages in the Gospels and 1 Corinthians touching on Jesus' teaching about divorce to show that the New Testament, like Shammai, allowed some dissolution divorces where immorality was involved.

However, we have endeavoured to show that this interpretation is quite foreign to the thought of Mark, Luke and Paul who give no hint that anyone may remarry after divorce. All their explicit remarks condemn such remarriage as adultery or in Paul's case as forbidden by the Lord. But more than this the Erasmian view makes Jesus express himself quite imprecisely on this issue, using the word 'divorce' in two quite different senses in Matthew 19:9. It also makes the whole development of his debate with the Pharisees in Matthew 19:3–12 incoherent, with Jesus first rejecting their approach and then partially accepting it. Further it makes the disciples' interjection inexplicable and Jesus' reply inconsequential. Similarly the Erasmian attempt to show that Paul allowed some divorcees to remarry overrides the canons of sound contextually sensitive exegesis.

These exegetical gymnastics finally meet their Waterloo in the teaching of the early church Fathers which cannot be reinterpreted to permit remarriage after divorce. If the Erasmians are right we must believe that Hermas or some unknown early Christian Father, persuaded the church to take this drastic step. Frankly it seems unlikely that such a revolution in social attitudes could have been foisted on the entire church on the authority of a minor figure. It is more credible to ascribe it to someone like Jesus or Paul. And Paul of course saw himself, in this area at least, as simply following his Lord's teaching. The early church view makes Jesus the great revolutionary who broke with the Jewish consensus about marriage and divorce. The Erasmian view makes him merely a disciple of Shammai.

In many Protestant churches Erasmian exegesis of these texts has held sway for so long that some will no doubt feel this is proof that there must be something in it. This does not follow. Unfortunately we see another example of well-intentioned but inaccurate exegesis in some contemporary feminist reinterpretations of the Bible. Erasmus was motivated by a desire to help those trapped in miserable marriages; feminists want to alleviate the lot of women. So starting from Galatians 3:28 'there is neither male nor female. . . You are all one in Christ Jesus', the feminist argues not simply for equality between the sexes, but for substantial identity of roles. All the other texts in Scripture setting out a differentiation of roles are then reinterpreted so that they do not contradict feminist goals. Yet until the twentieth century no branch of the church would ever have suggested Scripture supported feminism. It is simply incompatible with a plain reading of the text. Feminists have a serious case, but it is not advanced by inaccurate exegesis however sincerely argued. We do not question the sincere compassion that underlies the Erasmian position, but we cannot accept that it receives any support from a fair reading of the New Testament divorce texts.

CHAPTER SEVEN
The Unlawful Marriages View

Dissatisfied with both the early church and the Erasmian views of the Matthean exception clauses, many modern scholars have advocated what we term the unlawful marriages view. Matthew 5:32 and 19:9 mention impediments to a true marriage, not reasons for dissolving a valid marriage. In this way Jesus' total rejection of divorce and remarriage is maintained: He is not simply reduced to the Shammaite Pharisee of the Erasmian view, and the disciples' surprise at His teaching in Matthew 19:10 is understandable. Often this interpretation of the Matthean clauses is combined with the suggestion that they were in fact Matthew's addition to Jesus' original teaching, and this becomes a version of the traditio-critical view which we shall consider later. However, in the unlawful marriages interpretation Matthew cannot be accused of contradicting Jesus' teaching. He is simply applying it to the problems of the early church. He still maintains Jesus' absolute rejection of ordinary divorce and remarriage.

Two Major Variations

Leaving aside the traditio-critical variant, there are three ways of understanding 'immorality' (*porneia*) on this interpretation. The one with little support and not to be considered here understands that *porneia* in Matthew's clauses refers to marriages with non-Christians which could be a form of spiritual idolatry and hence unlawful.[1] The other variations of this view both understand the meaning of the term *porneia* in the Matthean exception clauses and in the Jerusalem Council decree (Acts

15: 20, 29; 21: 25) to bear the same nuance, yet each variation understands *porneia* differently.

The Rabbinic View

The first variation of the unlawful marriages view received authoritative support through the study of J. Bonsirven, *Le divorce dans le Nouveau Testament* (1948), later developed and refined by the studies of H. Baltensweiler.[2] Called by some the 'rabbinic' view, this variation understands *porneia* in Matthew 5: 32 and 19: 9 to be the equivalent of Hebrew $z^e n\hat{u}\underline{t}$, which in the context of the divorce sayings refers to illegitimate marriages within the prohibited degrees of consanguinity and affinity found in Leviticus 18: 6–18.[3] F.F. Bruce, J.A. Fitzmyer and others find support for this restricted nuance of *porneia* in 1 Corinthians 5: 1, Acts 15: 20, 29 and 21: 25.[4] Textually genuine, the exception clauses are believed by a few to have been spoken by Jesus Himself,[5] but most believe that they were added by Matthew who authoritatively dealt with a problem that confronted his largely Jewish-Christian readers. The problem facing Matthew's audience concerned Gentile converts who found themselves in an untenable situation: they were involved in a 'marital' relationship prohibited by the Levitical law, yet were unable to eliminate the problem because of Jesus' absolute prohibition of divorce. The problem is eliminated by Matthew through his qualifying phrase. At least one writer believes that once these illegitimate marriages were severed, remarriage was prohibited in light of the eunuch-saying, which refers to the state of singleness that arises after the separation in verse 9.[6]

The Intermarriage View

The second variation of the unlawful marriages view understands that *porneia* is a reference to intermarriages between Jews and Gentiles prohibited by the law (Deut. 7: 1–5; cf. Exod. 34: 16). This variation understands that Matthew's clauses stem from Christ Himself, still under the directives of the Mosaic covenant when He spoke these words to the Pharisees. Support for the 'intermarriage' meaning of *porneia* among the Jews is found in Jubilees 30: 7, 10–11, where a daughter of Israel's 'marriage with a Gentile is no better than fornication'.[7] The Septuagint uses the word *ekporneuō* to describe Israel's 'playing the harlot' with the daughters of Moab (Num. 25: 1). Furthermore, the Temple Scroll from the Qumran community, regarded by them as quintessential Torah, prohibits the king from marrying a foreigner and extends this prohibition to all the people.[8] Acts 15: 20, 29 and 21: 25 appear to make excellent sense with this meaning also. The marriage of a Jewish-Christian with a Gentile-Christian in the early stages of the church's growth would have caused many problems for a Jewish-Christian, conscience-bound to the teaching of the Mosaic law. Though Gentile-Christians were apparently 'free' (cf. 1 Cor. 10: 23 – 11: 1; Rom. 14) to indulge in the four prohibitions mentioned in the decree, the leaders of the church asked them not to take these liberties lest they offend their Jewish-Christian brethren's developing Christian scruples. The decree appears provisional and localised, sent only 'to the brethren in Antioch and Syria and Cilicia who are from the Gentiles' (Acts 15: 23; cf. v. 30). Some believe Antioch is the most likely destination for Matthew's Gospel, thus establishing another link between it and the meaning of the decree.[9]

Support for the Unlawful Marriages View

The Prohibition of Porneia in the Jerusalem Decree

Acts 15: 5 makes it clear that an acute problem arose in the early church over the presence of Gentile believers among their Jewish brethren. Would Gentile believers be required to observe the law of Moses? F.F. Bruce captures the emotional backdrop of the problem at hand:

> For many Jewish Christians, who may have felt nothing but good will for their Gentile fellow-believers, the problem of table fellowship was much more acute than it was for such emancipated souls as Peter and Paul. Centuries of devotion to the laws governing food and purity had bred in them an instinctive revulsion from eating with Gentiles which could not be immediately overcome. Gentiles quite happily ate certain kinds of foods which Jews had been taught to abominate, and the laxity of Gentile morals, especially where relations between sexes were concerned, made the idea of reciprocal hospitality between them

and Jewish Christians distasteful. An attempt was therefore made to remove some of these obstacles to fellowship.[10]

Peter's testimony made it clear that the stricter Jewish element should not place a yoke upon the disciples which neither they nor their fathers could bear (Acts 15: 10). James, as president of the council, agreed that Gentile believers should not be troubled with these matters (v. 19).

Nevertheless, it seemed good to the Holy Spirit and to the apostles and elders, with the whole church (cf. vv. 22, 28), that Gentile believers 'abstain from things sacrificed to idols (*eidōlothytōn*) and from blood and from things strangled and from fornication (*porneias*)'. If they kept themselves from these things they would do well (v. 29; cf. v. 20). The textual problems in this directive have been the occasion of numerous studies in the past. But it is generally accepted that the Western text, which mentions the three major offences of idolatry, fornication and bloodshed, to which the negative form of the Golden Rule is added, 'represents a revision of the original provisions at a time when they no longer had the relevance that they had in the early apostolic age'.[11] Idolatry, fornication and murder were the three cardinal sins in Jewish eyes, and the whole human race was bound by these from the time of Noah.

The four prohibitions of the original decree were largely ceremonial, however, and designed to promote peace between Jewish and Gentile believers in the early stages of the church's formation. Defenders of the unlawful marriage view ask what an ethical prohibition like *porneia* is doing in a largely ceremonial decree. This is really not a problem, though, because the differentiation between moral laws and ceremonial laws is foreign to biblical teaching as well as to primitive religions and even to classical Greek writers.[12] Defenders of the rabbinic view state that in the Jerusalem decree *porneia* is

. . . here intended not in the common sense of the word (for abstention from that was in any case stringently enjoined on all Christians), but in the sense of transgression of the degrees of consanguinity and affinity prohibited in Leviticus 18: 6–18. These marital prohibitions were basic to the Jewish marriage law and have been a part of Christian canon law from the time of the Jerusalem decree.[13]

Bruce notes further that *porneia* has this same nuance elsewhere in the New Testament in Matthew 5: 32; 19: 9; and 1 Corinthians 5: 1.

Additional support for this particularly Jewish concept of *porneia* is found in the actual order of the four prohibitions in the *written* decree (Acts 15: 29; 21: 25). Fitzmyer develops this observation:

> In Acts 15: 20, 29 (cf. 21: 25) *porneia* is used, however, in a specific sense, since it is lined up with several dietary tabus, which early Gentile Christians, living in close contact with Jewish Christians (i.e., in predominantly Jewish-Christian communities), were being asked to avoid: 'what has been sacrificed to idols, blood, and what is strangled.' The letter of James to the local churches of Antioch, Syria, and Cilicia forbids, in fact, four of the things proscribed by the Holiness Code of Lv 17–18, not only for 'any man of the house of Israel' but also for 'the strangers that sojourn among *them*' . . . These were the meat offered to idols (Lv 17: 8–9), the eating of blood (Lv 17: 10–12), the eating of strangled, i.e., not properly butchered, animals (Lv 17: 15; cf. Ex 22: 31), and intercourse with close kin (Lv 18: 6–18).[14]

The Sitz im Leben *of Matthew's Exception*

The point is often made that it is very unlikely that Jesus, in his controversy with the Pharisees, would have legislated for such an obscure case as this.[15] Why would Jesus have addressed a situation which the Jewish leaders knew was unlawful and would not have recognised as a valid marriage in the first place? Incestuous marriages were not dissolved with a letter of divorce. They were simply declared illegitimate.[16]

It is of interest that Tertullian sets Jesus' prohibition of divorce in the context of John's denunciation of Herod's unlawful and adulterous marriage with Herodias (*Against Marcion* 4. 34). J.C. Laney also feels this historical incident is important to consider: John the Baptist's denunciation of the 'unlawful' (Matt. 14: 4 = Mark 6: 18) union of Herod Antipas with the former wife of his brother Philip fits well with Jesus' confrontation with the Pharisees.[17] Perhaps the test with which the Pharisees confronted Jesus (Matt. 19: 3) was related to Herod's situation rather than simply to the rabbinic debate. But against this understanding we should note that this whole situation is usually connected with the order of events that Mark narrates,[18] and he does not include the reference to *porneia*. This connection might be possible in Mark's account since women might divorce their husbands in Greco-Roman culture (cf. Mark 10:12 also), but Matthew's account is consciously designed in the light of the Hillel-Shammai debate.

It must be admitted that the majority of scholars who propound the rabbinic view also recognise that it is unlikely that Jesus would have spoken the words of the exception clause in the original setting of the controversy with the Pharisees. Their approach to the presence of the exception clauses is quite different. 'Matthew is writing his gospel within the historical situation which gave rise to the decree of Acts 15, 20. 29; 21, 25.'[19] H.J. Richards has noted that Matthew appears to have a habit of adding explanations to the words of Jesus more than the other Gospels.[20] Similarly, R. Banks observes that 'Matthew's additions, omissions and alterations are not in such instances due to a judaistic bias, but rather to a desire for a clarification of the precise way in which the teaching of Jesus affects the oral and written Torah.'[21] Matthew's writing style in the light of the Jerusalem decree would suggest that

> . . . it is highly probable that we should understand it [the phrase about *porneia*] as his commentary rather than as part of the actual words of Christ, who, as we have seen, would have no reason to make any reference to it. It is Matthew who has to teach Christ's legislation on marriage to Christians who have already experienced the controversy which led to the Council of Jerusalem and are living by its decrees (Acts 15, A.D. 50–60). And it is Matthew who has to make it clear to them that Christ's words forbidding divorce are not to be taken to mean that the kinship marriage forbidden by that decree is indissoluble. It is not. It is *porneia*, and does not come under Christ's words about divorce.[22]

This qualification, of course, does not in any way affect Jesus' teaching of the indissolubility of marriage, since the 'marriages' in such cases are illegitimate or unrecognised to begin with.

Some may object that biblical inspiration argues against such an obscure and localised problem finding expression in a Gospel that is destined for readers in succeeding generations who will never face problems like those addressed by the Jerusalem decree. Yet the Gospels *do* record commands and sayings that are confined to a particular historical period (Matt. 5: 23–6; 10: 5–6; 16: 18–19; 24: 20–2; cf. Acts 1: 3–8; 8: 14–17, etc.). There is nothing in the doctrine of inspiration that guarantees for future generations the full application of potentially ambiguous teachings recorded in a first-century setting. Therefore, one should not reject too quickly the above construction of the origin of the Matthean exception clauses in the first century in the light of what is still unknown about how the evangelists constructed their accounts and applied Jesus' teaching in the light of peculiar circumstances.

Extra-biblical Lexical Evidence

Further lexical support for understanding *porneia* in Matthew's account as denoting a 'marriage' within the forbidden degrees of kinship has been marshalled by Fitzmyer. He writes concerning the text of the *Damascus Document* found in 4: 12b–5: 14a:

> . . . in this text we have a clear instance of marriage with degrees of kinship proscribed by Lv 18: 13 being labeled as *zĕnût*. In the OT *zĕnût* is used both of harlotry (e.g., Jer. 3: 2, 9; Ez. 23: 27) and of idolatrous infidelity (Nm. 14: 33). In the LXX it is translated by *porneia* (e.g., Jer. 3: 2, 9). Whatever one might want to say about the nuances of the word *zĕnût* in the OT, it is clear that among the Jews who produced the *Damascus Document* the word had taken on further specific nuances, so that polygamy, divorce, and marriage within forbidden degrees of kinship would be referred to as *zĕnût*. Thus, in CD 4: 20 and 5: 8–11 we have 'missing-link' evidence for a specific understanding of *zĕnût* as a term for marriage within forbidden degrees of kinship or for incestuous marriage; this is a specific understanding that is found among Palestinian Jews of the first century B.C. and A.D.[23]

We should note that the two most recent word study articles on the meaning of *porneia* in the New Testament agree that in the Matthean clauses it should be regarded as designating marriages within the forbidden degrees.[24]

Roman Incest Laws

Some writers contend that Roman incest laws were just as strict as those of the Jews, so it would be unlikely that the Jerusalem decree or Matthew's Gospel had to speak to these particular cases. It is also argued that 1 Corinthians 5:1 may be lexical support for understanding *porneia* as incest (Lev. 18:8 is the situation envisaged), but Paul goes on to say that this type of immorality is of such a kind 'as does not even exist among the Gentiles . . .' And Paul was correct. Roman law was as strict as the Mosaic law with respect to marriages between consanguines (those related by blood). But as far as relationships established through marriages (affinity) were concerned, the Roman law was not as stringent as the Mosaic regulations. Under Roman law, according to Gaius' *Institutes* (§58–67),[25] written about AD 161, one could marry one's former husband's brother (contra Lev. 18:16), or one's former wife's sister (contra Lev. 18:18), or if both parents were different, one's step-brother or step-sister (contra Lev. 18:9). For Roman law, affinity originally seems to have been no legal impediment to marriage.[26]

It *is* possible that the Jerusalem decree is formulated in the light of the situation in which Gentile converts, married to affines, were offending the conscience of Jewish believers. Nor does it take more than a few cases of such 'marriages' to cause church leaders, whether at the Jerusalem council or among Matthew's readers, to stand up and take note of it. This seems evident from the amount of space Paul devotes in 1 Corinthians to the proper course of action to be taken with the brother who was having relations with his step-mother (1 Cor. 5:1–13).

There are some good arguments in favour of this variation of the unlawful marriages view. The major one seems to be the historical context in which the Jerusalem decree prohibitions were formulated. It does seem unlikely that the reference to *porneia* includes illicit sexual relations in general, for this would have been wrong for any Christian, Jew or Gentile. It seems to have a more restricted nuance in this context. Yet the rabbinic variation of the unlawful marriages view is not without its problems. The intermarriage variation will be considered in the critique of the forbidden degrees version that here follows.

Critique of the Rabbinic View

Incestuous Marriages: Inconsequential or Prohibited?

An important issue confronts the defender of the forbidden degrees of kinship meaning of *porneia* in the Jerusalem decree: are marriages within the degrees prohibited by Leviticus 18: 6–18 really inconsequential, and hence to be treated as just another area of Christian liberty? In other words, is a Christian no longer bound by the moral principles upheld by the incest regulations of Leviticus 18 and therefore free today to marry a close relative should he so desire? Almost certainly the Christian does not have this freedom. The New Testament writers assume that the laws on incest (cf. 1 Cor. 5: 1ff.), adultery (cf. Rom. 13: 9), idolatry (cf. 1 Cor. 10: 7ff.), and homosexuality (cf. Rom. 1: 27; 1 Cor. 6: 9) still bind the Christian conscience. All of these are prohibited in Leviticus 18. So when Bruce says that these marital prohibitions have been a part of Christian canon law from the time of the decree, in all probability they were assumed to be operative even before the council met. We might ask why the eating of meats sacrificed to idols (which the Christian bought at the marketplace, cf. 1 Cor. 10: 23–11: 1) did not likewise become a part of Christian canon law. Are all four of these prohibitions still binding on all Christians today, or were they appropriate only for the historical problem confronting a largely Jewish-Christian church being flooded with Gentile converts?

The Meaning of Porneia in the Jerusalem Decree

If the prohibitions within the decree are matters of Christian liberty, designed by the early church leaders to promote social life among Jewish- and Gentile-Christians, then the second variation of the unlawful marriages view stands a better chance of being the correct one. The 'intermarriage' variation understands *porneia* as denoting marriages between Jews and Gentiles prohibited by the Mosaic law (Deut. 7: 3). Israel was to play a unique role in God's plan to bring blessing to all the peoples of the earth. They were to be a distinct people, separate from the religions of the land. The maintenance of a true relationship between Yahweh and His people could only be achieved through purity of race. It is significant that when the prophet of God addresses the problem of intermarriage in Malachi 2: 13–16, along with the rejection of divorce goes an emphasis on single marriage for the purpose of raising godly children (cf. Lev. 11: 44; Isa. 6: 13). Israel's history is a testimony to the fact that intermarriage led to idolatry and compromise (Judg. 3: 1–6; 1 Kings 11: 1–6; 16: 31–3; Ezra 9 – 10). This would not soon be forgotten, nor would it be easy to think of 'God's people' as Jew *and* Gentile in one single body.

Though the dividing wall between Jew and Gentile had been broken down by the cross of Christ (Eph. 2: 11–22), and the two were made into one new man, enmity still existed in Jewish- and Gentile-Christian relationships (so evident in Paul's letter to the Ephesians). The Jewish conscience, sensitised by the law, would still find marriage with a Gentile-Christian unthinkable. The decree's prohibition of *porneia* would then be regulating this aspect of social behaviour: the Gentile-Christian was asked not to marry a young Jewish girl lest a split occur within the community due to developing Christian scruples among Jewish brethren.

This may be the meaning of *porneia* in the Matthean exception clauses also. The question directed to Jesus by the Pharisees concerned a matter of Jewish law. Jesus' answer was given while His disciples were still under the authority of that law, hence the exception clauses could be a reference to the kind of 'divorce' that took place in Ezra's marriage reform (Ezra 9 and 10).

When Ezra arrived in Jerusalem from Babylon (*c.* 458 BC), he was informed about a serious problem: the people of Israel, including the priests and Levites, had not separated themselves from the peoples of the land and their abominations. Ezra 9: 2 states that this non-separation consisted in 'taking' daughters of the land for themselves and their sons 'so that the holy race has *intermingled* ('*ārab* "have fellowship") with the peoples of the lands'. This is described as 'unfaithfulness'. Ezra is so overcome with grief that he tears his garment and his robe and sits down appalled. In a prayer of confession he says, 'Shall we again break your commands and *intermarry* (*ḥtn* cf. Deut. 7: 3) with the peoples who commit such detestable practices? Would you not be angry enough with us to destroy us, leaving us no remnant or survivor?' (Ezra 9: 14, *NIV*). These very sins had caused God to give them into the hands of their enemies in the past, and Ezra feared for the future of Israel's existence if these sins were repeated. Shecaniah's proposal is accepted and carried out: 'Now let us make a covenant before our God *to send away* (*yāṣā'*) all these women and their children, in accordance with the counsel of my lord and of those who fear the commands of our God. Let it be done according to the Law' (Ezra 10: 3, *NIV*).

The situation described in Ezra 9 and 10 is often set forth as the classic example of one in which the lesser of two evils had to be chosen: divorce is a lesser evil than the destruction of the Jewish people. This can only be said, however, if Ezra looked upon these connections as real marriages. All the evidence indicates that he did not. As early as 1890, George Rawlinson observed:

> It is quite clear that [Ezra] read the Law as absolutely prohibitive of mixed marriages (Ezra ix. 10–14) – *i.e.*, as not only forbidding their inception, but their continuance. Strictly speaking, he probably looked upon them as unreal marriages, and so as no better than ordinary illicit connections. For the evils which flow from such unions, those who make them, and not those who break them, are responsible.[27]

In Ezra's eyes this was not a question of breaking up legitimate marriages but of nullifying those which were contrary to the law. This is further suggested by the two Hebrew words Ezra chose to describe these 'marriages' (*nāśā'* and *yāšab*)[28] and the 'divorce' terminology he employs.[29] Ezra 'was a scribe skilled in the law of Moses' (Ezra 7: 6). He studied, practised and taught it in Israel (v. 10). Yet he employs out-of-the-ordinary terminology to describe the 'marrying' ('taking') and the 'divorcing' ('sending away') of these women. Furthermore, how could these Israelites have made a covenant with God (Ezra 10: 3) to put away their legal 'wives' if it is true that Scripture portrays marriage as a covenant made between husband and wife in the presence of God? Ezra's prayer seems to indicate further that 'intermarriage' had not yet actually taken place (cf. Ezra 9: 2 with 9: 14).

We make these extended comments about Ezra's marriage reform for two reasons. First, because here is an Old Testament illustration of what we mean by 'marriages' illegally contracted: unlawful marriages. And second, because some contemporary writers point to Ezra's action to show that God allows divorce and remarriage under certain circumstances. Ezra's actions are usually looked upon as cruel and harsh; but the most serious cases of unlawful unions could be punished by the death of both parties, just like adulterers (Lev. 20). Numbers 25: 6–15 records the case of an Israelite who took a foreign wife and was summarily executed.[30] It could be significant that Ezra only demanded 'divorce' of the foreigners, not their execution. This would parallel the development at Elephantine where divorce was substituted for death in cases of adultery.[31]

The intermarriage interpretation of *porneia* also has its problems. Even though Jewish leaders formulated the prohibition against *porneia* in the decree, it was delivered to brethren from among the Gentiles. Would they have readily perceived this particularly Jewish nuance of *porneia*? Also, there is nothing in the context of Matthew 5: 32 or 19: 9 to suggest that *porneia* denotes intermarriages between Jews and Gentiles. The law's prohibition of intermarriage may have been as equally binding upon the nation of Israel as were the forbidden degrees of kinship, and both unlawful, but this is not the case in Christianity. For though the incest laws still apply, Paul forbids a Christian from leaving an unbeliever and considers mixed marriages as binding as marriages in the faith. Thus if the four prohibitions in the decree are mixed – some moral and some ceremonial – it is possible that *porneia* does denote incestuous marriages, and particularly those marriages with affines within which Gentile converts were trapped and Leviticus 18 forbade. There is still yet another possibility.

The alternative we ought to consider is that all four restrictions in the Jerusalem decree *are* binding on all Christians for all time. Though the letter carried by Paul and his companions was addressed 'to the brethren in Antioch and Syria and Cilicia who are from the Gentiles' (Acts 15: 23), this does not mean the injunctions were not applied elsewhere. The wording of Acts 15: 28 suggests that these were not matters of indifference: 'For it seemed good to the Holy Spirit and to us to lay upon you no greater burden than these *essentials* (*tōn epanankes*).' And Acts 16: 4 seems to indicate that Paul and his companions were now 'delivering the decrees . . . for them to observe' everywhere they travelled. On this understanding, 'things sacrificed to idols' (*eidōlothytōn*) is the equivalent of 'idolatry' (*eidōlolatria*) which Paul castigates in 1 Corinthians 10: 14; 'fornication' would denote any and all immorality, abhorred by Paul in 1 Corinthians 6: 12–20 and elsewhere; abstention from 'blood' (*haima*) would refer, as Tertullian thought (*Monogamy* 5), to the prohibition of eating blood with meat, an apparently universal ordinance found in Genesis 9: 4; and 'things strangled' (*pniktos*) would denote the improper preparation of animal meat resulting in the presence of too much blood, again falling under the prohibition of Genesis 9: 4. These suggestions are an attempt to give to the four elements of the critical text an ethical interpretation binding on all Christians down to the present. The Western text with its three cardinal sins of idolatry, fornication and murder, to which the negative form of the Golden Rule is added, may be an early witness to the entirely ethical nature of the Jerusalem decree. Despite the widespread consensus against an ethical interpretation of the decree, there is some evidence for understanding it this way, and in particular, for understanding *porneia* in another specific sense. This is potentially devastating to the rabbinic interpretation of the divorce texts for this view is virtually founded on the belief that *porneia* in the Jerusalem decree denotes incestuous 'marriages'.

In a recent article examining the problems in 1 Corinthians 8: 1 – 11: 1,[32] G.D. Fee has taken issue with the widespread assumption that things sacrificed to idols (*eidōlothyta*, our word in Acts 15: 29) in 1 Corinthians 8 merely denotes sacrificial food sold at the marketplace (which happens to be the issue in 10: 23 – 11: 1). Fee attempts to show that in 8: 1–13 Paul is not treating an issue of Christian liberty – sacrificial food sold in the marketplace which Christians are free to eat – but is in fact dealing with the eating of sacrificial food at the temple itself in the presence of idol demons (cf. v. 10). What is more, the Corinthians were arguing for the 'right' to continue this practice as they seem to have been arguing for the right to continue their immorality (cf. 6: 12–20). Paul's approach to the problem is first to deal with the deeper issue of their misunderstanding of the Gospel (9: 1 – 10: 13), but then he forthrightly says: 'flee from idolatry (*eidōlolatria*)'. The 'idolatry' which Paul tells them to flee from is the eating of sacrificial meat *at the temple*, the very matter which he began discussing in chapter 8 and simply called 'things sacrificed to idols', the word found in Acts 15: 29 and 21: 25.

The significance for our discussion lies in the fact that 'things sacrificed to idols' (*eidōlothyta*) and 'immorality' (*porneia*) are two sins coupled together in Acts 15: 29, 21: 25, Revelation 2: 14 and 20 (cf. 1 Cor. 10: 6–8). Fee explains the implications of these texts:

> It is highly probable, therefore, that in each case these two sins really belong *together*, as they did in the OT [Num 25: 1–2] and pagan precedents. And *eidōlothyta* and *porneia* go together *at the temples*. There is evidence, in fact, that sacred meals and sexual immorality were still a part of the temple cults of the first century c.e. Thus in all these texts the sins are probably *not* the eating of sacrificial food sold in the market place and sexual promiscuity in general, but sacred meals and sexual immorality at the temples.[33]

Yet Fee noted earlier in his article the totally non-Jewish character of 1 Corinthians 8: 1–13, very different from the problems the Jerusalem council addressed. He states we must 'seek the meaning of *eidōlothyta* in 1 Corinthians not in the Jewish abhorrence of idolatry but in the nature of idol-worship in pagan antiquity'.[34] It is still possible, then, that 'things sacrificed to idols' in the Jerusalem decree *is* a matter of indifference like the case that Paul discusses in 1 Corinthians 10: 23 – 11: 1 where Jewish presence is lacking. One thing appears certain, if *porneia* in the decree denotes incestuous relationships, immorality in general or sexual immorality at the temples, Paul does not use the decree's decision and the apostolic authority behind it when he treats these problems in Corinth (1 Cor. 5: 1–5; 6: 12–20; 8: 1 – 10: 22). And this may be due to the missing Jewish element. The problem is certainly complicated.

It is possible that the practice of eating sacred meals at pagan temples and the immorality that accompanied this was an especially weak point for Gentile-Christians amid their Jewish brothers; but if the decree is not ethical, why couple idolatry and immorality with abstaining from blood and from things strangled? The problem of the exact meaning of *porneia* in the Jerusalem decree does not have a simple solution. Many will not be convinced that it has the 'clear meaning' of either prohibiting marriages within the forbidden degrees of kinship or 'intermarriage' between Jews and Gentiles. The two variations of the unlawful marriages view virtually stand on these two possibilities.

Lexical Support for the Unlawful Marriages View

Defenders of the rabbinic variation should be cautious of appealing to certain nuances of *porneia* in other contexts as evidence that the word carries this same semantic flavour in Matthew 5: 32 and 19: 9. In 1 Corinthians 5: 1 it is clearly Paul's further description of the sin of *porneia* ('that someone has his father's wife') that specifies incest. Likewise, when Fitzmyer cites the *Damascus Document*, it is the context and description of $z^e n\hat{u}\underline{t}$ nine lines later[35] that makes it clear that $z^e n\hat{u}\underline{t}$ can denote an incestuous relationship, not the word in and of itself. No such further clarification occurs either in Acts 15: 20, 29, 21: 25 or in the Matthean exception texts. Does the context of Matthew's account suggest that *porneia* has the meaning of either incestuous marriages or intermarriage between Jew and Gentile? It does not seem to, though the context *does* suggest that both divorce and remarriage are contrary to God's creation directives and are forbidden by Jesus.

Thus the unlawful marriages view must go to a wider historical framework and cultural context to obtain these nuances of *porneia* in Matthew. This is not impossible, but another view may offer greater possibilities of being the correct one. In the light of the almost unanimous scholarly consensus that *porneia* in Acts 15: 20, 29 and 21: 25 denotes intercourse with close of kin, that no great problem exists in lining up a moral regulation with several ceremonial restrictions, and that the four things prohibited by the decree are the same four prohibited by the Holiness Code of Leviticus 17–18 for both Israelites and strangers among them, it seems that the rabbinic variation of the unlawful marriages view has the better chance of being the correct one. On this view, Gentiles who had 'married' within the categories forbidden by Leviticus 18: 6–18, upon becoming Christians, found themselves in a double-bind: caught by Jesus' absolute prohibition of divorce. Matthew solves their dilemma by inserting the clauses which indicated such unions were in fact non-marriages. They did not fall under Jesus' absolute prohibition of divorce where a valid marriage is concerned.

The Hebrew Words Alluded to in the Exception Texts

Another critical problem with the view that *porneia* in the Matthean exception texts corresponds to Hebrew $z^e n\hat{u}\underline{t}$ is the near certainty that the *logou porneias* (thing, or matter of unchastity) of Matthew 5:32 is a cryptic reference to the school of Shammai's reading of the *'erwa$\underline{t}$ dā$\underline{b}$ār* (nakedness of a thing) in Deuteronomy 24:1. The school of Shammai transposed Deuteronomy's words into $d^e\underline{b}ar$ *'erwāh* (*m. Gi$\underline{t}$.* 9:10), which corresponds almost exactly to the wording of Matthew 5:32.[36] *Porneia* in Matthew 19:9 is most likely an abbreviated form intended to be understood like the earlier statement.

E. Lövestam is one of the most recent writers to state his opinion that the unlawful marriages view is far from being without complications. One of his criticisms is that apart from contextual indications it has yet to be shown 'that *zenut/porneia* during the time in question had such a character as a technical term for this type of illegal relations that the expression would on that ground have been spontaneously interpreted in this way'.[37]

Conclusion

The unlawful marriages view has many attractions. It resolves the conflict between the Gospels' accounts of Jesus' teaching without resorting to the tortuous logic of the Erasmian view. In its rabbinic variation it assigns a meaning to *porneia* (incest) that is clearly attested elsewhere in the New Testament. Nevertheless, it must remain open to question whether such a broad term as *porneia* should be narrowed down to just one type of sexual misconduct as this view demands.

CHAPTER EIGHT
The Betrothal View

The betrothal view is similar to the unlawful marriages view in agreeing that Matthew 5: 32 and 19: 9 allow for the dissolution of an invalid marriage, but not for divorce with the right of remarriage after a legitimate marriage. But whereas the unlawful marriages view regards the obstacle to a valid marriage as incest (or intermarriage), this view says that it is infidelity to one's fiancé during the betrothal period.

This view is often summarily dismissed and considered impossible in the context of Matthew 5: 31–2, 19: 3–12 and Mark 10: 2–12 because 'explicit reference is made to the provisions of Deuteronomy 24: 1–4, where the wife in question cannot be simply a betrothed woman'.[1] Such a statement not only misunderstands the betrothal view but betrays a misunderstanding of the status of a betrothed woman in biblical and Talmudic law. The theology of Matthew's Gospel and its attention to particularly Jewish concerns are significant factors in favour of giving careful consideration to this interpretation.

Statement of the Betrothal View

The betrothal view has received its most authoritative defence in the work of A. Isaksson, *Marriage and Ministry in the New Temple* (1965).[2] This view begins with an understanding of the term 'betrothal' in Jewish law. Unlike the modern sense of engagement as an agreement to marry which does not definitely bind the couple and which may be broken without formal divorce, in Jewish society a betrothed or engaged couple were already considered 'husband' and 'wife' (Gen. 29: 21; Deut. 22: 23–4; 2 Sam.

3: 14; Matt. 1: 18–25).[3] In Israel, as in its Near-Eastern neighbours Babylonia and Assyria, 'from the time of betrothal and the presentation of gifts and the payment of the Purchase Price, the woman was called "wife," and the man a "husband," and a mutual obligation of marriage was then in existence'.[4] 'Betrothal was a formal act by which the woman became legally the man's wife; unfaithfulness on her part was adultery and punishable as such; if the relation was dissolved a bill of divorce was required.'[5] A period of twelve months (*m. Ketub.* 5: 2) separated the formal agreement to marry from the marriage ceremonies, though the interval varied and may have been fixed at the time of betrothal (cf. Gen. 24: 54–5; Deut. 20: 7).[6]

Proponents of this view[7] understand the 'unchastity' (*porneia*) in Matthew 5: 32 and 19: 9, consistent with its usual meaning of premarital or radically unlawful sexual intercourse, to denote 'the same kind of unchastity as that [which] Joseph suspected Mary of, i.e. premarital unchastity'.[8] Matthew, like Mark, has recorded Jesus' absolute prohibition of divorce with the right to remarry after a legitimately consummated marriage. But in the light of his largely Jewish audience, Matthew is faithful to include an exception which, very probably, Jesus would have had to make in the original controversy with the Pharisees if His teaching was not to be misunderstood.[9] This exception made reference to the possibility, even the necessity (cf. Matt. 1: 19), of dissolving the betrothal agreement in an unconsummated marriage where one of the partners had violated the agreement by engaging in sexual relations with a third party. If Jesus had not made this exception to His teaching of 'no divorce', the Pharisees could have accused Him of siding not with the swindled party, but with the swindler who had pledged his daughter in marriage as a virgin. As Isaksson points out, this is actually not a divorce, though a legal bill of divorce was required by the Jews in such cases; but 'it is more accurate to say that it was a matter of cancelling an unfulfilled contract of sale, because one of the parties had tricked the other as to the nature of the goods, when the price was fixed . . .'[10] Thus Jesus avoided the danger of saying divorce was forbidden 'even in the case in which no marriage was ever consummated, because one party had swindled the other and the swindled husband was obliged to accuse the girl and her father before a court and thus get the marriage properly annulled'.[11]

Isaksson further argues that Jesus is not speaking about the legal aspect of marriage when He states that marriage is indissoluble. Rather than quote Deuteronomy 24:1 like Hillel and Shammai, Jesus quotes the saying of Genesis 2:24 that husband and wife become one flesh. This one flesh is brought about by their sexual union, and this sexual union within a covenanted agreement before God is what results in a unity that 'cannot be dissolved by the legal formality of writing out and handing over a bill of divorce to the wife. A marriage consummated by sexual union still exists, even after the legal contract has been annulled.'[12] But this is not the case in the dissolution of an unconsummated marriage agreement when it is found that one's betrothed has violated the agreement by engaging in sexual relations with a third party. This is the divorce Jesus permitted to his hearers so familiar with the Jewish laws of marriage and divorce. Mark and Luke, writing to largely Gentile audiences, had no need to record such an exception relating to binding betrothal agreements. In Roman law, bride-money to guarantee that a betrothal agreement would be honoured was only introduced in Byzantine times.

Support for the Betrothal View

The Theology of Matthew's Gospel

One of the considerations in favour of the betrothal view is the Jewishness of Matthew's Gospel.[13] A comparison of Matthew's and Luke's record of Joseph and Mary's engagement reveals Matthew's familiarity with the Jewish betrothal custom. Though Luke briefly mentions the engagement (Luke 2:5), he gives none of the details of Matthew's account (Matt. 1:18–25). The distinction between the period of betrothal and the time when the husband would 'take' (*paralambanō*; cf. Deut. 20:7 LXX) his betrothed to his father's home and consummate the marriage is evident in Matthew's account. More significantly, Matthew 1:19 reflects the fact that 'a charge of adultery would have to be public, and tried before the central court',[14] whereas 'it was not necessary for a divorce by mutual consent to come before a regular court or Beth Din of three Rabbis, as later became the practice'.[15]

And so Joseph could have avoided publicly disgracing Mary and 'put her away secretly' by taking upon himself, without public trial, the responsibility of the act of divorce. Matthew also uses the same divorce term here (to put away = *apolyō*) as Jesus and the Pharisees use in the synoptic divorce texts. If Matthew had explicitly called Mary's sin 'unchastity' (*porneia*), a link with Jesus' use of 'unchastity' in the exception clauses would almost certainly be established.

Some may be tempted to draw the conclusion from Matthew 1: 19 that the death penalty for betrothal unfaithfulness (cf. Deut. 22: 13–24; *m. Sanh.* 7: 4, 9) was no longer applied in Jesus' time: that either Roman law had prohibited it,[16] or divorce through a public shaming had replaced it. But Angelo Tosato notes that

> The case of a woman's lack of fidelity to her betrothed in the period of time between the stipulation of the marriage contract and the consummation of the marriage is treated in Deut 22: 23–27. Two cases are distinguished: that of seduction (vv 23–24) and that of violation (vv 25–27). In the first case the woman is consenting; seducer and seduced are both reckoned to be guilty and are liable to death. In the second case the woman is not consenting; the violator is guilty and is, therefore, liable to death. The violated woman is an innocent victim and is exempt from punishment.[17]

So in the light of this legislation Mary's pregnancy can signify one of two things: either she has been seduced or she has been violated. Only in the first case is she judged as an adulteress. Until the facts are established she is only a suspected adulteress (cf. Num. 5: 11–31).

J.M. Ford appeals to the account of the woman caught in adultery in John 7: 53–8: 11 as evidence that Jesus would have similarly forgiven and prohibited the dismissal of a non-virgin betrothed wife;[18] but this is a misunderstanding of the woman-caught-in-adultery episode. Jesus, in obedience to the law which He was bound to fulfil (Matt. 3: 15), would have possibly required that she be stoned if the case had not been contrived.[19] Furthermore, it is unlikely that Jesus would have sided with the swindler in the case of a violated marriage contract and completely set Himself against what both the law and His opponents would have required in this situation in the first century. The fact that Jesus' debate with the Pharisees took place under the Old

Covenant somewhat affects our interpretation of these incidents.[20]

Isaksson feels it is important to note that Joseph, the legal father of Jesus, also belongs to the Old Covenant. Matthew 1: 19 states: 'And Joseph her husband, being a righteous man, and not wanting to disgrace her, desired to put her away secretly.'[21] Not only does Matthew portray Joseph as a just (*dikaios*) man, a man who observes the requirements of the law, but he records that Joseph also received a special revelation about the child his betrothed would bear (Matt. 1: 20–5) and obeyed angelic directives given for the protection of the divine child (Matt. 2: 13–15, 19–23). Isaksson explains the significance of this:

> Thus Joseph is described as a presumptive Christian, one who believes that Jesus is the Son of God. In view of this it is very unlikely that it would be related of him that he decided to do something which clearly conflicted with the teaching that Jesus gave, according to the account later in the Gospel, concerning a man's right to divorce his wife. We may assume that, when it is related that Joseph thought of divorcing Mary because he believed she was guilty of unchastity (*porneia*), what he planned to do is not to be understood as being at variance with what Mary's son later taught, according to Mt. 19. 9, since this teaching also permitted divorce on the ground of *porneia*.[22]

We should note, however, that Isaksson, not Matthew, describes Mary's suspected sin as 'unchastity' (*porneia*). Though the actual presence of the word 'unchastity' is not necessary in Matthew 1: 18–25 in order to bring this incident alongside Matthew's later exceptions, one could possibly argue that had Matthew wanted to make this identification apparent he would have included the appropriate description of Mary's suspected sin as 'unchastity'. But he does not.

It is also of interest that in the Jewish marriage customs great concern appears to be attached to the bride's virginity in both the Old Testament and in rabbinic Judaism.[23] Though the sayings concerned in the rabbinical sources cannot in each case be proved to derive from the time of Jesus, since marriage customs change quite slowly, they are of great importance for understanding views prevailing among the Jews of Jesus' time and the later readers of Matthew's Gospel.[24] *Ketubot* 1: 1 requires that marriages with virgins be celebrated on a Wednesday and with widows on Thursday. This is because the courts sit twice a week on Monday and Thursday. So if it becomes evident to the bridegroom on his wedding night that his bride is not a virgin (cf. Deut. 22: 13–21), he may go directly to the court on Thursday after their wedding night and bring suit against her and her father. We have found, perhaps by chance, that Keil and Delitzsch list among those sins which break the ninth commandment ('You shall not bear false witness') the case of Deuteronomy 22: 13–21 in which a man who had betrothed a woman found out after their wedding that his wife did not have the tokens of her virginity.[25] The crime she had committed is described as 'unchastity' ($z^e n\hat{u}\underline{t}$, LXX *ekporneusai*). The intensified form of *porneuō* (to commit fornication) is used to describe shameful behaviour that occurred during the period of betrothal before the actual consummation of the marriage. In this connection, it is Matthew, not Mark, who records among the list of sins that defile the man and reside in the heart, the sin of 'false witnessings' (*pseudomarturiai*, Matt. 15: 19 = Mark 7: 21–2).

In sum, these appear to be indications that Matthew is concerned with Jewish customs and Old Testament laws that affect the lives of those to whom he is writing. It is possible that the divorce which Jesus permits in Matthew's exception clauses is that divorce for betrothal unfaithfulness which only the Jews would have been attentive to.

One of the reasons why Matthew records in such detail the birth of Jesus and the status of his parents when Mary was found to be with child, is surely to correct the widespread opinion among the Jews of Jesus' illegitimate birth. We shall briefly consider this idea, the word which the Jews used to describe this illegitimate birth and its possible bearing on the meaning of 'unchastity' in Matthew's exception clauses.

The Use of Porneia in John 8: 41

In John 8: 34, in the midst of a discussion on freedom and enslavement, Jesus makes the statement that 'every one who commits sin is the slave of sin'. In the progress of the argument the Jews claim to be Abraham's offspring. To this Jesus responds that they should then do the deeds of Abraham and listen to the truth which He, Jesus, communicated. As Jesus was about to tell them they were of their father, the devil (John 8: 44), the Jews employed the classical *ad hominem* argument and said: 'We were not born of fornication (*porneias*); we have one Father, even God' (John 8: 41b). R. Brown, in his commentary on John's Gospel, writes:

> He has been talking about his heavenly Father and about their father, but were there not rumors about his own birth? Was there not some question of whether he was really the son of Joseph? . . . The Jews may be saying, 'We were not born illegitimate [but you were].' There is an early witness to Jewish attacks on the legitimacy of Jesus' birth in Origen *Against Celsus* I 28 (GCS 2: 79); and the *Acts of Pilate* II 3, has the Jews charging Jesus: 'You were born of fornication.'[26]

What should we make of the above use of 'unchastity'? It seems most natural to understand it as an *ad hominem* reference to Jesus' birth out of wedlock, yet other interpretations have been offered. The term *porneia* is clearly appropriate for such an unlawful act if the illegitimate birth is the intended reference. But that John 8: 41 can be cited as support for the use of *porneia* as a technical term for unchastity during the betrothal period is doubtful. The possibility, however, cannot be ruled out.

Isaksson's admirable word study of *porneia*, and the fact that Matthew used it and not 'adultery' (*moicheia*) to denote the sin for which separation is permitted, further suggests that the wife's adultery is *not* the (only?) sin Jesus had in view when He used the term *porneia*. He concludes:

> Thus we cannot get away from the fact that the distinction between what was to be regarded as *porneia* and what was to be regarded as *moicheia* was very strictly maintained in pre-Christian Jewish literature and in the N.T. *porneia* may, of course, denote different forms of forbidden sexual relations, but we can find no unequivocal examples of the use of this word to denote a wife's adultery. Under these circumstances we can hardly assume that this word means adultery in the clauses in Mt. The logia on divorce are worded as a paragraph of the law, intended to be obeyed by the members of the Church. Under these circumstances it is inconceivable that in a text of this nature the writer would not have maintained a clear distinction between what was unchastity and what was adultery: *moicheia* and not *porneia* was used to describe the wife's adultery. From the philological point of view there are accordingly very strong arguments against this interpretation of the clauses as permitting divorce in the case in which the wife was guilty of adultery.[27]

Critique of the Betrothal View

The Technical Meaning of Porneia

The major critique of this view, like the technical meaning given to *porneia* in the incestuous marriages view,[28] is that the betrothal unchastity meaning of *porneia* is far too restricted and 'such a specialized meaning of the term would not have been readily comprehended'.[29] The criticism which Isaksson brings against the use of *porneia* to denote a wife's adultery may be similarly used against the use of *porneia* to denote betrothal unchastity: we can find no unequivocal examples of this word as denoting unchastity during the betrothal period. Though a term like *moicheia* ('adultery') clearly and unambiguously denotes the act of adultery, *porneia*, in and of itself, does not signify any one particular sexual sin. It is a wide expression, and the context in which it appears determines its meaning. Hence, it may be used to denote *any and every* form of sexual misconduct contrary to the will of God.

To strengthen his case Isaksson noted further that he was 'unable to find in the rabbinic literature any example of the word *znut* being used to denote adultery'.[30] In the light of the recent essay by E. Lövestam this must surely be in error, for he observes that 'If we turn to the Rabbinic literature the use of *zanah* (*porneuein*) (with its derivatives) about a wife's unfaithfulness to her husband is well in evidence.'[31] Lövestam's conclusion, after noting the work of Isaksson, rejecting the interpretation of Matthew's *porneia* in the light of the Jerusalem decree, and citing numerous rabbinic texts where *zanah* refers to the sexual unfaithfulness on the part of the wife, is this: 'Against this background the most plausible interpretation is without doubt that *porneia* in the exceptive phrases in Mt. 5: 32 and 19: 9 means sexual unfaithfulness. If the intended meaning was any other the term used would have been highly open to misunderstanding.'[32]

When we consider that *porneia* can be used to denote unlawful intercourse in general; that Jesus would have used *moicheia* if the sin of adultery alone was intended; that *pornē* (prostitute, cf. Matt. 21: 31) would have been the better word to use if flagrant adultery bordering on prostitution was the exceptional sin permitting divorce; and that Matthew 19: 4–8 is surely an absolute prohibition of divorce within a legally contracted and consummated marriage, what alternatives are left? The historical-cultural reconstruction in the light of the Jerusalem decree that understands *porneia* as denoting forbidden degrees of kinship and believes that Matthew added the clause due to problems with Gentile converts is by no means air-tight. That *porneia* refers to intermarriages between Jews and Gentiles which the law prohibited is possible, but we have been unable to find this suggestion taken seriously elsewhere. Yet if we consider the Jewish marriage customs and the particular interests of Matthew's Gospel, the restricted nuance of *porneia* denoting that kind of sexual sin which Joseph suspected of Mary is a definite possibility and should not be dismissed lightly. If the *Sitz im Leben* of the exception clauses is the life of Jesus then the betrothal view has even a better chance of being correct than has the unlawful marriages view. This is because no divorce was needed for unlawful unions. They were considered null and void from the start.

Questionable Support from Patristic Texts

Isaksson has found a single patristic text in Ignatius' letter to Polycarp 'in which it is possible that Ignatius is explaining just how this clause in Matthew is to be applied in church discipline'.[33] The passage in *Ad Polycarpum* 5.2b is as follows: 'But it is right for men and women who marry to be united with the consent of the bishop, that the marriage be according to the Lord and not according to lust. Let all things be done to the honour of God.'[34] Isaksson believes that the phrase 'to be united' is a euphemism for the first sexual intercourse between a couple which was not to take place until the bishop had given his consent. He thinks it is 'probably not impossible that the reason for this rule was that, when the marriage was contracted, the leading men of the church were to be informed whether the clause on unchastity in Mt. was to be considered applicable, in case the question of divorce should arise in the future'.[35] The qualifications Isaksson himself adds to the 'probability' of this view renders it suspect, besides the fact that the phrase 'to be united' or 'enter into a union' usually denotes getting married. E. Schillebeeckx says this about Ignatius' statement:

Clerical intervention was regarded only as desirable and did not include a jurisdictional act of any kind. What is more, Ignatius' affirmation stands in almost complete isolation in the ancient church and was in fact never put to any great extent into practice. We may safely assume that his statement was in accordance with his 'episcopalism.'[36]

Of course it is possible that the Fathers misunderstood the particularly Jewish flavour of this betrothal exception, as they misconstrued other particulars in the Gospels. Various textual changes witness to this phenomenon. But the widespread testimony of the early Christian writers makes it less probable that the betrothal view can best account for the biblical and patristic evidence.

Conclusion

The betrothal view has much to commend it: the use of the word 'fornication' and not 'adultery' in the exception clauses may indicate a specific premarital sexual sin; the theology and interests of Matthew's Gospel suggest the exception clause is to be interpreted in the light of Jewish marriage customs; and if Jesus had absolutely prohibited divorce He would have had to make such an exception to avoid the danger of saying divorce was forbidden even in the case where no marriage was consummated, because one party had swindled the other by promising a virgin bride who had in fact already defiled herself and thereby violated the marriage agreement. The only major objection to this view is the restricted nuance given the word *porneia*. Without specific contextual indicators would Matthew's readers have understood it to mean betrothal unchastity? It is surely possible; but how possible?

CHAPTER NINE
The Preteritive View

This view understands the exception clauses in Matthew quite differently from the views we have considered so far. The other interpretations take the exception clause as giving a reason for separation (the early church view), or complete divorce (the Erasmian view) or for nullity (the unlawful marriages and betrothal view). The preteritive view understands Jesus' remarks to be refusing to take 'unchastity' as a cause for separation, divorce, or nullity. It is argued that in fact the addition of the exception clause alters the sense of Jesus' condemnation of divorce and remarriage very little at all. The phrase is just inserted to deal with the Pharisees' problem. From the point of view of the remarriage question then, this view is identical with the early church, forbidden marriages and betrothal views. Remarriage is always wrong following a valid marriage.

This view should not be confused with the 'inclusive' interpretation,[1] which translates Matthew 19:9, *'not even in the case of* unchastity'*, and means that divorce and remarriage are forbidden 'even inclusive of the case of unchastity'. The preteritive view may perhaps be more readily understood if it is designated the 'no comment' view. It is closely tied in with the phenomenon of Jesus' public teaching in parabolic speech which is often followed by private instruction for the disciples. This is especially clear in Mark's Gospel, the pattern of which is 'illustrated in Ch. 4 and assumed throughout the Gospel . . .'[2]

Statement of the Preteritive View

This view holds that the purpose of the Pharisees' question in Matthew 19:3 was to get from Jesus a decision on a much-disputed text of the Bible, namely, Deuteronomy 24: 1. In Bruce Vawter's words:

> The reference to 'any reason whatever' can be nothing except an allusion to the well known Shammai-Hillel controversy over the meaning of Dt 24, 1, whether the grounds of divorce were to be restricted to adultery (*moicheia*) alone, or were to be extended to what was, practically speaking, in the perhaps ironical description of the Pharisees, any reason whatever. The Pharisees were not asking whether divorce was lawful – a fact taken for granted and explicit in the Law – but what were the lawful grounds for divorce according to the Law.[3]

Christ would give no direct answer to this question posed by 'outsiders'. Instead He responds with a counterquestion intended to expose the Pharisees: they would never have asked that question had they understood the absolute indissolubility of marriage from the standpoint of the law itself as recorded in Genesis 1: 27 and 2: 24 (Matt. 19: 4–6). The Pharisees are astonished with this response and so abandon their question about Hillel's interpretation of the law only to ask another catch question concerning the law itself: why the command to give the bill of divorce then (v. 7)? Jesus plainly states that Moses' concession was 'an interim legislation in the true sense, contrary to the ideal of the Law and to the antecedent will of God'.[4]

Jesus' final retort, good enough for the hostile questioning outsiders but not revealing the full truth of the matter later provided for the disciples (Mark 10: 10–12; cf. Matt. 19: 10–12), is given in Matthew 19: 9: '*Whoever divorces his wife – not on the grounds of unchastity – and marries another, commits adultery.*' This view understands that 'unchastity' is a reference to the 'some indecency' of Deuteronomy 24: 1, but also states that Jesus refused to comment on the meaning of this cryptic reference.[5]

> The Pharisees had begun by asking that it be interpreted; they had clung to it as the divine authority which contradicted Christ's construction of the lesson of the creation narrative, as the opposition of 'law against law' so familiar to the rabbis. Christ had reinterpreted its significance in its historical context. It is only natural that the final elucidation of his teaching should conclude, in effect: 'I say to you, whoever dismisses his wife – Dt 24, 1 notwithstanding – and marries another, commits adultery.'[6]

The 'no comment' view understands the exception clauses as preteritions, or exceptions to the proposition itself, not simply to the verb 'to put away'. Vawter says the phrases are parenthetical to their respective contexts and could be translated as follows:

> 5, 32: *I say to you, however, that everyone who dismisses his wife – setting aside the matter of* porneia *– makes her become an adulteress; and whoever marries her who has been dismissed, commits adultery.*
>
> 19, 9: *I say to you, however, that if anyone dismisses his wife –* porneia *is not involved – and marries another, he commits adultery; and whoever marries one who has been dismissed, commits adultery.*[7]

The full answer, that not even unchastity constitutes an exception, is given by Christ to the disciples in private (Mark 10: 10) where they asked Jesus about the case upon which He had just reserved judgment. Though they had been granted to know such mysteries of the kingdom (Matt. 13: 11) and were better disposed than the Pharisees to hear it, even to them it was a shock (Matt. 19: 10).

Support for the Preteritive View

We will examine four main lines of support for this view: (1) the linguistic evidence for the semantic content given to the prepositions in the exception clauses (*parektos* and *epi*); (2) the reference to 'unchastity'; (3) Matthew's redactional activity; and (4) the pattern of Jesus' teaching ministry.

The Linguistic Evidence

Proponents of this view feel that the phrase 'except for unchastity' (*parektos logou porneias*) in Matthew 5: 32 is clearer than the 19: 9 phrase (*mē epi porneia*), and so its meaning should be considered first.[8] The word *parektos* is an improper preposition with the genitive. It 'occurs in the NT once as an adverb (II Cor. xi. 28) and two or three times as a preposition, with [the] Gen. = *apart from, except*'.[9] Besides its occurrence as a variant reading in Matthew 19: 9,[10] the only other place it occurs in the New Testament is in Acts 26: 29 where Paul, a prisoner, prays that not only King Agrippa, but all who heard him that day might be as he is (i.e., a believer) *'except for'* or *'apart from* these chains'. In 2 Corinthians 11: 28, *chōris tōn parektos* (apart from such external matters) refers to the troubles which came to Paul from outside, in contrast to the mental anxieties which came from within. Besides these texts, the word appears in only two other places in the Greek literature of the period.[11]

Thus *parektos* in Matthew 5: 32 must be given an *ex*clusive, not an *in*clusive sense. Though some have argued that a stronger exceptive force should be given to *parektos*, Robert Banks feels that 'a consideration of the other passages in which it is used in the NT and in apocalyptic literature indicates that "apart from" is probably the more basic meaning of the term'.[12] In Matthew 5: 32 *parektos* 'governs the *logos porneias* as an exception not to the absolute prohibition against dismissing a wife, but to the very consideration itself of the question of dismissal'.[13]

This brings us to a consideration of the phrase *mē epi porneia* in Matthew 19: 9. The usual translation of the exception phrase in this verse, where *epi* is followed by the dative case, is *'except for* immorality'. Yet nowhere else in Matthew's Gospel is *epi* translated 'for' when followed by the dative, or for that matter, in any of its 124 occurrences in Matthew's Gospel.[14] One of the most common ways Matthew uses *epi* followed by the dative is to denote the basis or grounds for an action.[15] The reason this preposition continues to be translated by 'for' in Matthew 19: 9 seems to be linked with the translation of the negative particle *mē* by 'except' from the Reformation to this day.[16] Advocates of the preteritive view say that the particle *mē* (not) should be understood simply as the negative particle nullifying *epi*,[17] the latter signifying the basis or grounds for the action, so the phrase should be translated *'porneia* is not involved'.[18] This is supposedly similar to the Matthean expression 'not during the festival' (*Mē en tē heortē*) in 26: 5 considered in relation to the whole preceeding verse.[19] Matthew 26: 3–5 reads:

> Then the chief priests and the elders of the people were gathered together in the court of the high priest, named Caiaphas; and they plotted together to seize Jesus by stealth, and kill Him. But they were saying, *'Not during the festival*, lest a riot occur among the people.'

The plot to seize and kill Jesus was excluded from taking place during the festival. This is supposed to be similar to Jesus' excluding from His consideration of the grounds for divorce the whole matter of 'some indecency' in Deuteronomy 24: 1.

The Reference to 'Unchastity'

One of the most important considerations in the preteritive or 'no comment' view concerns the significance of *logos porneias* ('a matter of unchastity') in Matthew 5: 32 and *porneia* in 19: 9. R. Banks, who prefers this view over all others, writes in his study of *Jesus and the Law in the Synoptic Tradition* (1975):

> As for *porneia* itself, in keeping with its most general meaning, i.e., 'uncleanness', it should be regarded as a reference to the *'rwt dbr* [some indecency] of Deut. 24. 1. These sayings may then be generally translated: 'I say to you, whoever dismisses his wife – the permission in Deut. 24. 1 notwithstanding – and marries another, commits adultery.' This means that the emphasis upon indissolubility (already present in *gamēsē allēn*) that is the thrust of Mark and Luke is also preserved in Matthew.[20]

Two lines of evidence argue for the understanding that Matthew's clauses make a reference to the 'some indecency' of Deuteronomy. First, there is no direct relationship between the divorce vocabulary in the Septuagint and the terms used in the New Testament.[21] The verb *chōrizō* is used in the New Testament for 'divorce' but never means this in the LXX even when the LXX uses it in other senses. *Apolyō* means 'divorce' in Matthew 1: 19, 5: 31–2, etc., and is used with many other nuances in the New Testament. But in the divorce passages it replaces the LXX *exapostellō* (Deut. 22: 19, 29; 24: 1, 3; Jer. 3: 1, 8; Isa. 50: 1; Mal. 2: 16), which is never used in this sense in the New Testament. Other examples could be cited, but the point is that it may not be so unusual to find *aschēmon pragma* (Deut. 24: 1 LXX, 'some indecency') rendered by the *logos porneias* of Matthew 5: 32.[22] A glance at Hatch and Redpath's *Concordance* reveals that the LXX translates the Hebrew *dābār* (word, matter, thing, etc.) by either *logos* or *pragma*, but that *logos*, the word which appears in Matthew 5: 32, appears eight times as often.

The second consideration in favour of seeing the matter of 'unchastity' in Matthew 5: 32 as a reference to the 'some indecency' in Deuteronomy 24: 1 we have already discussed.[23] This is the near certainty that the phrase in Matthew 5:32 and the abbreviated form in 19:9 correspond to Shammai's transposition of the Hebrew words in Deuteronomy 24:1 (cf. *m. Giṭ.* 9:10).

This identification has significant implications because it excludes from our consideration the unlawful marriages view and the betrothal view, both of which unnecessarily restrict the meaning of the broad term *porneia*. Shammai's transposition most likely denoted 'all the marriage and sexual prohibitions specified in Leviticus ch. 18. It embraces not only incest, but also adultery, buggery and homosexuality . . .'[24] But it must be remembered that in Jewish marriage customs the wife's sexual unfaithfulness does not give the husband the *right* to divorce her, as if he could choose to or not. He *had* to divorce his wife. She was prohibited to him for ever (*m. Soṭa* 1:2; 5:1; 6:1–3)! Here we find our earlier remarks on this subject masterfully articulated by E. Lövestam's recent essay:

> Against this background the clause of exception stands out in sharp relief. It is only found in passages on divorce which are formulated with reference to the Old Jewish marital laws, and it applies to the situation that arose when within this framework *the wife* [who could *not* make out a bill of divorce] had caused irreparable damage to the marriage, which was the case when she had been guilty of sexual unfaithfulness.[25]

We want to say again that this does not mean that Jesus condones Jewish marriage laws.

> This is where the exceptive phrase comes in. According to Jewish marital laws the wife could cause the break-up of a marriage by being unfaithful and the man had no say in the matter. If the wife was unfaithful, it was thus she and not the man who was responsible for the divorce. When the teachings in question are intended for people with this background, they relieve the man in this case of the responsibility for the divorce and its consequences. The wife bears it. That is what the exceptive clause means.[26]

All of this means that whether the preteritive view is correct or not, the practical application of Matthew's exception clauses amounts to the view which we find in the early church Fathers.

Matthew's Redactional Activity

Banks adds a third observation in support of the preteritive view of the Matthean clauses:

> Here [Matt. 19: 9], in the climactic saying of the narrative, it is perfectly in accord with Matthew's redactional method that he should round the encounter off with a reference to the provision around which the controversy revolved. This is precisely his procedure in the controversy over defilement that has just been examined (15. 20b). Though it may seem that it would have been more appropriate for the clause to have been placed earlier if it was meant to qualify the whole statement, its present position is the one in which a *parenthesis* is most likely to be inserted.[27]

We only wish to note here the major difference (and we believe the major error) between the preteritive and the early church view. Whereas the early church view understands the exception phrases as elliptical *clauses* with the verb 'to put away' understood, the 'no comment' view understands these clauses as *parenthetical phrases* functioning independently of the introductory conditional formula (*hos an*). As we shall see, the major problem with the preteritive view is a grammatical one.

The Pattern of Jesus' Teaching Ministry

The last point we wish to make in favour of the preteritive view is the phenomenon of Jesus' teaching ministry in the Gospels. Jesus said to His disciples, 'To you has been given the mystery of the kingdom of God; but those who are outside get everything in parables' (Mark 4: 11 = Matt. 13: 11). The circle of the disciples in the Gospels receives a different 'level' of teaching from that given 'to those who are outside', the unbelieving multitude.[28] This distinction is found in each of the synoptics.[29] Jesus allows His disciples to see and hear things which others are either not capable of understanding or do not want to understand. Besides examples unique to each Gospel (cf. Matt. 13: 36–43), there are three parallel instances in Mark and Matthew where this phenomenon of public teaching in parabolic speech is followed by private instruction for the disciples. This distinction affects our interpretations of the remarks which Jesus makes in the hearing of the public.

Each of these subjects – (1) the explanation of the parable of the sower (Matt. 13: 1–23; Mark 4: 1–20); (2) the question of defilement (Matt. 15: 1–20; Mark 7: 1–23); and (3) the question of divorce (Matt. 19: 3–12; Mark 10: 2–12)[30] – involved a significant issue for Jesus' audience. But for today's reader these episodes are much like watching an involved plot on the television screen. The actual characters participating are not aware of all that is transpiring (like those whom Jesus taught in parables), while the viewer is aware of both sides of the plot (like the disciples whom Jesus instructed more completely in private). In a similar fashion we see in the Gospels Jesus teaching publicly in parabolic speech[31] and then privately instructing His disciples. We are able to perceive both sides of the issue.

In two of the three episodes parallel in Matthew and Mark the present-day reader can unemotionally accept Jesus' private explanation to His disciples of a public precept He had just given enigmatically. Jesus clarifies for them and for us what He intentionally left unclear in the minds of the unbelieving public. There is one instance, however, that even today's reader can and does emotionally get involved in as did the disciples: Jesus' pronouncement on the matter of divorce and remarriage. Mark 10: 11–12 must 'be put on the same level as the explanations of the "sower" and of spiritual defilement'.[32] Unlike the other two examples of public teaching which Jesus explains more clearly in private (and the reader understands quite clearly), the emotional side of the divorce problem tends to obscure what, at least in Mark, is a clear example of public teaching in parabolic speech followed by private elucidation for the disciples. The teaching in Mark's Gospel is made obvious: divorce followed by remarriage in every case amounts to adultery. Though Matthew records the exact same controversy with the Pharisees, the absence of the Marcan place of private instruction (the house, cf. 7: 17; 9: 18, 33; 10: 10), the addition of the (enigmatic?) exception clause, and the possible change from the question of divorce to singleness for the sake of the kingdom as the topic of private instruction (Matt. 19: 10–12),[33] all combine to complicate the very clear teaching of Mark on the subject.

If, however, the 'no comment' view is correct, and the Matthean phrases are functioning as enigmatic references to the point of controversy which Jesus refuses to address, then Matthew's account communicates the same teaching so clear in Mark: divorce followed by remarriage amounts to adultery. Matthew's inclusion of the eunuch-saying, a 'proof', so to speak, that His disciples are able to remain single after divorce, further heightens the contrast between the teaching of the Pharisees and the teaching of Jesus. Whereas Jewish custom said, 'Behold, thou art permitted to any man' after divorce (*m. Giṭ.* 9: 3), Jesus states that His disciples must remain single after divorce (Matt. 19: 10–12).

If Matthew's exception is construed within the pattern of Jesus' public teaching in enigmatic speech, then those Erasmians, who contend that in Matthew Jesus spells out in detail when such a divorce and remarriage would be acceptable, could not be more mistaken. How could it be possible to derive a *specific* teaching of our Lord on divorce and remarriage from a text in which Jesus is being deliberately obscure in light of the state of unbelief exhibited by the Pharisees who asked the question to trap Him? In at least two other situations in Matthew's Gospel[34] the religious leaders ask Jesus specific questions designed to trap Him. Jesus, however, never answered them in the way they expected, but instead He 'carved clean through the controversy, and had forced his questioners to re-examine their own principles'.[35] It *is* possible that Jesus did not give a direct answer in Matthew 19: 9 as defenders of the preteritive 'no comment' view contend. Mark would obviously omit the 'unchastity' phrase in his account. The allusion to Deuteronomy 24: 1 would have no bearing on his Gentile audience who would not know about or have any interest in the Shammai-Hillel controversy which sparked its inclusion in Matthew. Banks summarises:

> Thus, in this controversy . . . Matthew and Mark by their alterations, omissions and additions have each shaped the original encounter according to the character of their respective tendencies and audiences. Particularly noteworthy have been Matthew's desire to draw out the implications of Christ's teaching for the Mosaic commandment and Pharisaic requirement to which it is most relevant, as well as Mark's desire to give that teaching its widest possible application, while once again Matthew's tendency to focus on the authority of Jesus and the opposition of the Pharisees has come into view.[36]

Much more could be said about Jesus' pattern of public teaching in parabolic speech and private instruction of the disciples,[37] as well as a discussion of the divorce pericopae in the light of rabbinic controversy forms attested in Jewish sources

from the first century AD onwards;[38] but it should be evident that
the preteritive view is both linguistically and pedagogically defensible.

Critique of the Preteritive View

The major problem with this view is grammatical. It was argued
above that in Matthew 19:9 the particle *mē* in *mē epi porneia* is
simply a negative particle nullifying *epi* and that a similar construction appears in Matthew 26:5. The problem with this is
twofold. First, this fails to see that *mē* here is not a simple negative
particle, but is governed by the introductory conditional formula
and thus no different than *ean mē* (if not, unless).[39] Second, the
example cited as parallel to this in Matthew 26:5 does not occur in
a conditional relative clause as is the case in Matthew 19:9. M.
Zerwick discusses the use of *mē* in the exception clause:

> Can *mē* mean 'except'? The question has a certain importance in
> connection with the 'divorce clauses'; for it is obviously likely that the
> two expressions (Mt 5,32 and 19,9) have the same meaning, i.e. that
> *mē epi porneia* means the same thing as the previous *parektos logou
> porneias*. The meaning would of course be the same if *mē* could mean
> 'except', but this is with good reason denied by many scholars. In this
> passage however, *mē* not only may but should mean 'except', not that
> *mē* = 'except' is of itself admissible, but because *mē* is here dependent
> upon the introductory *hosoi an* which is equivalent to *ean tis* ('whoever
> = if anyone dismisses his wife *mē epi porneia* . . .') and thus we have
> (*ean*) *mē* = 'unless', i.e. 'except'. Both expressions, therefore, lay down
> the same true exception; . . .[40]

Much of the same point is made by J. Dupont who argues that
the only way to understand *mē epi porneia* is as an ellipsis for a
longer conditional clause, 'if he does not put her away for
unchastity'. We should then have: 'Whoever puts away his wife,
if he does not put her away for unchastity, and marries another,
commits adultery.' Thus whereas the major problem with the
unlawful marriages and betrothal views is lexical, in that they
assign an unusually narrow meaning to *porneia*, the biggest
problem with the preteritive view is grammatical: can the phrases
really be interpreted parenthetically as this view demands?

We should also mention that it is probably wrong to understand Matthew's exception clause enigmatically in the light of a teaching pattern that is clearly followed through in Mark, but is not as clear in Matthew. Furthermore, what is stated privately in Mark 10:11–12 is made public in Matthew 19:9. As Banks observes, Matthew focuses on Jesus' authority over and above that of the Pharisees, so he brings them in open conflict and introduces Jesus' final pronouncement with the solemn 'And I say to you.'

We only note again, that if the preteritive view is correct, it would amount to the early church view in practical application. This is because in the time of Jesus, Jews, Romans and Greeks alike would have *required* the wife or husband of an adulterer to divorce the partner. The same principles apply here as discussed in chapter 6 in the critique of the Erasmian view. We stated that in all probability the exception clauses do not give 'grounds' for divorce, but refer to those who would be forced to put away their adulterous partners by the mores of the society around them. We believe that Lövestam, quoted earlier in this chapter, has clearly articulated the precise meaning of the exception clauses in Matthew's Gospel where Jewish marriage customs lie in the background. Thus both Matthew and Mark's accounts record Jesus' absolute prohibition of divorce *and* remarriage. Should a divorce be required because of one of the partners' sexual unfaithfulness, both evangelists make it clear that Jesus would regard any remarriage as adulterous.

CHAPTER TEN

The Traditio-Historical View

The traditio-historical view does not offer any new exegetical options which have not been reviewed so far. It is really an attempt to understand how the evangelists composed their Gospels and arranged the material out of the traditions at their disposal. But whereas the views we have already looked at harmonise all the accounts of Jesus' teaching by arguing that every passage teaches much the same, the traditio-historical view admits that the different texts have different meanings. However, it is argued that these differences reflect the special interests of the evangelists' adapting Jesus' teaching for the needs of the church they were writing for. As far as the divorce sayings are concerned, it is the exception clauses that stand out as peculiar to Matthew and which are often held to be this evangelist's addition to the original teaching found in the other Gospels.

On the older traditio-historical view the exception clauses tended to be understood in the Erasmian sense. But this view has several disadvantages over the straight Erasmian interpretation in that it starts from the premise that Jesus taught the absolute indissolubility of marriage, but that Matthew deliberately contradicted Him. This approach also views Matthew as a very inept editor of the gospel stories with Jesus apparently changing His mind in successive verses. For these reasons there is a clear tendency among more modern tradition critics to favour the unlawful marriages interpretation as it avoids the contradictions of the Erasmian view. But since many of the older critical works assume the Erasmian view we shall examine it here in detail.

Statement of the Traditio-Historical View

This view concludes from studying the various sayings on divorce in the New Testament that all of them cannot go back to

Jesus. The obvious point in conflict with the other sayings is the Matthean exception clauses. 'Mt. uses both Mk. and Q [a source Matt. and Luke supposedly used alongside Mark's Gospel as they composed their own], but in both cases introduces a qualification which blunts the saying and is obviously designed to justify the practice of the Early Church: Mt. 19: 9: *mē epi porneia*, and Mt. 5: 32: *parektos logou porneias*.'[1] The phrase 'for any cause at all' in Matthew 19: 3 is also added by Matthew (or the final editor of Matthew) to Mark's more primitive account and prepares the reader for the qualification in verse 9.[2] Both of these insertions into Mark's account are inconsistent with Jesus' otherwise absolute prohibition of divorce and hence clearly must be Matthean interpolations.

The exception in Matthew 5: 32 is also confusing because 'if a man divorced his wife for *porneia*, he would not then cause her to commit adultery, because she would already be guilty of this crime'.[3] The author of Matthew 'has so shaped Christ's teaching about divorce as to make it consonant with the permanent validity of the Pentateuchal law, and harmonious with the stricter school of Jewish theologians'.[4] Thus Jesus, like Shammai, allows divorce and remarriage in the case of 'unchastity'.

Finally, verses 11–12 of Matthew 19 are understood in traditional fashion as treating the question of celibacy.

> They are, however, introduced by verse 10, in which the disciples infer that what Jesus has just said (cf. *houtōs*) implies that it is not appropriate or advantageous or expedient to marry. Yet nothing in verses 3–9 contains the slightest hint that avoidance of marriage is the best policy: indeed there is nothing which might give grounds even for misunderstanding. . . . So yet more evidence suggests that Matthew's account is somewhat dislocated.[5]

Protestants cite Matthew's account as another example of the historical development and amplification that took place in the early church as Jesus' teachings (tradition) were transmitted among the faithful. Catholics who hold this view find support for their belief 'that the Church has the power, not to abrogate the fundamental laws restated by its Founder, but to regulate their application taking personal situations into account.'[6]

Support for the Traditio-Historical View

It must be admitted that if the Erasmian interpretation of the exception clauses is assumed, critical scholars cannot be faulted for excising the clauses or attributing their presence to the hand of Matthew who supposedly found the absolute nature of Jesus' teaching inapplicable in his church. Though at times they have accused the gospel text of confusion where none exists,[7] scholars holding the traditio-historical view have done evangelicals a great service: they have provided the pressure needed to see that either the Erasmian interpretation must be abandoned or that a new view of inspiration should be adopted to take account of the historical developments that have supposedly taken place in the transmission of Jesus' teaching.[8] The latter option, however, confronts the evangelical with problems of a still more serious nature.

Tradition critics such as D.R. Catchpole hold that in remodelling Mark's account of Jesus' discussion with the Pharisees, Matthew has introduced a great deal of confusion. He finds four points of incoherence in Matthew's pericope.

(a) Verses 10–12 do not arise out of verses 3–9. (b) Verse 9 does not cohere with verses 4–8. (c) Verses 4–8 do not cohere with verse 3b [v. 3b contains a question of content, not a catch (*peirazō*) question]. (d) Verse 3b does not cohere with 3a [i.e., if the discussion is wholly within the Pharisaic schools ('for any cause at all') as v. 3b suggests, why does this merit *peirazō* language as in v. 3a?].[9]

Catchpole then asks what adjustments, if any, would remove these awkwardnesses. He feels that (a) is not a problem because two separate traditions on a different topic are combined. He says (b) however, cannot be solved simply by separating verse 9 from verses 4–8 because in Matthew's narrative verse 8 is not decisive enough to function as an ending. Tampering with verses 4–8 to bring them in line with verse 9 would be so far-reaching that another solution is preferred: 'either verse 9 has replaced another conclusion that followed verses 4–8, or the trouble is intrinsic to verse 9, i.e. its cause is *mē epi porneia*, which would then be secondary'.[10] These two solutions are felt to be very close alternatives.

In the case of (c) Catchpole feels that a drastic remodelling of verses 4–8 must occur to make them cohere with verse 3b, or we must modify verse 3b itself. 'This latter could hardly be other than the excision of *kata pasan aitian*.'[11] Finally, in case (d) either the removal of *peirazontes* (testing) or *kata pasan aitian* (for any cause at all) would solve the problem Catchpole perceives.

Two options emerge: (1) either a drastic remodelling of verses 4–8 and the excision of 'testing' which leaves only verses 3b and verse 9 of the actual debate; or (2) a retention of verses 4–8 and of 'testing', but the excision of 'for any cause at all' and 'except for immorality'. Catchpole feels overwhelming probability favours the second of these alternatives.

Especially interesting is Catchpole's argument that Mark 10: 12, which assumes divorce proceedings initiated by a woman, is not impossible on Jesus' lips in a Palestinian society. He points to Paul's remark in 1 Corinthians 7: 11a where he seems to be drawing on a tradition prohibiting the remarriage of a woman who carries through divorce proceedings (cf. Salome and Herodias),[12] and Paul associates that tradition with Jesus.[13] The bipartite form in Mark 10: 11–12 (directed to men and women who may divorce) is extremely similar to the bipartite form in 1 Corinthians 7: 10 and 11b, and a tradition branding the remarriage of a divorced woman as wrong is reflected in verse 11a.[14] Despite these possible parallels the vast majority of scholars agree that in a Jewish environment the right to divorce was in principle restricted to the man. The passage in Mark is clearly formulated with the Greco-Roman situation in mind.[15]

The remainder of Catchpole's article consists of a defence of the two-document hypothesis where he answers all the objections that have been raised against it in the light of the unique features of Matthew 19 and Mark 10.[16] Some of the ardent defenders of the two-document hypothesis have conceded that Matthew's version seems more original than Mark and this has created some problems.[17] But Catchpole does an excellent job of defending the priority of Mark.

Critique of the Traditio-Historical View

In responding to Catchpole's understanding of Matthew 19: 3–12, we can hardly see the internal problem he sees in verse

3. The Pharisees were not merely asking for information or clarification but were trying to elicit a response by which they could accuse Jesus. The disappointing thing about Catchpole's article was his failure to consider the fine article by Q. Quesnell[18] on the close relationship between verses 3–9 with what follows in verses 10–12. We have discussed this fully in chapter 2 of our study, and though we do not agree completely with Quesnell, he rightly challenged the disjuncture that commentators saw between verses 3–9 and 10–12. We understand verses 10–12 to continue Jesus' teaching on the indissolubility of marriage. On this understanding Matthew's account is every bit as authoritative and powerful as the Marcan account and the critical problems vanish.

Furthermore, this older critical approach makes Matthew a very poor editor of the divorce sayings. The difficulties have been fully set out earlier in chapter 6 in the critique of the Erasmian view. Particularly one should note the two different senses of 'put away' in 19:9, and the way that Jesus contradicts Himself. Having totally condemned the Pharisaic positions in verses 3–8, He suddenly retracts in verse 9 accepting the validity of the Shammaite stance. What is more, on this view Matthew took it into his own hands to change his Lord's teaching; unlike Paul who carefully transmitted what Jesus had said. Even without a high view of biblical inspiration, it is surely poor exegesis which portrays Matthew as so inept in his handling of Jesus' traditions. As B. Vawter has said:

> The most telling argument against this position is its plain *arbitrariness*. It may be rightly asked whether the respect accorded to the Lord's logia elsewhere in the gospels has prepared us to believe that an evangelist could have introduced into one of them, on whatever authority, a clause which is surely not an adaptation or an extension of Christ's teaching, but, as the interpreters themselves affirm, a formal contradiction of it. Interpolations should be presumed with difficulty. This is wholly *a priori*. For laudable theological reasons they do not permit Jesus to contradict himself, thus they lay the blame on his recorder. Would not the more critical approach lie in first determining whether the alleged contradiction exists in fact? There is no great show of evidence that this approach has been pursued, or that these exegetes have examined very thoroughly their own premises before bowing in the ultimate refuge, the tampered text.[19]

When it comes to the differences in the synoptic accounts of Jesus' divorce sayings we believe A. Isaksson's analysis is more plausible than the reorganisation suggested by Catchpole. Isaksson begins with an incredibly uncomplicated, yet sound approach. 'The different versions of the logion must be adjudged to be different formulations of a common original tradition and not deliberate changes which an individual evangelist made from two different sources (Mk and Q).'[20] He continues with sound reasoning based upon what is clear in all the synoptic accounts:

> If we regard the original form of the logion as being the one which says that the husband makes himself guilty of adultery if he divorces his wife and marries another woman, the other forms of the logion can quite simply be understood as examples of the applications and expositions of this original form which the Christian churches felt the need to make. From this original formulation it was clear to the disciples that Jesus maintained the indissolubility of marriage. What conclusions could they draw from this?[21]

Starting with the saying that a man who divorces his wife and marries another commits adultery, we can see that the following conclusions were drawn from Jesus' pronouncement on divorce:

> (1) If the husband commits adultery by divorcing his wife and re-marrying, the wife also commits adultery if she divorces her husband and re-marries (Mk 10. 12). (2) Since marriage is indissoluble, it is against the divorced wife that the husband commits adultery, since this first marriage still subsists (Mk 10. 11). (3) Since marriage is indissoluble, the man who marries a divorced woman commits adultery (Lk. 16. 18b, and Mt. 5. 32b). (4) Since marriage is indissoluble, it is also forbidden for a man to divorce his wife, even though he himself does not re-marry. It may happen that his divorced wife may re-marry and in that case he is morally guilty of the fact of adultery in respect of this still subsisting marriage (Mt. 5. 32a).[22]

Catchpole's view makes Matthew a ham-fisted botcher of Mark's material. It is much better to see both evangelists as intelligent, coherent authors, adapting, but not distorting, the traditions of Jesus for the particular needs of their readers in the way Lohmeyer and Schmauch have suggested:

Mark's composition is carried out in three parts; he begins with Moses' legislation concerning divorce, primarily in order to set it aside, then sets forth the fundamental Law of Creation which makes marriage indissoluble, and in his supplement for the disciples he adds two prohibitions for husband and wife, that if divorced they may not marry again. *This composition is determined throughout by interest in the reader for whom the Mosaic divorce-practice is unimportant. Hence it is set aside at the outset before the positive command follows. Then an explanation is given to the disciples which appears to interpret this fundamental law for them, as the future missionaries to the Gentiles.*

For the audience of Matthew, on the other hand, the marriage and divorce regulations of Moses are completely familiar. *Thus there is no need to describe what Moses had commanded* and what, therefore, would be the consequence if one divorced one's wife.

Instead, it is possible to begin immediately by citing the decision according to the law of Genesis. The Mosaic regulation then appears next as an objection to this decision, and this is quite properly placed in the mouth of the antagonists. Moses is then authoritatively set aside, and it is possible in a conclusion to state definitively that any new marriage by a divorced man is adultery. *It is a Controversy-dialogue which lies before us, following the plan: Question/Answer, Objection/ Refutation, Conclusion.*[23]

From this perspective it is unnecessary to determine which account is more original. Each record stands on its own and communicates the teaching of Jesus on divorce and remarriage to their respective audiences.

Conclusion

For the above reasons more recent tradition critics have given up the Erasmian interpretation of the exception clauses. The problem of viewing the exception clauses as a special Matthean addition is greatly diminished if they are understood along the lines of any of the other interpretations we have examined, whether early church, unlawful marriages, betrothal or preteritive views. In the latter cases all that Matthew is doing is making explicit something taken for granted by Jesus' first hearers. But simply because the Matthean exception clauses taken in one of these senses is so congruent with the rest of our Lord's teaching on divorce, we do not see any difficulty in Isaksson's view that Matthew 19:9 contains the precise original form of Jesus' teaching.

CHAPTER ELEVEN
Conclusions and Implications

Considering the brevity of Jesus' recorded remarks about divorce, the quantity of literature that they have generated is truly remarkable. This survey has tried to present the current scholarly theories as fairly as possible, to show their strengths and weaknesses, so that the reader can decide for himself or herself which is the most probable view. Though it appears certain that Jesus did not permit remarriage after divorce for any reason, the question remains as to how the exception clause should be precisely understood. The betrothal view seems mutually exclusive of all the others, and its simplicity and purity in permitting the divorce of an unconsummated marriage, while upholding the absolute indissolubility of a consummated marriage, is attractive. Yet we have problems with the restricted lexical nuance of 'unchastity'. The same is true of the unlawful marriages view. The interpretation that is hard to get a feeling for, perhaps because Jesus Himself was speaking in somewhat obscure terms (at least in Mark 10) to His unbelieving questioners, is the preteritive or 'no comment' view. This understanding could possibly have given rise to each of the other views in practical application, but we find its grammatical construction faulty.

It seems unlikely to us that Jesus 'permitted' divorce for a particular sexual sin via the exception clauses, for this would conflict with His absolute prohibition of divorce in Matthew 19: 4–8 and the loyal covenant love exhibited by Hosea for unfaithful Gomer. It seems safest to say that Jesus gave an absolute prohibition of divorce *and* remarriage. Should a man be forced to put away his unfaithful wife, as the Jewish readers of Matthew's Gospel would have been, Jesus does not hold him responsible for breaking His command not to divorce. The guilt and the blame lie with the woman who is an adulteress by reason of her offence. And should the hard-heartedness of one of the partners result in an unfortunate divorce, lack of forgiveness and a refusal to be reconciled, Jesus requires His disciples to remain single.

One thing appears certain from this study: the New Testament and the early church as a whole are *not* vague or confusing when it comes to the question of remarriage after divorce. It is clear that Jesus said that a man may have one wife or no wife, and if someone puts away their partner for whatever reason they must remain single.

Some of the precepts of Scripture are difficult to accept and often make the Christian uncomfortable as he considers the implications of these teachings for his own life and the lives of those to whom he ministers. This is certainly true with respect to the conclusions we have reached in this study. One of the most difficult problems facing a minister of the Gospel is counselling the divorced and those already remarried. How does one move from a careful exegesis of the relevant texts to the heartbreaking problems of those who seek his counsel in this matter? Carefully exegeting the texts is one thing, but the manner in which God's word is conveyed to believers facing divorce and the issue of remarriage is quite another. There are ethical problems involved, certainly,[1] but there are also standards involved for those who by faith desire to be Christ's disciples and experience His joy in fullest measure (John 14: 20; 15: 1–11; 17: 13). Jesus' disciples *did* object to His firm stand on divorce and remarriage. They said, 'If the relationship of the man with his wife is like this, it is better not to marry' (Matt. 19: 10). This attitude makes the attractiveness of marriage contingent upon the possibility of divorce and remarriage to another. The disciples had an anthropocentric outlook. They felt that their designs for their own 'well-being' *had* to be better than their Creator's design just communicated to them via the Messiah Himself. But remarriage was clearly not better for them in His teaching. He said it was adultery.

Jesus then responded to their objections: 'Not all men can accept this statement, but only those to whom it has been given.' This does not mean that Jesus' standard for the marriage relationship applies to *some* Christians but not to *all* Christians. 'Those to whom it has been given' *are* Jesus' disciples, the ones to whom He granted the knowledge of 'the mysteries of the kingdom of heaven' (Matt. 13: 11 = Mark 4: 11, cf. vv. 33–4). All who would be Christ's disciples are called to this standard of marriage just as they are called to lay down their lives for their friends (John 15: 13); to cut off hand and foot and pluck out their eye to avoid sin (Matt. 5: 29–30); to take up their cross, which is God's will for their life, and follow Christ no matter what it may cost (Mark 8: 34); and to believe that 'whoever wishes to save his life shall lose it, but whoever loses his life for My sake shall find it' (Matt. 16: 25).[2] Though the standards appear to be impossible our Lord would say to us, 'With men this is impossible, but with God all things are possible' (Matt. 19: 26). He calls each of His disciples to a life of grace and faithful dependence upon Him so that He might bring about His own image in us whether He uses a good marriage or a broken marriage to accomplish this end.

It is essential to hold before our people continually the ideal that human marriage should reflect the union between Christ and the church. As Christ loved us sinners and gave Himself for us, so Christian husbands and wives are called to love their partners even if their love is inadequately responded to. As God remains faithful despite our frequent faithlessness, so even a divorced believer who remains single out of loyalty to Christ and the former partner can be a vivid, powerful symbol of the enduring love of God for sinful mankind. When the world sees this quality of love they, too, may wish to know the God who so loved them while they were yet sinners.

Those couples who have already remarried after divorce may be wondering how their situation fits into all of this. We believe that you should see that your present marriage is now God's will for you. You should seek to be the best husband or wife you can be, rendering to each other your full marital duty. If you come to the realisation that Jesus calls remarriage after divorce the sin of adultery, then call sin 'sin' rather than seek to justify what you have done. We believe this will bring great freedom to your marriage and will break down barriers to ministry you may have encountered before. As one divorced and remarried couple responded to the apologetic attitude of the dean of a Bible Institute as he explained their policy of not granting degrees to those who remarry after divorce: 'Don't apologize for your policy. We know now that what we have done is wrong; but that isn't going to keep us from preparing to serve the Lord as best as we possibly can.'

We also have theological reasons for believing that maintaining your present marriage will accomplish the greatest good. First, Deuteronomy 24: 1–4 clearly forbids restoration of marriage to a divorced partner after one of the partners has consummated a second marriage. Such a restoration of marriage is called 'an abomination before the Lord' (Deut. 24: 4). Now according to our understanding,[3] this Deuteronomic regulation is based on the idea that marriage creates a permanent relationship between the spouses – 'the two become one flesh' – a principle endorsed by the New Testament. Ideally, where Jesus' principles have been understood and obeyed, the situation envisaged by Deuteronomy should never arise for His followers. But where it has arisen and remarriage following divorce has occurred, it would seem wisest to adhere to the Deuteronomic provision. To act otherwise and seek to return to your former partner may or may not succeed, but it will surely bring great grief to your second partner. Secondly, all Christians, from the apostle Peter onward, recognise that their past sins have inevitable consequences which we cannot alter. But however blatant our past denials, Christ still offers us forgiveness and the opportunity to love and follow Him in the future (John 21: 15–19). If this study has perturbed you, because of your own past failures or because of the way you have counselled divorcees, do not forget that Christ came to *save sinners*. None of us can pretend to be above reproach in the realm of sexual morality when we measure ourselves by our Lord's standards (Matt. 5: 27–30; John 8: 1–11). All of us need to claim His daily forgiveness and grace if we are to be transformed into His likeness. 'If we say that we have no sin, we are deceiving ourselves, and the truth is not in us. If we confess our sins, He is faithful and righteous to forgive us our sins and to cleanse us from all unrighteousness' (1 John 1: 8–9). So let us praise Him for His mercy and dedicate ourselves anew to serve Him more faithfully in the future.

We wish to conclude our study with some penetrating words from Geoffrey Bromiley's little book *God and Marriage* (1980). He reminds us that marriage belongs to the temporal and not to the eternal order. Jesus told the cynical Sadducees that in the resurrection people neither marry nor are given in marriage (Matt. 22: 30). And even though marriage may be a fulfilling and wonderful relationship between one man and one woman in this life, marriage has an eschatological limit.

Life *can* go on apart from marriage; and those whose marriages have been broken must remember their citizenship in God's kingdom. Bromiley writes:

> In the world of the fall the redemptive work of God carries with it a service of God – not necessarily a technical ministry but a service according to God's will, by God's appointment, and in God's discipleship – which means that some part of life, if not all, must be lived temporarily outside the regular patterns of God's created order.
>
> This reminds us of the order of priorities which Jesus demands in the calling of his disciples. What God requires must come before all else, the good as well as the bad. The followers of Jesus must be ready, should he will, to renounce even marriage for the sake of the gospel. They must be ready to obey God and not remarry after separation even though they might plead, as they often do, that they have a right to happiness or to the fulfillment of natural desires. To talk of a right to happiness is to delude onself. Happiness, when it is attained, is a gift from God and it cannot be attained, nor can human life be fulfilled, where there is conflict with God's stated will or a defiant refusal to see that true happiness and fulfillment lie only in a primary commitment to God's kingdom and righteousness. For God's sake some people may have to forego marriage, some may have to put it in a new perspective, and some who have broken their marriage may have to refrain from remarriage. Marriage is a good thing but it is not 'the one thing needful' (Luke 10: 42). Hence it may be – and in some instances it may have to be – surrendered.[4]

Jesus did not come to lay down a new 'law' on His disciples, one too strict for them to bear. He gave them a moral standard which, by God's grace, He expected His disciples to fulfil. He said that one of the distinguishing characteristics of His disciples is that they do not remarry after divorce. Christ came to give freedom, not for divorce and remarriage, but for marriage in its creational design. Jesus' disciples have the power of the indwelling Spirit of life and no longer have hearts of stone, nor are they subject to hard-heartedness when it comes to fulfilling God's commands. Though man will never perform perfectly, he is able to live on a plane far above that of failure. And if one thing or another leads to the tragedy of divorce, Christ's disciple has available that grace which is needed to remain single or be reconciled. The death of Christ itself has implications for the Christian husband and wife. It has resulted in Christ's taking upon Himself the cost of human unfaithfulness. He has broken its power. In Bromiley's words: 'Living with *divine* reconciliation as a constant fact in human life means living with *mutual* reconciliation as a constant fact. This makes indissoluble union a practical and attainable goal even for sinners.'[5]

APPENDIX

J.D.M. Derrett's
'No Further Relations View'

This view originated with J.D.M. Derrett and is presented in his work, *Law in the New Testament*. Derrett's fundamental consideration is the need to go to Genesis first in order to construe the provisions of Deuteronomy. In Genesis 2: 24 God established the doctrine of 'one flesh' that derives from the mating of two beings. The text shows that one is not entitled sexually to enjoy a woman who is not 'his', and 'his' means exclusively his. No interpretation of Moses (esp. Deut. 24: 1–4) which conflicts with this fundamental can possibly be right. Nor did Jesus abrogate or disapprove of the legislation of Moses. Furthermore, the seventh commandment, 'You shall not commit adultery' (*lō' tin'āp*, Exod. 20: 13 [14]), is in Derrett's opinion an inaccurate rendering of the root *nā'ap*, which, in other contexts, is associated with fornication or sexual irregularity in general (Jer. 3: 3–8; Ezek. 23: 37; Josh. 7: 4). A man's adultery is forbidden in Leviticus 18: 20, and Exodus 20: 17 forbids coveting a neighbour's wife, while incest and harlotry are distinctly forbidden elsewhere. Thus the seventh commandment is understood to forbid any kind of sexual intercourse between unmarried people who will not or cannot marry.

As for Deuteronomy 24: 1–4, it is concerned solely with the fact that a divorced wife can *not* be taken back by her former husband 'since she has been defiled' (Keil and Delitzsch). The wife's intercourse with a third party has for ever defiled the original and still remaining 'one flesh'. Deuteronomy 24: 1–4 prohibits divorce *and* remarriage – a prohibition which, contrary to Moses' original intent, Jewish practice contravened. Moses permitted divorce for 'hardness of heart' (Matt. 19: 8), which has nothing to do with human compassion but implies human weakness in the face of moral temptation (i.e., if the original husband continues living with a defiled wife he is tempted to continue sexual relations which would, in turn, defile him, and he, too, would commit *nā'ap*). Likewise, the stress in Jesus' divorce teaching lies on the prohibition of remarriage. Mark 10: 11 is literally correct and Luke 16: 18 agrees: one who divorces and marries again is an adulterer vis-à-vis his first wife, because he breaks the commandment against *nā'ap* in that the original one flesh cannot be broken.

Matthew is equally correct, though it gives rise to what Derrett calls the 'incorrect (soft) interpretation . . . the superficial view' (his description of the evangelical Protestant or Erasmian view). Matthew says one who divorces *for unchastity* is avoiding 'adultery' at home, which would be committed if he were to continue sexual relations within this now defiled, yet still remaining, 'one flesh' monstrosity (now three in one). Matthew permits the innocent man to clean his home, to avoid temptation, though the welfare of the divorced wife should be a righteous Jewish husband's concern. But the husband must remain unmarried whether his wife marries her lover or not – for as long as she lives the 'one flesh' (though now a defiled plurality) still remains – and any sexual relations on his part = *nā'ap*. As the response of the disciples indicates (Matt. 19: 10), Jesus proved that the *Torah* taught a stricter way of righteousness than anyone could have desired. Derrett finds support for his view in Hermas *Mandate* 4.1.4–10. [Cf. *TDNT* 6: 592 lines 2–5]

Abbreviations

The abbreviations of the works cited in the notes correspond to the listing in the 'Instructions for Contributors', in the *Journal of Biblical Literature* 95 (1976) 339–46. Abbreviations from that listing that are used here, as well as abbreviations for works not listed in the *JBL* article, are identified below.

AB	Anchor Bible
ACR	*Australian Catholic Record*
ACW	Ancient Christian Writers
AER	*American Ecclesiastical Review*
AfER	*African Ecclesiastical Review*
AnBib	Analecta biblica

ANF   The Ante-Nicene Fathers
APOT   R.H. Charles (ed.), *Apocrypha and Pseudepigrapha of the Old Testament*
ASNU   Acta seminarii neotestamentici upsaliensis
ATANT   Abhandlungen zur Theologie des Alten und Neuen Testaments
BA   *Biblical Archaeologist*
BAGD   W. Bauer, W.F. Arndt, F.W. Gingrich, and F.W. Danker, *Greek-English Lexicon of the New Testament*
BDB   F. Brown, S.R. Driver, and C.A. Briggs, *Hebrew and English Lexicon of the Old Testament*
BDF   F. Blass, A. Debrunner, and R.W. Funk, *A Greek Grammar of the New Testament*
BGBE   Beiträge zur Geschichte der biblischen Exegese
Bib   *Biblica*
BJRL   *Bulletin of the John Rylands University Library of Manchester*
BLE   *Bulletin de littérature ecclésiastique*
BR   *Biblical Research*
BSac   *Bibliotheca Sacra*
BT   *The Bible Translator*
BTB   *Biblical Theology Bulletin*
CBQ   *Catholic Biblical Quarterly*
CD   Codex Damascus, Cairo (Genaizah text of the [Damascus] document)
CGTC   Cambridge Greek Testament Commentary
CH   *Church History*
ChM   *The Churchman*
CleR   *Clergy Review*
CTJ   *Calvin Theological Journal*
CTM   *Concordia Theological Monthly*
DTC   *Dictionnaire de théologie catholique*
EGT   W.R. Nicoll (ed.), *The Expositor's Greek Testament*
EncJud   *Encyclopaedia judaica* (1971)
ERE   J. Hastings (ed.), *Encyclopedia of Religion and Ethics*
ETL   *Ephemerides theologicae lovanienses*
EvQ   *Evangelical Quarterly*
Exp   *Expositor*
ExpTim   *Expository Times*
FC   Fathers of the Church
GGNT   A.T. Robertson, *A Grammar of the Greek New Testament in the Light of Historical Research*
GKC   *Gesenius' Hebrew Grammar*, ed. E. Kautzsch, tr. A.E. Cowley
Greg   *Gregorianum*
HeyJ   *Heythrop Journal*
HNTC   Harper's New Testament Commentaries

HTR	Harvard Theological Review
ICC	International Critical Commentary
IDB	G.A. Buttrick (ed.), Interpreter's Dictionary of the Bible
IDBSup	Supplementary volume to IDB (1976)
Int	Interpretation
ITQ	Irish Theological Quarterly
JAOS	Journal of the American Oriental Society
JBC	R.E. Brown et al. (eds.), The Jerome Biblical Commentary
JBL	Journal of Biblical Literature
JE	The Jewish Encyclopedia
JEH	Journal of Ecclesiastical History
JES	Journal of Ecumenical Studies
JETS	Journal of the Evangelical Theological Society
JJS	Journal of Jewish Studies
JLA	The Jewish Law Annual
JPsT	Journal of Psychology and Theology
JSNT	Journal for the Study of the New Testament
JSOT	Journal for the Study of the Old Testament
JSS	Journal of Semitic Studies
JT	Journal of Theology
JTS	Journal of Theological Studies
KJV	King James Version
LCC	Library of Christian Classics
LCL	Loeb Classical Library
LSJ	Liddell-Scott-Jones, Greek-English Lexicon
MHT	J.H. Moulton, W.F. Howard, and N. Turner, A Grammar of New Testament Greek (4 vols.)
NASB	New American Standard Bible
NCBC	New Century Bible Commentary
NEB	New English Bible
NICNT	New International Commentary on the New Testament
NICOT	New International Commentary on the Old Testament
NIDNTT	C. Brown (ed.), The New International Dictionary of New Testament Theology
NIV	New International Version
NovT	Novum Testamentum
NovTSup	Novum Testamentum, Supplements
NRT	La nouvelle revue théologique
NPNF	Nicene and Post-Nicene Fathers
NTA	New Testament Abstracts
NTS	New Testament Studies
OTL	Old Testament Library
PAAJR	Proceedings of the American Academy of Jewish Research
PCB	M. Black and H.H. Rowley (eds.), Peake's Commentary on the Bible

PCTSA Proceedings of the Catholic Theological Society of America
PG   J. Migne, Patrologia graeca
RefJ   Reformed Journal
RestQ Restoration Quarterly
RevQ   Revue de Qumran
RHE   Revue d'histoire ecclésiastique
RSV   Revised Standard Version
Scr   Scripture
SJT   Scottish Journal of Theology
SCM   SCM Press
SNTSMS Society for New Testament Studies Monograph Series
TBT   The Bible Today
TCGNT B.M. Metzger, A Textual Commentary on the Greek New
       Testament (1971)
TD   Theology Digest
TDNT   G. Kittel and G. Friedrich (eds.), Theological Dictionary of the
       New Testament
TDOT   G. J. Botterweck and H. Ringgren (eds.), Theological Dictionary
       of the Old Testament
Theol Theology
Them   Themelios
ThW   Third Way
TOTC   Tyndale Old Testament Commentaries
TS   Theological Studies
TZ   Theologische Zeitschrift
UBSGNT United Bible Societies Greek New Testament
VT   Vetus Testamentum
ZNW   Zeitschrift für die neutestamentliche Wissenschaft

NOTES

Introduction

1. See, for example, C.G. Montefiore, *The Synoptic Gospels* (2nd ed.; London: Macmillan, 1927) 1: 225–36; 2: 65–7, 257–65, 535–6; T.W. Manson, *The Sayings of Jesus* (London: SCM, 1957) 135–8; D. Crossan, 'Divorce and Remarriage in the New Testament', in *The Bond of Marriage* (ed. W.W. Bassett; Notre Dame, Ind.: Univ. of Notre Dame Press, 1968) 1–33; R.N. Soulen, 'Marriage and Divorce: A Problem in New Testament Interpretation', *Int* 23 (1969) 439–50; P. Hoffmann, 'Jesus' Saying about Divorce and its Interpretation in the New Testament Tradition', trans. J.T. Swann, in *Concilium* 55: *The Future of Marriage as Institution* (ed. F. Böckle; New York: Herder and Herder, 1970) 51–66; B. Vawter, 'Divorce and the New Testament', *CBQ* 39 (1977) 528–42.
2. Major doctoral works that evidence familiarity with the literature and problems involved, none of which opt for the Erasmian exegesis, include A. Isaksson, *Marriage and Ministry in the New Temple: A Study with Special Reference to Matt. 19. 13 [sic]-12 and 1. Cor. 11. 3–16*, trans. N. Tomkinson with J. Gray (ASNU 24; Lund: Gleerup; Copenhagen: Munsgaard, 1965); D.L. Dungan, *The Sayings of Jesus in the Churches of Paul: The Use of the Synoptic Tradition in the Regulation of Early Church Life* (Philadelphia: Fortress, 1971) 81–135; R. Banks, *Jesus and the Law in the Synoptic Tradition* (Cambridge: Univ. Press, 1975) 146–59; J.P. Meier, *Law and History in Matthew's Gospel: A Redactional Study of Mt. 5: 17–48* (Rome: Biblical Institute Press, 1976) 140–50. The two most learned studies on this subject appear to be those of J. Dupont, *Mariage et divorce dans l'évangile: Matthieu 19, 3–12 et parallèles* (Bruges: Desclée de Brouwer, 1959) and H. Baltensweiler, *Die Ehe im Neuen Testament: Exegetische Untersuchungen über Ehe, Ehelosigkeit und Ehescheidung* (ATANT 52; Zürich: Zwingli Verlag, 1967).
3. There are a few exceptions, but even these have failed to interact

with the vast body of literature available in journals and numerous other studies. Worthy of mention is the small, yet theologically significant, book by G. Bromiley, *God and Marriage* (Grand Rapids: Eerdmans, 1980) esp. pp. 38–46. Bromiley is the translator of many German volumes including the *Theological Dictionary of the New Testament*. There is also the unpublished work by G.J. Wenham, 'Marriage and Divorce: The Legal and Social Setting of the Biblical Teaching', a memorandum submitted to the Church of Ireland Committee on the remarriage of divorced persons (Queen's Univ., n.d.). This 60-page study is summarised in *Third Way*, Oct. 20th, 1977, pp. 3–5; Nov. 3rd, 1977, pp. 7–9; and Nov. 17th, 1977, pp. 7–9.

4. All translations are from the *New American Standard Bible* unless indicated otherwise.

5. Here Jesus connects the prohibition of coveting found in the tenth commandment (Exod. 20: 17; Deut. 5: 21) with the prohibition of adultery found in the seventh (Exod. 20: 14; Deut. 5: 18).

6. This is structurally suggested by the shortening of the formula 'You have heard that . . .' (*Ekousate hoti errethē*; Matt. 5: 21, 27, 33, 38, 43) to 'It was said' (*Errethē*) in 5: 31 and the link between 5: 27–30 and vv. 31–2 established by *de* (and). The formula is resumed by *Palin* (furthermore, BAGD, *palin*, 3) in v. 33. This is lexically suggested by the occurrence of *moicheuō* (to commit adultery) and its cognates (Matt. 5: 27, 28, 32a, 32b). Cf. R.H. Gundry, *Matthew: A Commentary on His Literary and Theological Art* (Grand Rapids: Eerdmans, 1982) 89.

7. Cf. A.B. Bruce, 'The Synoptic Gospels', in *EGT* (ed. W.R. Nicoll) 1: 109; R.H. Charles, *The Teaching of the New Testament on Divorce* (London: Wms. & Norgate, 1921) 25 n.1; Montefiore, *Synoptic Gospels*, 2: 66; Hoffmann, 'Jesus' Saying about Divorce', 60: 'But if she has already committed adultery he is not guilty, for she has herself broken the marriage by her deed.'

8. See chapter 2.

9. See chapter 7.

10. The most recent defenders of the Erasmian view contend for this broader understanding of *porneia* in Matthew's exception clauses. See further chapter 4.

11. Six are treated extensively in this study. J.D.M. Derrett's (*Law in the New Testament* [London: Darton, Longman & Todd, 1970] 363–88) very interesting 'no further relations' view is summarised in the Appendix. It may be subsumed under the early church view. The 'inclusive' and 'interpretative' interpretations are not sufficiently supportable to warrant discussion in this study. On these last two views see B. Vawter's ('The Divorce Clauses in Mt 5, 32 and 19, 9,' *CBQ* 16 [1954] 160–2) discussion and critique.

12. That this interpretation still reigns in evangelical circles is evident by articles like J.R.W. Stott's, 'The Biblical Teaching on Divorce', *ChM* 85 (1971) 165–74, and P.H. Wiebe's 'The New Testament on Divorce and Remarriage: Some Logical Implications', *JETS* 24 (1981) 131–8. The latter article makes no attempt to exegete the texts and assumes the correctness of the Erasmian exegesis.

13. One of the primary motivations for publishing our research is the realisation that no layman or pastor would have the time or resources to pursue a comprehensive study of the subject of divorce and remarriage. Evangelical works in print on this issue have also failed to accomplish this task.

14. See chapter 4, n.4.

Chapter 1

1. E. Flesseman-van Leer, *Tradition and Scripture in the Early Church* (Van Gorcum's Theologische Bibliotheek 26; Assen, Neth.: Van Gorcum, 1954) 9.

2. For a superb illustration of this where Granville Sharp's rule is checked with the interpretations of the Greek writers, see C. Kuehne, 'The Greek Article and the Doctrine of Christ's Deity (Part III)', *JT* 14 (March 1974) 11–20. Daniel B. Wallace brought this to our attention.

3. J.T. McNeill, ed., *Calvin: Institutes of the Christian Religion* (LCC 20–1; Philadelphia: Westminster, 1960) 1: 18. Cf. A.N.S. Lane, 'Calvin's Use of the Fathers and the Medievals', *CTJ* 16 (1981) 149–205.

4. D.F. Wright, ed., *Common Places of Martin Bucer* (Courtenay Library of Reformation Classics 4; Abingdon: Sutton Courtenay, 1972) 40–1.

5. John Jewel, *An Apology of the Church of England* (ed. J.E. Booty; Ithaca, N.Y.: Cornell Univ., 1963) 41.

6. Ibid , 135.

7. H. Crouzel, *L'église primitive face au divorce du premier au cinquième siècle* (Paris: Beauchesne). Also J.P. Arendzen, 'Ante-Nicene Interpretations of the Sayings on Divorce', *JTS* 20 (1919) 230–41; G.H. Joyce, *Christian Marriage: An Historical and Doctrinal Study* (2nd ed.; Heythrop Series 1; London: Sheed and Ward, 1948) 304–31. Others who find the early church view most convincing but are unable to speak as confidently as Crouzel, include: E. Schillebeeckx, *Marriage: Human Reality and Saving Mystery* (New York: Sheed and Ward, 1965) 145–55; A.J. Bevilacqua, 'History of the Indissolubility of Marriage', *PCTSA* 22 (1967) 253–308; W. Rordorf, 'Marriage in the New Testament and in the Early Church', *JEH* 20 (1969) 193–210. Another good survey of early Fathers may be found in J.

Bonsirven, *Le divorce dans le Nouveau Testament* (Paris: Desclée, 1948) 61–75.

8. Cf. T.P. Considine, 'The Pauline Privilege', *ACR* 40 (1963) 111–13; Schillebeeckx, *Marriage*, 283 n.72; Crouzel, *L'église primitive*, 274.

9. See the articles on 'Adultery' and 'Marriage' in Hastings *Encyclopedia of Religion and Ethics* and *The Jewish Encyclopedia*.

10. Contra N. Turner, 'The Translation of *Moichatai ep' Autēn* in Mark 10: 11', *BT* 7 (1956) 151–2; B. Schaller, '"Commits adultery with her", not "against her", Mk. 10^{11}', *ExpTim* 83 (1972) 107–8. Mark never uses the preposition *epi* c. acc. to mean 'with'. He often uses it to mean 'against' (3: 24, 25, 26; 13: 8, 12; 14: 48).

11. Cf. F.L. Cross, *The Early Christian Fathers* (London: Gerald Duckworth, 1960) 23–4. J.A.T. Robinson (*Redating the New Testament* (Philadelphia: Westminster, 1976] 319–22) would date Hermas about AD 85 at the latest.

12. Cf. Arendzen, 'Ante-Nicene Interpretations', 231; Schillebeeckx, *Marriage*, 145–6.

13. Cf. 1 Cor. 7: 11, *menetō agamos* (let her remain unmarried). Paul's and Hermas' addition of 'remain single' seems to indicate clearly that legal divorce is involved, not simple separation.

14. The translation is our own from the Greek text in *The Apostolic Fathers* (LCL; Cambridge: Harvard Univ.; London: Wm. Heinemann, 1913) 2: 78, 80.

15. Bevilacqua, 'History', 254. On the *Lex Julia* see P. Corbett, *The Roman Law of Marriage* (Oxford: Clarendon, 1930) 133–46.

16. Crouzel, *L'église primitive*, 51.

17. Ibid., 50. This was also observed by K. Lake, 'The Earliest Christian Teaching on Divorce', *Exp* 10 (1910) 425–7.

18. J.A. Sherlock, Review of *L'église primitive face au divorce*, by H. Crouzel, *TS* 33 (1972) 334–5. R.H. Charles (*The Teaching of the New Testament on Divorce* [London: Wms. & Norgate, 1921] 106) counters his own argument to this effect when he adds: 'Yet, according to the use he makes of the saying of our Lord . . . remarriage after divorce appears to be absolutely forbidden.'

19. V. 6d reads: *can de apolysas tēn gynaika heteran gamēsē, kai autos moichatai*.

20. A.J. Bellinzoni, *The Sayings of Jesus in the Writings of Justin Martyr* (NovT Sup. 17; Leiden: Brill, 1967) 1. Cf. C.C. Richardson's remarks in LCC 1: 232–3.

21. Bellinzoni, *Sayings of Jesus*, 140. D.A. Hagner (*The Use of the Old and New Testaments in Clement of Rome* [NovT Sup 34; Leiden: Brill, 1973] 283n.2, 302–3) criticises Bellinzoni's attempt to find a Gospel harmony behind similar sayings. Yet Tatian, Justin's pupil, did produce a full Gospel harmony.

22. Crouzel, *L'église primitive*, 54 (cf. ANF 1: 167; FC 6: 48; LCC 1: 250).

23. Trans. by C.C. Richardson, LCC 1: 230. Cf. Rordorf, 'Marriage in the New Testament', 204.

24. *Legatio Pro Christianis* 33 (*PG* 6. 965 ff.). Trans. by J.H. Crehan, ACW, 23: 74–5. Richardson's (LCC 1: 337) translation following the Scripture quote is as follows: 'Thus a man is forbidden both to put her away whose virginity he has ended, and to marry again. He who severs himself from his first wife, even if she is dead, is an adulterer in disguise. He resists the hand of God, for in the beginning God created one man and one woman. But the adulterer breaks the fellowship based on the union of flesh with flesh for sexual intercourse.' The text and meaning at the very end is doubtful.

25. Arendzen, 'Ante-Nicene Interpretations', 232–3; Joyce, *Christian Marriage*, 591; Bevilacqua, 'History', 271; etc.

26. Crouzel, *L'église primitive*, 60. Rordorf ('Marriage in the New Testament', 204, 205 n.2) leans toward Crouzel's view but is in doubt.

27. Arendzen, 'Ante-Nicene Interpretations', 233.

28. Such feelings may also have been influenced by the prevailing asceticism and abstinence that characterised both philosophy and religion in Roman society (P.E. Harrell, 'The History of Divorce and Remarriage in the Ante-Nicene Church' [Th.D. dissertation, Boston University, 1965] 10–18, 167–9). It also seems clear that there was a fairly strong feeling that a second marriage, though not forbidden, was not altogether creditable. 'This feeling was apparently shared by pagans and Christians without much distinction' (C.H. Dodd, 'New Testament Translation Problems II [1 Tim. 3: 2, 12; Titus 1: 6]', *BT* 28 [1977] 115). Did Christians find in the Roman ideal of single marriage an apparent similarity with their own religious tenets and thereby go beyond what is written? (cf. M. Lightman and W. Zeisel, 'Univira: An Example of Continuity and Change in Roman Society', *CH* 46 (1977) 19–32.) Against linking the 'husband of one wife' phrases in the Pastorals with the Roman *univira* see the articles summarised in *NTA* 3: 415; 12: 314; 16: 276.

29. Joyce, *Christian Marriage*, 584–600. Cf. E. Valton, 'Bigamie', *DTC* 2 (1905) 878–88; Wm. P. Le Saint, ACW 13: 112 n.4; Crouzel, *L'église primitive*, 374–6.

30. *Ad Autolycum* 3.13. Trans. by R.M. Grant (*Theophilus of Antioch: Ad Autolycum*. Oxford Early Christian Texts [Oxford: Clarendon, 1970] 119). Cf. ANF 2: 115.

31. Cf. Bellinzoni, *Sayings of Jesus*, 70–1. The relationship of Theophilus' text to Luke 16: 18b seems certain. The only change is the transfer of the participle *gamōn* (marries) to the beginning of the saying.

32. Note the *NIV* and *NEB* trans. of Matt. 5: 32b: 'And anyone who marries a woman *so* divorced commits adultery' [italics ours]. This

implies the qualification 'unjustly divorced' – i.e., not for unchastity – is to be understood from v. 32a (cf. *KJV*). Perhaps Theophilus *did* invert the two halves of Matt. 5: 32 to prevent confusion! Cf. Bonsirven, *Le divorce*, 64.

33. *Adversus Haereses* 3.3.4 (ANF 1: 416; LCC 1: 373–4). Cf. A.C. Perumalil, 'Are not Papias and Irenaeus competent to report on the Gospels?' *ExpTim* 91 (1980) 332–7.

34. *Adversus Haereses*, 4.15.2 (ANF 1: 480).

35. *Stromata* 2.23.145.3ff. Trans. by W. Wilson, ANF 2: 379.

36. Crouzel, *L'église primitive*, 71. Clement's exception clause is *plēn ei mē epi logō porneias* (PG 8: 1096). In *Stromata* 3.6.47 (LCC 2: 62; PG 8: 1149, 1152) Clement conflates the Matt. 19 and Mark 10 accounts, first reflecting Mark 10: 2b–5 then Matt. 19: 4–5. Then he writes: *Hōste ho apolyōn tēn gynaika chōris logou porneias poiei autēn moicheuthēnai* (Matt. 5: 32)! If we can learn anything from the patristic citations of the Matthean texts it is that they interpreted Matt. 19: 9 in the light of 5: 32. Cf. J. MacRory, 'Christian Writers of the First Three Centuries and St. Matt. xix. 9', *ITQ* 6 (1911) 172–85; H. Crouzel, 'Le texte patristique de Matthieu v. 32 et xix. 9', *NTS* 19 (1972) 98–119; 'Quelques remarques concernant le texte patristique de Mt 19, 9', *BLE* 82 (1981) 83–92. Also Bonsirven, *Le divorce*, 61–3.

37. *Commentary on Matthew* 14.24. Trans. by J. Patrick, ANF 10: 511.

38. *Stromata* 3.6.50. Trans. by J.E.L. Oulton and H. Chadwick, LCC 2: 63.

39. Q. Quesnell, '"Made Themselves Eunuchs for the Kingdom of Heaven" (Mt 19, 12),' *CBQ* 30 (1968) 347–9, esp. p. 348 n.23. We shall return to this possibility in the next chapter.

40. J.M. Ford, 'St Paul, the Philogamist (1 Cor. vii in Early Patristic Exegesis)', *NTS* 11 (1965) 327. Cf. J. Schneider, '*Eunouchos*', *TDNT* 2 (1964) 768.

41. J. Kodell, 'The Celibacy Logion in Matthew 19: 12', *BTB* 8 (1978) 21. Cf. T.V. Fleming, 'Christ and Divorce', *TS* 24 (1963) 113.

42. *Stromata* 3.1.4; 3.7.57. Cf. Augustine, *Adulterous Marriages* 2. 18–20 (FC 27: 126–32); Oulton and Chadwick, LCC 2: 42 n.9.

43. *Stromata* 3.12.82 (LCC 2: 78–9). Cf. Crouzel, *L'église primitive*, 74. For a synthesis of the bad and good aspects of Clement's view of marriage, see Oulton and Chadwick, LCC 2: 33–9; Rordorf, 'Marriage in the New Testament', 206–8.

44. Ford, 'St Paul, the Philogamist', 329.

45. *Commentary on Matthew* 14.23 (ANF 10: 510). Cf. Crouzel, *L'église primitive*, 83.

46. *Commentary on Matthew* 14.24 (ANF 10: 511). Cf. Crouzel, *L'église primitive*, 86.

47. *Commentary on Matthew* 14.16. Trans. by J. Patrick, ANF 10: 505.

48. 'Origen on 1 Corinthians', *JTS* 9 (1908) 500–14 (cf. Fragment in §33,

p. 501, line 47; Fragment in §35, p. 505, line 50). Cf. Crouzel, *L'église primitive*, 89.

49. *Commentary on Matthew* 14.24 (ANF 10: 511).

50. Crouzel, *L'église primitive*, 92.

51. Quite complete treatments in English of Tertullian on divorce and remarriage may be found in Arendzen, 'Ante-Nicene Interpretations', 233–6; Joyce, *Christian Marriage*, 306–8; and most importantly A.J. Bevilacqua, 'History', 254–9. Very helpful is *Tertullian: Treatises on Marriage and Remarriage*, trans. and annotated by W.P. Le Saint (ACW 13; Westminster, Maryland: Newman, 1951).

52. Le Saint, ACW 13: 67.

53. *De Patientia* 12. Trans. by S. Thelwall, ANF 3: 714–15. Cf. Crouzel, *L'église primitive*, 94–5.

54. *Ad Uxorem* 2.1. Trans. by Le Saint, ACW 13: 23.

55. So V.J. Pospishil, *Divorce and Remarriage: Towards a New Catholic Teaching* (New York: Herder and Herder, 1967) 143–4; W.W. Bassett, 'Divorce and Remarriage – The Catholic Search for a Pastoral Reconciliation: Part I', *AER* 162 (1970) 32–3. Contrast Le Saint's cautious discussion, ACW 13: 124 n. 76; 162 n.134; 163 n.136.

56. *Ad Uxorem* 2.2. Trans. by Le Saint, ACW 13: 27. Bonsirven (*Le divorce*, 68) comments: 'We also understand these lines to refer to an incomplete divorce, which seems to be indicated by the last sentence . . .'

57. *Adversus Marcionem* 4.34 (ANF 3: 405). The other texts in which Tertullian treats our subject include: *Adversus Marcionem* 5.7 (ANF 3: 443); *De Exhortatione Castitatis* 5 (ACW 13: 50–1); *De Monogamia* 5 (ACW 13: 78–80), 9 (ACW 13: 88–90), 11 (ACW 13: 93–8); *De Pudicita* 16.

58. Crouzel, *L'église primitive*, 103–8.

59. Studies antedating Crouzel's consider the teaching of a few of the Fathers to be ambiguous. Cf. W.T. Celestine-Sheppard, 'The Teaching of the Fathers on Divorce', *ITQ* 5 (1910) 402–15; MacRory, 'Christian Writers'; O. Rousseau, 'Divorce and Remarriage: East and West', *Concilium* 24 (1967) 113–38.

60. Quoted in Crouzel, *L'église primitive*, 269.

61. See S.B. Clark, *Man and Woman in Christ: An Examination of the Roles of Men and Women in Light of Scripture and the Social Sciences* (Ann Arbor, Mich.: Servant Books, 1980) 281–97.

62. A. Ott, *Die Auslegung der neutestamentliche Texte über die Ehescheidung* (Münster, 1911) 97, quoted in Crouzel, *L'église primitive*, 273.

63. Pospishil, *Divorce and Remarriage*, 17.

64. W.R. O'Connor, 'The Indissolubility of a Ratified, Consummated Marriage', *ETL* 13 (1936) 692–722. Pospishil's bibliography incorrectly dates this article in 1963.

65. J.A. Fitzmyer, 'The Matthean Divorce Texts and Some New Pales-

tinian Evidence', *TS* 37 (1976) 225 n.98. One wonders what kind of homework the Church of England's Commission did in their preparation for their report, *Marriage, Divorce and the Church* (London: SPCK, 1971), when in section 18 (p. 11) they call Pospishil's book one of the 'more scholarly studies' on the subject of divorce and remarriage!

66. Crouzel reviewed Pospishil's book in *ITQ* 38 (1971) 21–41, and Pospishil reviewed Crouzel's book in *ITQ* 38 (1971) 338–47.
67. Crouzel, *L'église primitive*, 87.
68. J.J. Hughes, *JEH* 24 (1973) 61.
69. A reading of the Introduction in *The Bond of Marriage* (ed. W.W. Bassett; Notre Dame: Univ. Press, 1967) ix–xxi, and pp. 11–18 of Pospishil's book will reveal this on the Catholic side. For a glimpse of this on the evangelical Protestant side, see C. Brown, *'Chōrizō: Divorce, Separation and Remarriage'*, *NIDNTT* 3 (1978) 535–43.
70. G.W. Bromiley, *God and Marriage* (Grand Rapids: Eerdmans, 1980) 41.
71. Cf. Augustine, *Adulterous Marriages* 2. 1–4 (FC 27: 101–5).
72. Crouzel, *L'église primitive*, 141 (cf. FC 28: 109; *Saint Basil: The Letters*, LCL 3: 248–9).
73. Crouzel, *L'église primitive*, 352.
74. Origen, *Commentary on Matthew* 14.23, cited by Crouzel, *L'église primitive*, 83 (cf. ANF 10: 510). For a summary of indications of pastoral lenience in the early church, see Crouzel, 372–4.
75. Quoted in Joyce, *Christian Marriage*, 310. Cf. C.J. Hefele, *A History of the Christian Councils* (trans. and ed. W.R. Clark; Edinburgh: T. & T. Clark, 1894) 1: 189–90; Crouzel, *L'église primitive*, 121–3.
76. Cf. G.W.H. Lampe, 'Church Discipline and the Interpretation of the Epistles to the Corinthians', in *Christian History and Interpretation: Studies Presented to John Knox* (eds. W.R. Farmer, C.F.D. Moule, R.R. Niebuhr; Cambridge: Univ. Press, 1967) 337–61.

Chapter 2

1. We do not intend in this chapter to develop fully the exegetical arguments in favour of this view over the others we shall discuss. We shall return to a number of these points in chapter 6 where we critique the Erasmian view's handling of the NT data. Chapters 7–10 also contain exegetical discussions which strengthen the probability that a modified form of the early church view, at least in our opinion, has the best chance of answering to all of the available evidence.
2. On the whole matter of Jewish divorce and the possible figurative

aspect of Hillel's language, see I. Abrahams, *Studies in Pharisaism and the Gospels* (2 vols in 1; Cambridge: Univ. Press, 1917–24; reprint ed., New York: KTAV, 1967) 66–78. M. Mielziner (*The Jewish Law of Marriage and Divorce* [Cincinnati, Ohio: Bloch, 1884] 119 n.1) writes: 'The highly noble and humane tendencies of the founder and followers of this school [i.e., Hillel's] are too well known to permit us to ascribe this, their extension of the causes of divorce, to a loose view of the marriage relation.'

3. J. Jeremias, *New Testament Theology* (London: SCM, 1971) 1: 225. R. Le Déaut ('Targumic Literature and New Testament Interpretation', *BTB* 4 [1974] 251) suggests that if a certain Palestinian targumic interpretation of Gen. 1: 27 forms the background of Matt. 19, 'then the force of the argumentation appears even more clearly: the institution of the *couple* . . . the union of *one* man and of *one* woman corresponds to the intentions of the Creator and, in addition, for each marriage it is God himself who intervenes for the formation of this new couple'.

4. J. Dupont, *Mariage et divorce dans l'évangile: Matthieu 19, 3–12 et parallèles* (Bruges: Desclée, 1959) 55.

5. Ibid., 57.

6. Ibid., 65–6.

7. Ibid., 69.

8. Ibid., 100–2. We find it difficult to adopt the suggestion that the exception clause in Matt. 5: 32 (*parektos logou porneias*) stems from a pre-Matthean tradition and meant one thing, while the clause in Matt. 19: 9 (*mē epi porneia*) is Matthew's redaction and that he understood it and Matt. 5: 32 to mean something else. Cf. R.A, Guelich, *The Sermon on the Mount: A Foundation for Understanding* (Waco, Texas: Word, 1982) 204–11.

9. Dupont, *Mariage et divorce*, 149 n.3. Cf. Matt. 9: 2//Mark 2: 5 which requires Mark 2: 4 for understanding; cf. Mark 9: 43, 45, 47 with Matt. 5: 29–30 and 18: 8–9. For other examples see W.C. Allen, *A Critical and Exegetical Commentary on the Gospel according to S. Matthew* (3rd ed.; ICC; Edinburgh: T. & T. Clark, 1912) xvii–xix.

10. R.H. Gundry, *Matthew: A Commentary on His Literary and Theological Art* (Grand Rapids: Eerdmans, 1982) 90.

11. The comments of P.P. Levertoff and H.L. Goudge ('The Gospel according to St. Matthew', in *A New Commentary on Holy Scripture* [eds C. Gore, H.L. Goudge, A. Guillaume; New York: Macmillan, 1928] 174) on this point are interesting: 'The view that adultery dissolves the marriage bond not only degrades the conception of marriage by making its physical side the dominant consideration; it involves two absurdities. First, a man may cease to be married and yet be unaware of the fact. Secondly, it makes adultery, or the

pretence of having committed it, the one way to get rid of a marriage which has become distasteful, and so it puts a premium on adultery. If marriage is to be dissoluble at all, it should be also dissoluble upon other grounds than this, as sensible opponents of the Christian law recognize. The suffering which an unhappy marriage involves is not in the least confined to that caused by unfaithfulness . . .'

12. Some writers have argued from the Babylonian Talmud's Gemara on the tractate Gittin 90a–b that Shammaites allowed divorce for reasons other than adultery. But I. Sonne's study ('The Schools of Shammai and Hillel Seen from Within', in *Louis Ginzberg Jubilee Volume* [New York: American Academy for Jewish Research, 1945] 275–91) of the school of Shammai on Deuteronomy 24: 1 led him to say 'The cause of divorce . . . can be only a matter which affects the very basis of the marital bond, and such a cause can be only unfaithfulness' (288).

13. Dupont, *Mariage et divorce*, 102–3.

14. Supplying the elided elements in the Greek text we have: *hos an apolysē tēn gynaika autou, (ean) mē epi porneia (apolysē autēn), kai gamēsē allēn, moichatai*. Cf. M. Zerwick, *Biblical Greek* (adopted and trans. from the 4th Latin ed. by J. Smith; Rome, 1963) §442.

15. Gundry, *Matthew*, 90–1. It seems that Gundry must have read Dupont.

16. 'To suppose that the exception, "except for unchastity", is valid not just for the putting away, but also for the new marriage, it would be necessary to recognize that its place in the sentence is not well chosen. Matthew ought to have placed it after the second verb of the relative [i.e., after "marries"]. If, on the other hand, he wants only to specify the valid motive for putting away, he could not have constructed his sentence another way. To move forward the exception phrase [e.g., *hos an mē epi porneia apolysē* . . .] or move back the verb *apolysē* [e.g. *hos an tēn gynaika autou mē epi porneia apolysē kai gamēsē allēn*] would be to risk making the putting away obligatory: "If someone does not put away his wife for unchastity . . ."' (Dupont, *Mariage et divorce*, 148–49). See further chap. 6.

17. There remains the possibility that sexual sin is indeed a *de facto* exception to Jesus' teaching on the indissolubility of marriage. Thus when the genuine exception of sexual sin comes into play perhaps Jesus *does* use 'divorce' with the meaning of divorce with the right of the innocent party to remarry – the Gen. 2: 24 'one flesh' foundation of marriage having been annulled by a violation of that upon which it is predicated. We have already noted some problems with permitting the innocent but not the guilty partner to remarry. The OT understanding and use of the 'one flesh' concept to be considered in chap. 5 will present even greater problems for the exegete

who wishes to offer a biblical precedent for allowing the offended innocent party to remarry.

18. See further chap. 9.

19. Dupont, *Mariage et divorce*, 161–220.

20. There is a possible answer for the origin of the shorter reading in Matt. 19:9: the scribal error of homoioteleuton. *TCGNT* (48) argues against this probability by saying that B C* f^1 *al* read *moichatai* only once at the conclusion of the combined clauses. But this, however, involves the assumption that homoiotelenton had to come off the B etc. texts; but this scribal error could have occurred in one of B's ancestors. It is not certain that the longer reading in Matt. 19:9 simply arose through harmonisation with 5:32 (cf. Dupont, *Mariage et divorce*, 51–2 n.3 and pp. 81–5). J.K. Elliott ('The United Bible Societies' Textual Commentary Evaluated', *NovT* 17 [1975] 145–6) points out that homoiotelenton regularly caused the accidental shortening of texts and that scribes are more likely to omit accidentally than to add deliberately. Notice also the significant split in the Alexandrian readings: א (4th cent.) alone supports the shorter reading. The longer reading is supported by C W (both 5th cent.) p^{25} (4th cent.) and B (4th cent.). The longer reading is further supported by f^1 f^{13} the Majority text, lat sy^{ph} and bo. C (3rd corrector) D L a few Itala MSS and a few Latin Fathers of the 4th–5th centuries also support the shorter text. The other Fathers, including the ante-Nicene prior to all our present MSS, word it like Matt. 5:32. Recent scholarship on this issue may point to Tatian's *Diatessaron* (*c.* 160) as playing an important role in shaping the reading of the critical text (cf. chap. 1, n.36).

21. The *NASB* omits this possessive and the critical text brackets *autou* (his). The use of possessives with 'disciples' to distinguish the disciples of Jesus from the disciples of the Pharisees, of John, and so on, were most likely deleted by scribes as the church developed and 'disciples' came always to signify Jesus' disciples (cf. Elliott, 'Textual Commentary', 140)

22. For a discussion of the rabbinic texts attesting these two categories of eunuchs, see C. Daniel, 'Esséniens et Eunuques (Matthieu 19, 10–12)', *RevQ* 6 (1968) 380–9. Daniel argues in his article (353–90) that the second category of eunuchs are the Essenes.

23. Allen, *Matthew*, 204–6; T. Matura, 'Le célibat dans le Nouveau Testament d'aprés l'exégèse récente', *NRT* 97 (1975) 487–96 [= 'Celibacy in the New Testament', *TD* 24 (1976) 41–2]; J. Kodell, 'The Celibacy Logion in Matthew 19:12', *BTB* 8 (1978) 19–23.

24. W.D. Davies, *The Setting of the Sermon on the Mount* (Cambridge: Univ. Press, 1964) 393; D.R. Catchpole, 'The Synoptic Divorce Material as a Traditio-Historical Problem', *BJRL* 57 (1974) 95.

25. Davies, *Setting*, 393–4.

26. A.H. McNeile, *The Gospel According to St. Matthew* (London: Macmillan, 1915) 275; E. Stauffer, '*Gameō*' *TDNT* 1 (1964) 652; H.B. Green, *The Gospel according to Matthew* (New Clarendon Bible; Oxford: Univ. Press, 1975) 169.

27. For discussions of the causal or final sense of *dia* in Matthew 19: 12, see R. Balducelli, 'The Decision for Celibacy', *TS* 36 (1975) 226–8; Kodell, 'The Celibacy Logion', 21–2.

28. At least one writer argues that 'celibacy is probably not one of the charisms which is either there or not, but one of those which may also be striven for, according to the counsel of the Apostle Paul (1 Cor. 12: 31)'. Thus it is a challenge to all. Cf. L.M. Weber, 'Celibacy', in *Encyclopedia of Theology: The Concise Sacramentum Mundi* (ed. K. Rahner; New York: Seabury, 1975) 183.

29. G. Bornkamm, G. Barth, and H.J. Held, *Tradition and Interpretation in Matthew* (trans. P. Scott; Philadelphia: Westminster, 1963) 96.

30. Allen, *Matthew*, 205.

31. Q. Quesnell, '"Made Themselves Eunuchs for the Kingdom of Heaven"' (Mt 19, 12)', *CBQ* 30 (1968) 335–58. Gundry (*Matthew*, 381–3) follows the Dupont-Quesnell interpretation almost to the letter.

32. Dupont, *Mariage et divorce*, 161.

33. Ibid., 194–6, 198. Cf. Daniel, 'Esséniens et Eunuques', 380–9; J. Galot, 'La motivation évangélique du célibat', *Greg* 53 (1972) 744. Exegetes who continue to follow the reasoning of J. Blinzler ('*Eisin eunouchoi*: Zur Auslegung von Mt. 19, 12', *ZNW* 48 [1957] 254–70) in making the 'eunuch' the equivalent of the 'celibate', or who continue to assert that the eunuch metaphor *must* signify the irreparable incapacity for marriage, should again read Dupont, 198 n.3.

34. Dupont, *Mariage et divorce*, 162–3. Cf. BDF §§ 290, 3; 394.

35. McNeile, *Matthew*, 275; T.W. Manson, *The Sayings of Jesus* (London: SCM, 1949) 214–16. Cf. R.H. Charles, *The Teaching of the New Testament on Divorce* (London: Wms. & Norgate, 1921) 1 n.2, pp. 35–8; C.G. Montefiore, *The Synoptic Gospels* (2 vols.; 2nd ed; London: Macmillan, 1927) 2: 263. K. Weiss ('*Sympherō ktl.*', *TDNT* 9 [1974] 75 n.13) is unsure which context to choose.

36. Dupont, *Mariage et divorce*, 165.

37. Dupont himself (ibid., 168–70) is able to give a very good defence of this view in the face of its critics.

38. Cf. Stauffer, '*Gameō*', 651 n.20; K. Stendahl, 'Matthew', *PCB* §689c. For a comparison of Matthew's and Mark's treatment of the parable of the rich young ruler, see N.B. Stonehouse, *Origins of the Synoptic Gospels: Some Basic Questions* (Grand Rapids: Eerdmans, 1963) 93–112.

39. Dupont, *Mariage et divorce*, 173. Dupont is here following the

development of this parallel by P. Ketter, ' "Nicht alle fassen dieses Wort": Bemerkungen zu Mt 19, 10–12', *Pastor bonus* 49 (1938–9) 311–23.

40. F.J. Moloney, 'Matthew 19, 3–12 and Celibacy. A Redactional and Form Critical Study', *JSNT* 2 (Jan. 1979) 46.

41. Cf. Stonehouse, *Origins*, 107–8; J.B. Hurley, *Man and Woman in Biblical Perspective* (Grand Rapids: Zondervan, 1981) 95–6.

42. Moloney, 'Matthew 19, 3–12', 47. The ethic of Jesus is an ethic of grace in which the one who has accepted God's rule is placed under the gracious and demanding rule of God. Cf. W.D. Davies, 'Ethics in the NT', *IDB* 2: 167–76 (though an excellent article, we do not accept all of Davies' conclusions).

43. Dupont, *Mariage et divorce*, 178–9. Cf. Allen, *Matthew*, 206; G. Kittel, '*Legō*', *TDNT* 4 (1967) 108; G. Bornkamm, '*Mystērion*', *TDNT* 4 (1967) 817–19 and n.138; Gundry, *Matthew*, 254–5, 381–3.

44. J. Behm, '*Exō*', *TDNT* 2 (1964) 576. For this conception in the epistles see 1 Cor. 5: 12–13; 1 Thess. 4: 12; Col. 4: 5; 1 Tim. 3: 7. The fate of unfaithful 'disciples' who do not produce fruit is 'the outer darkness' (*to exōteron*; Matt. 8: 12; 22: 13; 25: 30).

45. BAGD, '*Syniēmi*'. Cf. H. Conzelmann, '*Syniēmi ktl.*', *TDNT* 7 (1971) 892–5. Synonyms are *nveō* (to understand, perceive, Matt. 15: 17; 16: 9, 11), *ginōskō* (to know, Matt. 13: 11) and *epiginōskō* (to know, recognise, Matt. 17: 12).

46. Dupont, *Mariage et divorce*, 178–87. Cf. J. Goetzmann, '*Synesis*', *NIDNTT* 3 (1978) 131–2.

47. BAGD, '*Chōreō*', 3bβ lists the meaning in Matt. 19: 11, 12 as '*grasp in the mental sense, accept, comprehend, understand*'. Why this word and not *syniēmi* is used here will be discussed in the following evaluation.

48. Guelich, *Sermon on the Mount*, 31.

49. Dupont, *Mariage et divorce*, 188.

50. Quesnell, 'Made Themselves Eunuchs', 341–2. One writer commends Quesnell for arguing 'with great erudition for Dupont's view', and another says that Quesnell's reading of Matt. 19: 12 'makes eminently good sense' when read in the context of a society which had long regarded *porneia* as making divorce mandatory, not optional.

51. Ibid., 343.

52. Ibid., 344. But assuming that Jesus' remark picks up on the disciples' words, 'It is better not to marry' (which seems to be less probable than the reference to v. 9), Jesus need not *agree* with this statement, just *correct* it and take up a different point raised by the shocked disciples.

53. Ibid., 357–8.

54. G. Bromiley, *God and Marriage* (Grand Rapids: Eerdmans, 1980) 41.

We would not, however, interpret the first two classes of eunuchs metaphorically. Only the third class is figurative, and Bromiley's interpretive paraphrase catches the intent of the Dupont-Quesnell exegesis quite well.

55. Quesnell, 'Made Themselves Eunuchs', 344–6. D.L. Balch ('Background of I Cor. vii: Sayings of the Lord in Q; Moses as an Ascetic *THEIOS ANÊR* in II Cor. iii', *NTS* 18 [1972] 351–64) draws on Quesnell's analysis of Matthew and Luke's use of the Q material pertaining to celibacy while discussing the possibility that Paul's opponents at Corinth made use of a sayings source like Q. Cf. W.H. Kelber, *The Oral and the Written Gospel* (Philadelphia: Fortress, 1983) 140–83.

56. Besides the textual problem in Matt. 19:29 where the variant reading includes 'wife' (contrast the *UBSGNT*[3] decision here and at Matt. 10:37!), G. Vermes (*Jesus the Jew: A Historian's Reading of the Gospels* [New York: Macmillan, 1973] 246 n.79) says that 'In the Marcan and Matthean recension, "home" is synonymous with "wife". In vernacular Aramaic "one belonging to his house" is the owner's wife'. This weakens Quesnell's argument if 'wife' is implied in Matthew and Mark.

57. Quesnell assumes that these are parallel passages. This assumption is questionable. Cf. Stonehouse, *Origins*, 35–42.

58. Quesnell, 'Made Themselves Eunuchs', 346. Balch ('Backgrounds', 354–5) feels Quesnell is mistaken here: Matthew still leaves room for the possibility that some may choose never to marry.

59. Cf. J.D. Quinn, 'Celibacy and the Ministry in Scripture', *TBT* 46 (1970) 3168.

60. Quesnell, 'Made Themselves Eunuchs', 341, n.10. Also R. Kugelman, 'The First Letter to the Corinthians', in *JBC*, 264. For a critique of the traditional distinction between commands and counsels in Pauline theology, see J.W. Glaser, 'Commands-Counsels: A Pauline Teaching?' *TS* 31 (1970) 275–87.

61. R. Scroggs, 'Marriage in the NT', *IDBSup*, 576–7; B. Vawter, 'Divorce and the New Testament', *CBQ* 39 (1977) 536; G.J. Wenham, 'The biblical view of marriage and divorce 3–New Testament teaching', *Third Way*, Nov. 17th, 1977, 7–9; R.F. Collins, 'The Bible and Sexuality II', *BTB* 8 (1978) 5–6; Moloney, 'Matthew 19, 3–12 and Celibacy', 46–8; J.J. Pilch, 'Marriage in the Lord', *TBT* 102 (1979) 2010–13; Bromiley, *God and Marriage*, 40–1; K. Condon, 'Apropos of the Divorce Sayings', *Irish Biblical Studies* 2 (1980) 40–51; cf. W.J. O'Shea, 'Marriage and Divorce: the Biblical Evidence', *ACR* 47 (1970) 101–2.

62. Matura ('Le célibat', 491 n.43; 493 n.48) lists a number of writers who attach v. 11 to v. 9: H. Baltensweiler, J.M. Lagrange, T.V. Fleming, H. Roux and P. Bonnard. He mistakenly lists D. Hill (*The*

Gospel of Matthew [NCBC; London: Marshall, Morgan & Scott, 1972] 281) in support of this understanding.

63. *Syniēmi* (13: 13, 14, 15, 19, 23, 51; 15: 10; 16: 12; 17: 13); *akouō* (to hear) (11: 15; 13: 9, 43; etc.). See further n.45.

64. P. Schmidt, *'Chōreō'*, *NIDNTT* 1 (1975) 742.

65. Cf. A. Isaksson, *Marriage and Ministry in the New Temple* (Lund: Gleerup, 1965) 104–112; D.L. Dungan, *The Sayings of Jesus in the Churches of Paul* (Philadelphia: Fortress, 1971) 132–4; and a forthcoming study by David Wenham, 'Paul's use of the Jesus tradition: three samples'.

66. J.A.T. Robinson, *Redating the New Testament* (Philadelphia: Westminster, 1976) 97.

67. Cf. K.L. Schmidt, *'Basileia'*, *TDNT* 1 (1964) 584–9; Dupont, *Mariage et divorce*, 207; B. Klappert, *'Basileia'* *NIDNTT* 2 (1976) 383–6.

68. Cf. chap. 1, n.41.

69. Balducelli, 'Decision', 225–6.

70. J.J. Kilgallen, 'To what are the Matthean Exception-Texts (5, 32 and 19, 9) an Exception?' *Bib* 61 (1980) 102–5.

71. The *NASB* and *RSV* translations correctly avoid the suggestion implicit in the *NEB* and *NIV* rendering of Matt. 5: 32b: that this unqualified conditional statement assumes the condition added in the previous statement, i.e., 'Whoever marries a woman divorced *for adultery* commits adultery'. Cf. chap. 1, n.32.

72. J.P. Lange, *The Gospel according to Matthew*, in *Commentary on the Holy Scriptures* (ed. J.P. Lange; 12 vols; n.p.; reprint ed., Grand Rapids: Zondervan, 1960) 8: 115; Manson, *Sayings of Jesus*, 137; Isaksson, *Marriage and Ministry*, 73–4; Green, *Matthew*, 84; I.H. Marshall, *'Apostasion'*, *NIDNTT* 1 (1975) 506–7.

73. Gundry, *Matthew*, 90. *poiei* in *poiei autēn moicheuthēnai* is not a simple active, but a *causative* active: the husband's divorce action is ultimately the cause of his wife's subsequent adulterous marriage. On the full passive force of *moicheuthēnai* see D.S. Deere, 'The Implied Agent in Greek Passive Verb Forms in the Gospel of Matthew', *BT* 18 (1967) 165.

74. F.W. Beare, *The Earliest Records of Jesus* (New York: Abingdon, 1962) 192–92 (Beare is following notes made available to him by C.R. Feilding). See also n.7 in Introduction.

75. Kilgallen, 'Matthean Exception-Texts', 103, Cf. Dupont, *Mariage et divorce*, 216–17 n.4; J.D.M. Derrett, *Law in the New Testament* (London: Darton, Longman & Todd, 1970) 371–2, 380–1.

76. J.A. Fitzmyer, 'The Matthean Divorce Texts and Some New Palestinian Evidence', *TS* 37 (1976) 203. We recognise that from a strictly grammatical perspective (MHT, 3: 107) the action of the relative clause is antecedent to the main action. But the context of Matt. 5: 32a, the causative active (*poiei*) and the passive infinitive

(*moicheuthēnai*) seem to warrant our understanding. The function of
the exception clauses we have noted (cf. n.74) is independent of our
postulate that Matthew presents unwarranted divorce as tantamount to adultery.
77. Kilgallen, 'Matthean Exception-Texts', 104.
78. Ibid., 105.

Chapter 3

1. We are dependent on V.N. Olsen (*The New Testament Logia on
   Divorce: A Study of their Interpretation from Erasmus to Milton* [BGBE
   10; Tübingen: J.C.B. Mohr, 1971] 2–149) for most of the material in
   this chapter. Cf. also J.B. Payne, *Erasmus: His theology of the Sacraments* (Atlanta: John Knox, 1970) 109–25.
2. Olsen, *New Testament Logia on Divorce*, 4. See also E. Schillebeeckx,
   Marriage: Human Reality and Saving Mystery (trans. N.D. Smith; New
   York: Sheed and Ward, 1965) 281–6.
3. These include baptism, confirmation, the Eucharist, penance,
   extreme unction and holy orders. For brief discussions of these see
   The Church Teaches: Documents of the Church in English Translation (eds
   J.F. Clarkson et al; Rockford, Ill.: Tan Books, 1973) 257–344.
4. Olsen, *New Testament Logia on Divorce*, 6.
5. Ibid., 7. Cf. Payne, *Erasmus*, 112–14.
6. Olsen, *New Testament Logia on Divorce*, 8, 43–6. Erasmus's NT was
   already read widely in England after its appearance in 1516; but it
   was not until the accession of Edward VI (1547–53) that the interpretation of Erasmus came to the forefront (p. 117).
7. T.F.C. Stunt, 'Desiderius Erasmus: Some Recent Studies', *EvQ* 42
   (1970) 233, 235.
8. Olsen, *New Testament Logia on Divorce*, 16–17. Payne (*Erasmus*, 124)
   states that Erasmus 'reveals himself not only as a historical, but also
   as something of an ethical, relativist and contextualist who thinks
   that love, which is the substance of the law of nature and the law of
   Scripture, is the only ultimate guide to human behavior – not
   human, historically conditioned laws'.
9. Olsen, *New Testament Logia on Divorce*, 21.
10. Ibid., 21–2. Luther also was influenced by the objective of securing
    an individual's salvation and by the judgment of charity (p. 47).
    Luther was probably unable totally to remove himself from the
    teaching of the Church of his day which said that no salvation was
    possible outside its doors.
11. Ibid., 23. Erasmus's humanistic reasons in his quest for an inter-
    pretation that permits remarriage should not go unnoticed.

12. Ibid., 26. Erasmus incorrectly understands the law mentioned here as Deut. 24: 1. C.E.B. Cranfield (*A Critical and Exegetical Commentary on the Epistle to the Romans* [2 vols; ICC; Edinburgh: T. & T. Clark, 1975–9], 1:333) argues that 'the law concerning the husband' in v. 2 refers to 'the law which (or, in so far as it) binds her to her husband'.

13. Olsen, *New Testament Logia on Divorce*, 30.

14. Ibid., 40. Cf. pp. 38–40.

15. Cf. R.J. Ehrlich ('The Indissolubility of Marriage as a Theological Problem', *SJT* 23 [1970] 297–306) for another discussion of this and the problems surrounding remarriage that confronted the Scottish reformers (who will not be surveyed here).

16. Olsen, *New Testament Logia on Divorce*, 53. Similar reasoning is advocated by J. Adams, *Marriage, Divorce and Remarriage in the Bible* (Phillipsburg, N.J.: Presbyterian & Reformed, 1980) 88–91. He correlates 1 Cor. 7: 15 with Matt. 18: 15–17 and thereby sanctions divorce and remarriage between two believers.

17. Olsen, *New Testament Logia on Divorce*, 53.

18. Here we skip over Philip Melanchthon (1497–1560), Zwingli (1484–1531), Bullinger (1504–75), Martin Bucer (d. 1551) and Peter Martyr (1500–62). There follows a progressively more liberal interpretation from Luther through Zwingli and Bullinger to Bucer.

19. Ibid., 104–5.

20. Ibid., 111. Tyndale combined 1 Cor. 7: 15 with 1 Tim. 5: 8 further to support desertion as a second cause for divorce and remarriage.

21. D. Atkinson, *To Have and To Hold: The Marriage Covenant and the Discipline of Divorce* (London: Collins, 1979) 62.

22. J. Lightfoot, *A Commentary on the New Testament from the Talmud and Hebraica: Matthew-I Corinthians* (4 vols; Oxford: Univ. Press, 1859; reprint ed., Introduction by R. Laird Harris, Grand Rapids: Baker, 1979), 2: 125, 261. Also W.R. O'Connor, 'The Indissolubility of a Ratified, Consummated Marriage', *ETL* 13 (1936) 706–10.

23. Ehrlich, 'Indissolubility of Marriage', 305.

24. R.H. Charles, *The Teaching of the New Testament on Divorce* (London: Wms. & Norgate, 1921) 3–34; J.B. Hurley, *Man and Woman in Biblical Perspective* (Grand Rapids: Zondervan, 1981) 102–4; C. Brown, '*Chōrizō*: Divorce, Separation and Remarriage', *NIDNTT* 3 (1978) 538, 540–1.

25. Bullinger, Bucer and Peter Martyr all appeal to 1 Cor. 7: 15 as proof that Christ's words should not be restricted to the cause of adultery alone (cf. Olsen, *New Testament Logia on Divorce*, 71, 83, 90). R.H. Stein ('Is it lawful for a man to divorce his wife?' *JETS* 22 [1979] 119) similarly appeals to Matthew's exception and 1 Cor. 7: 15 as evidence that Jesus' words in Mark 10 and Luke 16 are an overstatement. Cf. W.P. Paterson, 'Divorce and the Law of Christ', *Exp* [7th series] 10 (1910) 300–1.

26. Olsen, *New Testament Logia on Divorce*, 106 (indirectly quoting Beza). Beza also said that Matt. 5: 32b could not be used to support the argument against remarriage after adultery. He said the exception assigned to Matt. 5: 32a (the Reformers also used a Greek text with the longer reading at Matt. 19: 9) is added also to the latter. See chap. 2, n.71.

Chapter 4

1. J. Murray, *Divorce* (Phillipsburg, N.J.: Presbyterian & Reformed, [1953]). Cf. R.H. Charles, *The Teaching of the New Testament on Divorce* (London: Wms. & Norgate, 1921); A.T. Robertson, *Word Pictures in the New Testament* (6 vols; Nashville: Broadman, 1930–3), 1: 155; S.A. Ellisen, *Divorce and Remarriage in the Church* (Grand Rapids: Zondervan, 1977); M.J. Harris, 'Prepositions and Theology in the Greek New Testament', *NIDNTT* 3 (1978) 1195; probably D. Guthrie, *New Testament Theology* (Leicester, England; Downers Grove, Ill.: Inter-Varsity, 1981) 950; P.H. Wiebe, 'The New Testament on Divorce and Remarriage: Some Logical Implications', *JETS* 24 (1981) 131–8.

2. D. Atkinson, *To Have and To Hold: The Marriage Covenant and the Discipline of Divorce* (London: Collins, 1979). Cf. G. Duty, *Divorce and Remarriage* (Minneapolis, Minn.: Bethany, 1967); J.R.W. Stott, 'The Biblical Teaching on Divorce', *ChM* 85 (1971) 165–74; D.H. Small, *The Right to Remarry* (Old Tappan, N.J.: Revell, 1975); C. Brown, '*Chōrizō*: Divorce, Separation and Remarriage', *NIDNTT* 3 (1978) 535–43.

3. W.C. Allen, *A Critical and Exegetical Commentary on the Gospel according to S. Matthew* (3rd ed.; ICC; Edinburgh: T. & T. Clark, 1912) 52, 201–6. Cf. W. Harrington, 'Jesus' Attitude towards Divorce', *ITQ* 37 (1970) 199–209. Harrington has since changed his view. (See chap. 10, n.6.)

4. Atkinson, *To Have and To Hold*, 132 n.78; J. Adams, *Marriage, Divorce and Remarriage in the Bible* (Phillipsburg, N.J.: Presbyterian & Reformed, 1980) 53; Guthrie, *NT Theology*, 949–50 and n.154; J.B. Hurley, *Man and Woman in Biblical Perspective* (Grand Rapids: Zondervan, 1981) 103 n. 13; and others.

5. Murray, *Divorce*, 41. Cf. Duty, *Divorce and Remarriage*, 32–44; R.L. Saucy, 'The Husband of One Wife', *BSac* 131 (1974) 232–3; J. Job, 'The biblical view of marriage and divorce 4 – New Testament teaching', *ThW*, Nov. 17, 1977, 13; Ellisen, *Divorce and Remarriage*, 49.

6. Murray, *Divorce*, 42. Atkinson (*To Have and To Hold*, 103) writes: 'It is

important to note that Moses is talking about divorce (in the phrase "bill of divorcement") and not just separation . . . It indicates the severing of what was once a living union.'

7. Cf. J.A. Fitzmyer, 'The Matthean Divorce Texts and Some New Palestinian Evidence', *TS* 37 (1976) 212–13. Also Atkinson, *To Have and To Hold*, 121.

8. Murray, *Divorce*, 14. This statement alone seems to argue against Murray's contention that the relationship between the original couple can be dissolved. In fact, Murray here seems to anticipate the view of Deut. 24 that we shall set forth in the critique of his Mosaic 'dissolution divorce' idea.

9. Ibid., 15. A. Isaksson (*Marriage and Ministry in the New Temple* [trans. N. Tomkinson with J. Gray; ASNU 24; Lund: Gleerup, 1965] 22) thinks Murray's suggestion is rather far-fetched.

10. Murray, *Divorce*, 39. The partial quote is from J.G. Machen, *Christianity Today* [not the popular edition], Oct. 1931, 12.

11. Perhaps Murray chooses clauses with *ei mē* inserted because the *TR* includes the particle *ei* before the negated prepositional phrase in Matt. 19: 9 resulting in the construction *ei mē epi porneia*. Tischendorf (*Novum Testamentum Graece* [8th ed.; Lipsiae: Giesecke & Deverient, 1869], 1: 114) notes the particle *ei* is only supported by a few minuscules along with the Ethiopic version of Basil. The *TR* and Griesbach's 1827 ed. contain this reading. Murray would also have found this reading in his Moulton and Geden's *Concordance* under *epi* c. dat. (p. 357) and under *porneia* (p. 842).

12. Murray, *Divorce*, 39–40.

13. Note that Murray is trying to relate the exception clause to both halves of the conditional sentence (protasis and apodosis) rather than attempting to understand how this negated adverbial expression qualifies one or the other or both verbal actions in the protasis alone (the conditional relative clause).

14. Murray, *Divorce*, 40.

15. Ibid., 41.

16. Job, 'Marriage and divorce', 13. Cf. D. Atkinson, 'A Response [to G. Wenham's review of his book]', *ChM* 95 (1981) 163.

17. Murray, *Divorce*, 51.

18. Job, 'Marriage and divorce', 14.

19. We do not question that Mark's and Luke's Gospels might permit divorce for adultery, but that they also permit remarriage is a conjecture completely foreign to what they have plainly written.

20. Murray, *Divorce*, 52. C. Brown agrees with Murray's line of reasoning here. Note his additions to the article by H. Reisser, '*Porneuō*', *NIDNTT* 1 (1975) 500.

21. Brown, *NIDNTT* 3: 540.

22. Charles, *Teaching*, 58. Cf. D.W. Shaner, *A Christian View of Divorce* (Leiden: Brill, 1969) 65–6.
23. H. Ridderbos, *Paul: An Outline of His Theology* (trans. J.R. DeWitt; Grand Rapids: Eerdmans, 1975) 308–9 n.139.
24. BAGD, '*deō*', 3.
25. G.W. Peters, *Divorce and Remarriage* (Chicago: Moody, 1972) 18; M. Neal, 'The Christian and Marriage', *Biblical Viewpoint* 7 (1973) 105.
26. Cf. Murray, *Divorce*, 74–5. Atkinson (*To Have and To Hold*, 132 n.18) repeats Murray's assertion.
27. G.L. Archer, *Encyclopedia of Bible Difficulties* (Grand Rapids: Zondervan, 1982) 399. Cf. Ellisen, *Divorce and Remarriage*, 66–8.
28. Archer, *Encyclopedia*, 399–400.
29. Job, 'Marriage and divorce', 14. Cf. Duty, *Divorce and Remarriage*, 109; Adams, *Marriage*, 84–6.
30. Brown, *NIDNTT* 3: 537. Cf. G. Stählin, '*Chēra*', *TDNT* 9 (1974) 452 n.110; H. Conzelmann, *A Commentary on the First Epistle to the Corinthians* (Hermeneia; trans. J.W. Leitch; Philadelphia: Fortress, 1975) 132 n.15. Atkinson (*To Have and To Hold*, 124–5) more cautiously realises that this may apply to the person whose marriage was terminated by death. Nevertheless, he says that it 'can equally apply to those whose marriage has been broken by divorce'.
31. Brown, *NIDNTT* 3: 535, 537.
32. Charles, *Teaching*, 62. Cf. Murray, *Divorce*, 43.
33. Charles, *Teaching*, 68.
34. Brown, *NIDNTT* 3: 535. A quick perusal of key commentaries on 1 Cor. 6 will reveal that vv. 12–20 do *not* address 'the question of adultery' as Brown seems to believe.
35. Ibid., 539. Cf. N. Geisler's *(Ethics: Alternatives and Issues* [Grand Rapids: Zondervan, 1971] 199–200) statement: 'In brief, there is no such thing as premarital intercourse in the Bible. If the couple were not married, then intercourse with another person made them married. If they were already married, then intercourse with another person constituted a second, adulterous marriage for them. Harlotry is considered an illegitimate marriage.' Prof. Geisler no longer holds this view we are happy to note.
36. Cf. D.A. Carson, *Matthew* (The Expositor's Bible Commentary, 8; Grand Rapids: Zondervan), forthcoming.

Chapter 5

1. This has been treated in greater depth by G.J. Wenham, 'Marriage and Divorce: The Legal and Social Setting of the Biblical Teaching',

A Memorandum submitted to the Church of Ireland Committee on the remarriage of divorced persons (Queen's University, n.d.), 3–24, summarised in *ThW*, Oct. 20th, 1977, 3–5; Nov. 3rd, 1977, 7–9.

2. A. Isaksson, *Marriage and Ministry in the New Temple* (trans. N. Tomkinson with J. Gray; ASNU 24; Lund: Gleerup, 1965) 17. R. de Vaux (*Ancient Israel* [2 vols; New York: McGraw Hill, Paperback ed., 1965], 1: 35) believes that Jesus uses the same argument for indissolubility as Mal. 2: 14–16.

3. Isaksson, *Marriage and Ministry*, 19. Cf. BDB, '*dābaq*', 179–80; R.F. Collins, 'The Bible and Sexuality', *BTB* 7 (1977) 153–4.

4. E.S. Kalland, '*dābaq*', in *Theological Wordbook of the Old Testament* (ed. R. L. Harris; 2 vols.; Chicago: Moody, 1980), 1: 178. Cf. W. Brueggemann, 'Of the Same Flesh and Bone (Gn 2, 23a)', *CBQ* 32 (1970) 540.

5. Isaksson, *Marriage and Ministry*, 20. Cf. BDB, '*bāśār*', 142 (4); F. Baumgärtel, '*sarx*', *TDNT* 7 (1971) 106; N.P. Bratsiotis, '*bāśār*', *TDOT* 2 (1977) 327–8.

6. Brueggemann, 'Flesh and Bone', 533.

7. Isaksson, *Marriage and Ministry*, 21.

8. The preposition *le* with *hāyāh* here indicates '*Into* . . . of a transition into a new state or condition' (BDB, '*l*' 512 [4]). R.J. Williams (*Hebrew Syntax: An Outline* [2nd ed; Toronto: Univ. Press, 1976] §278) calls this a *lāmed* of product (cf. GKC §117ii; 119t). For example, Gen. 2: 7 reads: 'and the man became a living soul/living person . . .' This clearly shows that time is *not* involved. BDB ('*hāyāh*', 226 [II2e]) lists numerous examples of this, the vast majority of which, if not all, refer to a change of state without reference to development towards that state. This is further confirmed by the 'one flesh' denoting a new family unit (cf. n.5), which is clearly not a process but a change of state: it happens at the ratification of the marriage covenant (*dābaq*) and its consummation.

9. B. Vawter, 'The Biblical Theology of Divorce', *PCTSA* 22 (1967) 230.

10. P.F. Palmer, 'Christian Marriage: Contract or Covenant?' *TS* 33 (1972) 621 n.8. He cites P. Grelot, *Man and Wife in Scripture* (New York, 1964) 71.

11. J.A. Fitzmyer, 'The Matthean Divorce Texts and Some New Palestinian Evidence', *TS* 37 (1976) 204. Cf. P. Hoffmann, 'Jesus' Saying about Divorce and its Interpretation in the New Testament Tradition', *Concilium* 55 (1970) 55–6; R. Banks, *Jesus and the Law in the Synoptic Tradition* (SNTSMS 28; Cambridge: Univ. Press, 1975) 148–9.

12. E. Neufeld, *Ancient Hebrew Marriage Laws* (London: Longman's, Green & Co., 1944) 89.

13. The agreements were most likely verbal in normal marriages and

not written. Cf. S. Greengus, 'Old Babylonian Marriage Contract', *JAOS* 89 (1969) 505–32; D. Piattelli, 'The Marriage Contract and Bill of Divorce in Ancient Hebrew Law', in *JLA* 4 (ed. B.S. Jackson; Leiden: Brill, 1981) 66–78.

14. Palmer, 'Contract or Covenant', 618. A note at the end of this paragraph refers to K. Baltzer, *The Covenant Formulary in Old Testament, Jewish and Early Christian Writings* (Oxford, 1971) 14–15.

15. G.J. Wenham, *The Book of Leviticus* (NICOT; Grand Rapids: Eerdmans, 1979) 255. Cf. R.K. Harrison, *Leviticus: An Introduction and Commentary* (TOTC; Downers Grove, Ill.: Inter-Varsity, 1980) 186.

16. Wenham, *Leviticus*, 253.

17. Ibid., 254. Neufeld (*Hebrew Marriage Laws*, 193–4) concurs: 'The prohibitions, with one exception, are unqualified as to their duration, and hence one can only assume that they are permanent and are not terminated by the death of a person who forms a link in a chain of relationship by marriage.'

18. G. Wenham, 'May Divorced Christians Remarry?' *ChM* 95 (1981) 151. Cf. esp. pp. 154, 159–60 on the restriction of remarriage in the OT.

19. Cf. A. Phillips, 'Some Aspects of Family Law in Pre-Exilic Israel', *VT* 23 (1973) 349–61; 'Another Example of Family Law', *VT* 30 (1980) 240–5. Also, D.W. Amram, 'Divorce', *JE* 4: 624–8.

20. For an analysis and exegesis of Deut. 22: 13–29, see G. Wenham and J.G. McConville, 'Drafting Techniques in Some Deuteronomic Laws', *VT* 30 (1980) 248–52; Wenham, '*Bᵉtulāh* "A Girl of Marriageable Age"', *VT* 22 (1977) 330–6; Phillips, 'Aspects of Family Law', 351–6. For case comparisons, see J.J. Finkelstein, 'Sex Offenses in Sumerian Laws', *JAOS* 86 (1966) 355–72.

21. J.D.M. Derrett, *Law in the New Testament* (London: Darton, Longman & Todd, 1970) 377. Cf. Isaksson, *Marriage and Ministry*, 126. D. Atkinson (*To Have and To Hold* [London: Collins, 1979] 105) rejects Derrett's understanding for no good reason.

22. P.C. Craigie, *The Book of Deuteronomy* (NICOT; Grand Rapids: Eerdmans, 1976) 304–5. Also, Isaksson, *Marriage and Ministry*, 25; R. Yaron, 'The Restoration of Marriage', *JJS* 17 (1966) 3.

23. Isaksson (*Marriage and Ministry*, 25–7) quite convincingly argues that the indecency here is a matter of the wife's having exposed her pudendum voluntarily or involuntarily. This arouses the husband's loathing (cf. 2 Sam. 6: 12–20; Ezek. 23: 18; also Exod. 20: 26).

24. See Yaron, 'Restoration of Marriage', 1–11; G.J. Wenham, 'The Restoration of Marriage Reconsidered', *JJS* 30 (1979) 36–40; Isaksson, *Marriage and Ministry*, 21–5; Derrett, *Law in the NT*, 376–7.

25. J. Murray, *Divorce* (Phillipsburg, NJ: Presbyterian & Reformed, [1953]) 15. Murray here seems to be following the 1921 work by R.H. Charles. Cf. A.M. Rabello, 'Divorce of Jews in the Roman Empire', in *JLA* 4 (ed. B.S. Jackson; Leiden: Brill, 1981) 91.

26. Phillips, 'Aspects of Family Law', 351; Cf. R. Yaron, 'On Divorce in Old Testament Times', *Revue Internationale des Droits de l'Antiquité* 3 (1957) 127–8.

27. Cf. D. Daube, 'Concessions to Sinfulness in Jewish Law', *JJS* 10 (1959) 1–13, esp. pp. 10–11; W. Eichrodt, *Theology of the Old Testament* (trans. J.A. Baker; 2 vols; OTL; Philadelphia: Westminster, 1961–7), 2: 322–6. Interesting is Origen, *Commentary on Matthew* 14. 23 (ANF 10: 510).

28. J.A. Thompson, *Deuteronomy: An Introduction and Commentary* (TOTC; Downers Grove, Ill.: Inter-Varsity, 1974) 244. Cf. Collins, 'The Bible and Sexuality', 161. This was also true in the Greek world and Hellenism (cf. A. Oepke, '*Gynē*', *TDNT* 1 [1964] 778).

29. Craigie, *Deuteronomy*, 305. Also R.C. Campbell ('Teachings of the Old Testament concerning Divorce', *Foundations* 6 [1963] 175), who cites Driver (ICC, p. 272), who also approvingly quotes Keil (p. 418) in this connection. The 'adultery' view clashes with S.A. Kaufman's ('The Structure of the Deuteronomic Law', *Maarav* 1/2 [1978–9] 105–58) brilliant analysis of the structure of the Deuteronomic law. The Deut. 24: 4 remarriage regulation does not appear in the 22: 9 – 23: 19 section which expands the seventh Word, 'Thou shall not commit adultery.'

30. *NIV* translation. Cf. A.B. Davidson, *Hebrew Syntax* (3rd ed.; Edinburgh: T. & T. Clark, 1901) §145b.

31. Isaksson, *Marriage and Ministry*, 23. Also Derrett, *Law in the NT*, 363–88.

32. Yaron, 'Restoration of Marriage', 8.

33. Ibid.

34. Wenham, 'Restoration of Marriage Reconsidered', 40. This has been quoted with approval by A. Phillips, 'Another Look at Adultery', *JSOT* 20 (1981) 14, and C.-D. Stoll, *Ehe und Ehescheidung: Die Weisungen Jesu* (Giessen: Brunnen Verlag, 1983) 15, 44.

35. This understanding has been most recently defended by Y. Zakovitch, 'The Woman's Rights in the Biblical Law of Divorce', in *JLA* 4 (ed. B.S. Jackson; Leiden: Brill, 1981) 28–46. He prefers this view over the view that states the law's purpose was to prevent quick remarriage after divorce and Yaron's view that it protects the woman's marriage from the first husband. Zakovitch seems to be unaware of the view that understands Deut. 24: 4 in the context of legislation against 'incestuous' unions.

Chapter 6

1. On the textual problem here, see chap. 2 n.20.
2. J. Barr, *The Semantics of Biblical Language* (Oxford: Univ. Press, 1961) 222.
3. BDF §472.
4. K.J. Dover, *Greek Word Order* (Cambridge: Univ. Press, 1960) v.
5. G. Duty, *Divorce and Remarriage* (Minneapolis: Minn.: Bethany, 1967) 49. D.H. Small (*The Right to Remarry* [Old Tappan, NJ: Revell, 1975] 150) has virtually copied Duty's remarks but attributes them to the grammarian A.T. Robertson (who says no such thing in any of his writings)!
6. For a study of conditional sentences in the NT, see the unpublished work by R.L. Roberts, 'The Use of Conditional Sentences in the Greek New Testament As Compared with Homeric, Classical, and Hellenistic Uses' (Ph.D. Dissertation, University of Texas, 1955).
7. MHT 3: 349–50; A.T. Robertson, *GGNT*, 419; BDF §474.
8. A.C. Thiselton, 'Semantics and New Testament Interpretation', in *New Testament Interpretation: Essays on Principles and Methods* (ed. I.H. Marshall; Grand Rapids: Eerdmans, 1977) 83.
9. See chap. 2 n.16. J.P. Arendzen ('Another Note on Matthew xix, 3–12', *Clergy Review* 21 [1941] 26) also writes that in this position the exception clause means that the man is put 'under obligation of sending his wife away for this cause, so that if he continued to live with her he would commit adultery – which is nonsense'. But this is nearly the position of Derrett (see Appendix) and the *Shepherd of Hermas* Mandate 4.1.5–6.
10. Apart from the five examples of *ei mē* used in first class (logical) conditions and once in a third class (anticipatory; Luke 9: 13) condition, '*ei mē* is confined to the second class condition and to the elliptical use like *plēn* in the sense of "except" or the phrase *ei de mē* meaning "otherwise" without a verb' (Robertson, *GGNT*, 1016). Cf. BDF §§428, 3; 375; 448, 8; 480, 6.
11. Cf. Matt. 5: 13; 11: 27; 12: 4, 24, 39; 13: 57; 14: 17; 15: 24; 16: 4; 17: 8; 21: 19; 24: 22, 36. Only in 24: 22 in an unreal (2nd class) condition does *ei mē* introduce an actual conditional clause. As a rule in the NT *ei* goes with the indicative and *ean* with the subjunctive.
12. M. Zerwick, *Biblical Greek* (adapted and trans. from 4th Latin ed. by J. Smith; Rome, 1963) §329. Cf. Roberts, 'Use of Conditional Sentences', 249–51.
13. Zerwick, *Biblical Greek* §442; BDF §§380, 1; 376; BAGD, '*mē*', AI1. An examination of the 19 examples BAGD list in which *mē* is in a conditional clause after *ean* reveals that *mē* is immediately followed by a verb 14 times; in 4 cases a single word comes between *mē* and

the verb (*men, prōton, auto, pygmē*); and Mark 3: 27//Matt. 12: 29 adds *ton ischuon to prōton* before the verb. Of the 8 examples they list in which *mē* is in a conditional clause after *hos an* (= *ean*), of which Matt. 19: 9 is one, in each instance *mē* is immediately followed by a verb (Matt. 10: 14; 11: 6; Mark 6: 11; 10: 15; 11: 23; Luke 8: 18; 18: 17). Only in Matt. 19: 9 is *mē* followed by a prepositional phrase. It is a unique construction, and, as we have said, needs a verb supplied. All the evidence indicates that the verb to be supplied *comes before* the (*ean*)*mē* (= *apolyō* in Matt. 19: 9).

14. C.R. Feilding believes 'that in opposition to the Pharisees of his own day, Matthew attempted to bring together the attack on divorce which he found in Mark and the perfectly compatible doctrine of *v.* 32 [of Matt. 5: that the exception clause is a matter-of-fact recognition that if the wife has already committed adultery, her husband cannot be held guilty of driving her into it by divorcing her], and that in so doing he produced the awkward construction represented by xix. 9'. Quoted in F.W. Beare, *The Earliest Records of Jesus* (New York: Abingdon, 1962) 193. Cf. chap. 2, pp. 69–72.

15. This excludes those cases in which another grammatical or lexical category is operative (cf. Matt. 11: 23//Luke 10: 15; 11: 11; John 7: 35, 41, 52; 18: 17 – 18: 25; 1 Cor. 9: 8; Acts 27: 17, 29; 2 Cor. 12: 6; Acts 25: 27; Gal. 2: 2; 5: 15). Of course, for any norm to be established one should check the LXX and papyri and literary Koine as well as classical Greek, plus the semantic equivalent of our structure, *ou* plus the indicative.

16. P.H. Wiebe, 'The New Testament on Divorce and Remarriage: Some Logical Implications', *JETS* 24 (1981) 132.

17. J. Murray, *Divorce* (Phillipsburg, NJ: Presbyterian & Reformed, [1953]) 41.

18. R.F. Collins ('The Bible and Sexuality', *BTB* 7 [1977] 158) makes an important observation: the seventh commandment (Exod. 20: 14; Deut. 5: 18) makes it clear that the way in which man lives his sexuality is not independent of his relationship with Yahweh. The stories of Joseph and Potiphar's wife (Gen. 39) and David and Bathsheba (2 Sam. 11) 'indicate well that human sexuality is not an awesome force over which man has no control. These stories, told so often in Jewish tradition, clearly proclaim that man is responsible for the way in which he uses his sexuality, that God-given gift over which he exercises dominion in Yahweh's name and by Yahweh's power.' Thus remarriage *need* not take place after divorce.

19. Even if we are judged to be wrong in our postulate that Matthew presents unwarranted divorce as tantamount to adultery, the function of the exception clause noted above (n.14; cf. chap. 2 n.76) is still valid.

20. One of our critics has suggested to us a better illustration of the

Erasmian understanding of the syntax of Matt. 19:9 than the one offered by Wiebe.

'Anyone who kills a dog, unless the animal is diseased, and buries it in his garden, shall be fined by the city council.' Now of course it is true that in one sense the exception to the killing is the diseased animal; but it is also true that the killing of the animal and the burial of it are seen as two complementary conditions which stand or fall together. Such a statute would not address the problem of the person who buries his dog in his garden without first killing it! One could argue that the statute is not particularly well framed: is it primarily the killing or the burying of the dog that is being objected to? But I venture to suggest that as the statement stands, it is precisely the combination of *both taken together* that will win the displeasure of the city council. Perhaps the council has other statutes on the books dealing with killing of animals when the animals are not buried, or with the cruelty of burying animals alive. Nevertheless, as the statute stands, the two protases are taken as joint conditions upon the apodosis, and the exceptive phrase, though formerly linked with the first protasis, has bearing on both.

Since we also feel this illustration is not ideologically parallel to Matt. 19:9, perhaps we should offer an illustration of our own. The reader may be aware that cremation was, and maybe still is, suspect lest murderers attempt to destroy incriminating evidence by cremating instead of burying their victim. Burials may be exhumed and autopsied. Thus we might say:

To kill someone and cremate them is murder.
(cf. Luke 16:18; Mark 10:11, 12)
To kill someone, if it was not by accident, is murder.
(cf. Matt. 5:32)
To kill someone, if it was not by accident, and to cremate them is murder.   (cf. Matt. 19:9)

Thus killing as such and cremation are always murderous. Only accidental killing not followed by cremation is not murderous. Only divorce for immorality not followed by remarriage is not adulterous. (We apologise for our morbid example.)

21. G. Bromiley, *God and Marriage* (Grand Rapids: Eerdmans, 1980) 45.
22. Cf. N.B. Stonehouse, *Origins of the Synoptic Gospels: Some Basic Questions Answered* (Grand Rapids: Eerdmans, 1963) 56.
23. D.L. Dungan (*The Sayings of Jesus in the Churches of Paul* [Philadelphia: Fortress, 1971] 102–31) would say that there *is* a significant difference between saying Jesus taught 'no divorce' and that He taught 'no divorce *and* remarriage'.
24. Murray, *Divorce*, 40.
25. Augustine concluded his discussion of the synoptic teaching on divorce as follows: 'Therefore, since it is not proper for us to maintain that the Evangelists, in writing on one topic, disagree in

meaning and sense, although they may use different words, it follows that we are to understand Matthew as having desired to indicate the whole by the part, but, nevertheless [sic], as having held the same opinion as the other Evangelists . . . everyone who puts away his wife and marries another is most certainly guilty of adultery' (*Adulterous Marriages* 1.11.12. Trans. C.T. Hugelmeyer, FC 27:76).

26. F. Hauck, '*Moicheuō ktl.*', *TDNT* 4 (1967) 733. Cf. F.W. Hall, 'Adultery (Roman)', *ERE* 1:134–5.

27. Cf. E. Stauffer, '*Gameō*', *TDNT* 1 (1964) 650, lines 8–15. Stauffer's use of 'dissolution' is comparable to the Fathers'.

28. E. Lövestam, 'Divorce and Remarriage in the New Testament', in *JLA* 4 (ed. B.S. Jackson; Leiden: Brill, 1981) 60.

29. Cf. M. Mielziner, *The Jewish Law of Marriage and Divorce* (Cincinnati, Ohio: Bloch, 1884) 25–7, 124–5; D.R. Hillers, *Covenant: The History of a Biblical Idea* (Baltimore: John Hopkins Univ. Press, 1969) 92–4.

30. Cf. I. Abrahams, *Studies in Pharisaism and the Gospels* (2 vols in 1; Cambridge: Univ. Press, 1917–24; reprint ed., New York: KTAV, 1967) 70–6; B. Cohen, 'Concerning Divorce in Jewish and Roman Law', *PAAJR* 21 (1952) 31–2; A. Phillips, 'Another Look at Adultery', *JSOT* 20 (1981) 3–25.

31. D. Hill, *The Gospel of Matthew* (NCBC; London: Marshall, Morgan & Scott, 1972) 125.

32. A. Tosato, 'Joseph, Being a Just Man (Matt. 1:19)', *CBQ* 41 (1979) 547–51.

33. F. Hauck and S. Schulz, '*Pornē ktl.*', *TDNT* 6 (1968) 592. B. Vawter ('Divorce and the New Testament', *CBQ* 39 [1977] 531 n.4) approves of Hauck and Schulz's analysis. Also, K. Stendahl, 'Matthew', *PCB* §679g.

34. Lövestam, 'Divorce and Remarriage', 61. Lövestam earlier set forth this interpretation in his dissertation on marriage in the NT (*Äktenskapet i Nya Testamentet* [Lund, 1950]). A. Isaksson (*Marriage and Ministry in the New Temple* [ASNU 24; Lund: Gleerup, 1965] 89–90) reviews and criticizes Lövestam's reasoning; but it is Isaksson himself who seems to create the major problems he finds in Lövestam's position.

35. D.H. Small ('The Prophet Hosea: God's Alternative to Divorce for the Reason of Infidelity', *JPsT* 7 [1979] 133–40) lists 10 reasons why it cannot be said that Hosea 'divorced' Gomer. Cf. H.H. Rowley, 'The Marriage of Hosea', *BJRL* 39 (1956–7) 227–30; F.I. Andersen and D.N. Freedman, *Hosea* (AB; Garden City, NY: Doubleday, 1980) 124, 220–4.

36. From J.J. Kilgallen's perspective (see end of chap. 2), 'The attention to the Law, then, giving rise to a general legal atmosphere, can explain Matthew's concern to make explicit a particular exception

to the general law that divorce is an adulterous act' ('To what are the Matthean Exception-Texts (5, 32 and 19, 9) an Exception?' *Bib* 61 [1980] 105).

37. This same principle is operative in 1 Cor. 7: 15. See below.

38. Cf. D. Greenwood, 'Moral Obligation in the Sermon on the Mount', *TS* 31 (1970) 301–6, 308–9.

39. Cf. Josephus *Antiquities* 4. 253; *The Life* 415, 426–7; Philo *Special Laws* 3. 30; Hauck and Schulz, *TDNT* 6: 591 n.71.

40. The Essenes combined Gen. 1: 27 with Gen. 7: 9 and Deut. 17: 17 (CD 4.20–1) to forbid at least polygamy and remarriage after divorce and possibly both polygamy and divorce. Cf. J.R. Mueller, 'The Temple Scroll and the Gospel Divorce Texts', *RevQ* 38 (1980) 247–56.

41. Cf. Isaksson, *Marriage and Ministry*, 90–1.

42. D.R. Catchpole, 'The Synoptic Divorce Material as a Traditio-Historical Problem', *BJRL* 57 (1974) 120.

43. B.M. Metzger, *The New Testament: Its Background, Growth, and Content* (Nashville: Abingdon, 1965) 163 n.10.

44. Cf. J.B. Hurley, *Man and Woman in Biblical Perspective* (Grand Rapids: Zondervan, 1981) 100–3.

45. Ibid., 100. Cf. Isaksson, *Marriage and Ministry*, 45 n.1; J.P. Meier, *Law and History in Matthew's Gospel. A Redactional Study of Mt. 5: 17–48* (AnBib 71; Rome, Biblical Institute Press, 1976) 143 n.44.

46. D.W. Amram, 'Divorce', *JE* 4: 624–5; Abrahams, *Pharisaism and the Gospels*, 71; G.F. Moore, *Judaism in the First Centuries of the Christian Era: The Age of the Tannaim* (3 vols in 2; n.p.; Harvard Univ. Press, 1927–30; reprint ed., New York: Schocken, 1971) 2: 123–4; E. Neufeld, *Ancient Hebrew Marriage Laws* (London: Longman's, Green & Co., 1944) 178; Y. Zakovitch, 'The Woman's Rights in the Biblical Law of Divorce', in *JLA* 4 (ed. B.S. Jackson; Leiden: Brill, 1981) 28–46.

47. The school of Shammai transposed the *erwaṯ dāḇār* of Deut. 24: 1 into *deḇar 'erwāh* (*m. Git.* 9.10), which corresponds almost exactly with the wording of Matt. 5: 32. Cf. Abrahams, *Pharisaism and the Gospels*, 71; Moore, *Judaism*, 2: 124 n.4; J. Dupont, *Mariage et divorce dans l'évangile: Matthieu 19, 3–12 et parallèles* (Bruges: Desclée, 1959) 87, 129; and esp. B. Vawter, 'Divorce and the New Testament', *CBQ* 39 (1977) 534 n.12.

48. A. Plummer, *An Exegetical Commentary on the Gospel according to S. Matthew* (London: Robert Scott, 1909) 260. Cf. M. Thurian, *Marriage and Celibacy* (trans. N. Emerton; London: SCM, 1959) 25–6; E. Schillebeeckx, *Marriage: Human Reality and Saving Mystery* (trans. N.D. Smith; New York: Sheed and Ward, 1965) 153; and many others.

49. R.A. Dyson and B. Leeming, 'Except It Be for Fornication?' *Scr* 8

(1956) 76. Cf. B. Vawter, 'The Divorce Clauses in Mt. 5, 32 and 19, 9', *CBQ* 16 (1954) 158.

50. D. Field, 'Talking points: The divorce debate – where are we now?' *Them* NS 8: 3 (1983) 29. Cf. Murray, *Divorce*, 35–43; D. Atkinson, 'A Response', *ChM* 95 (1981) 163.

51. G.E. Ladd, *A Theology of the New Testament* (Grand Rapids: Eerdmans, 1974) 93.

52. Barr, *Semantics*, 124.

53. E.D. Hirsch, Jr., *Validity in Interpretation* (New Haven, Conn.: Yale Univ. Press, 1967) 85 n.10.

54. Thiselton, 'Semantics', 82.

55. Ibid., 78–9. Cf. G.B. Caird, *The Language and Imagery of the Bible* (Philadelphia: Westminster, 1980), chap. 2: 'The Meaning of Meaning'.

56. Many writers still fall into the mistaken notion that the details of Deut. 24: 1–3 somehow constitute legislation when in fact the only piece of legislation found here occurs in v. 4 (cf. H. Montefiore, 'Jesus on Divorce and Remarriage', in *Marriage, Divorce and the Church: The Report of a Commission appointed by the Archbishop of Canterbury to prepare a statement on the Christian Doctrine of Marriage* [London: SPCK, 1971] 79–95). Zerwick (*Biblical Greek*, § 458) has the correct analysis. See chap.5, n.22.

57. For lexical studies of *porneia*, see R.H. Charles, *The Teaching of the New Testament on Divorce* (London: Wms. & Norgate, 1921) 91–115; F. Gavin, 'A Further Note on *PORNEIA*', *Theol* 16 (1928) 102–5; Isaksson, *Marriage and Ministry*, 127–42; B. Malina, 'Does *PORNEIA* Mean Fornication?' *NovT* 14 (1972) 10–17; J. Jensen, 'Does *PORNEIA* Mean Fornication? A Critique of Bruce Malina', *NovT* 20 (1978) 161–84. Both Malina (11–13) and Jensen (174) believe that *porneia* in the Matthean passages designates an incestuous 'marriage'.

58. M.J. Harris, 'Prepositions and Theology in the Greek New Testament', *NIDNTT* 3 (1978) 1195.

59. Vawter, 'Divorce and the NT', 531 n.4.

60. Jensen, 'Does *PORNEIA* Mean Fornication?' 172–3.

61. Isaksson, *Marriage and Ministry*, 133–4.

62. Andersen and Freedman, *Hosea*, 157–63.

63. Cf. J.C. Hurd, Jr., *The Origin of 1 Corinthians* (New ed.; Macon, Georgia: Mercer Univ. Press, 1983) 63–74.

64. We wish to thank Dale M. Wheeler for his permission to use an abbreviated form of his exegetical outline of 1 Cor. 7.

65. Cf. Hurd, *1 Corinthians*, 158–65; G.D. Fee, '1 Corinthians 7: 1 in the *NIV*', *JETS* 23 (1980) 307–14.

66. Cf. W.F. Orr, 'Paul's Treatment of Marriage in 1 Corinthians 7', *Pittsburgh Perspective* 8: 3 (1967) 12; C.H. Giblin, '1 Corinthians 7 –

A Negative Theology of Marriage and Celibacy?' *TBT* 41 (1969) 2841.

67. Cf. J.K. Elliott, 'Paul's Teaching on Marriage in 1 Corinthians: Some Problems Considered', *NTS* 19 (1973) 219–25.

68. Cf. H. Vörlander and C. Brown, '*Katallassō*', *NIDNTT* 3 (1978) 172–3. Note Brown's 'redactional additions' to this article by Vorländer, who otherwise understands Paul's teaching on remarriage as we do.

69. Charles, *Teaching*, 51–2.

70. Ibid., 52.

71. For discussions of why Paul does not, if he knew of it, refer to the exception clause, see Isaksson, *Marriage and Ministry*, 78; Dungan, *Sayings of Jesus*, 132–3. B.A. Pearson, in a Review of Dungan's book (*Int* 26 [1972] 350–1), believes Paul's parenthesis in 1 Cor. 7: 11a may refer to Matthew's 'exception'.

72. Dungan, *Sayings of Jesus*, 89–93. Cf. P. Hoffman, 'Jesus' Saying about Divorce and its Interpretation in the New Testament Tradition', *Concilium* 55 (1970) 62.

73. Catchpole, 'Synoptic Divorce Material', 106. Cf. Pearson, 'Review', 350; J.A. Fitzmyer, 'The Matthean Divorce Texts and Some New Palestinian Evidence', *TS* (1976) 200.

74. For a study of these terms, see Fitzmyer, 'Matthean Divorce Texts', 210–11.

75. Josephus *Antiquities* 15. 259 (15.7.10). There were ways in which the Jewish wife could get round this. Cf. D. Daube, *The New Testament and Rabbinic Judaism* (London: Athlone, 1956) 365–6; Catchpole, 'Synoptic Divorce Material', 111–13.

76. For a discussion of the Corinthian attitude that lies behind Paul's directives in these verses and each of the problems in 1 Cor. 7, see Catchpole, ibid., 108; Fee, '1 Corinthians 7: 1', 312–14.

77. Cf. W.C. Kaiser, Jr., 'Legitimate Hermeneutics', in *Inerrancy* (ed. N.L. Geisler; Grand Rapids: Zondervan, 1979) 144 (yet Kaiser is a defender of the Erasmian view). B.K. Waltke ('1 Corinthians 11: 2–16: An Interpretation', *BSac* 135 [1978] 46–7) also makes a distinction between the Law and the creation directives.

78. Cf. A.F. Johnson, 'Is There a Biblical Warrant for Natural-Law Theories?' *JETS* 25 (1982) 191.

79. D. Atkinson, *To Have and To Hold* (London: Collins, 1979) 124.

80. A. Robertson and A. Plummer, *A Critical and Exegetical Commentary on the First Epistle of St Paul to the Corinthians* (2nd ed.; ICC; Edinburgh: T. & T. Clark, 1911) 143. Others who claim that remarriage is not in the scope of Paul's language include K. Lake, 'The Earliest Christian Teaching on Divorce', *Exp* 10 (1910) 416–17; P. Dulau, 'The Pauline Privilege: Is It Promulgated in the First Epistle to the Corinthians?' *CBQ* 13 (1951) 146–52; R.L. Roberts, 'The

Meaning of *Chorizo* and *Douloo* in I Corinthians 7: 10–17', *RestQ* 8 (1965) 179–84; C.K Barrett, *A Commentary on the First Epistle to the Corinthians* (HNTC; New York: Harper & Row, 1968) 167.·

81. J.A. Bengel, *New Testament Word Studies* (trans. C.T. Lewis and M.R. Vincent; 2 vols.; Philadelphia: Perkinpine & Higgins, 1864; reprint ed., Grand Rapids: Kregel, 1971) 2: 210.

82. Dungan, *Sayings of Jesus*, 97. Catchpole ('Synoptic Divorce Material', 108 n.3) lists four other writers who understand v. 16 in the optimistic sense. For a discussion of the question, see S. Kubo, 'I Corinthians vii. 16: Optimistic or Pessimistic?' *NTS* 24 (1978) 539 –44. On the use of *ei* in questions, see Zerwick, *Biblical Greek*, §§ 403–5. Calvin (C.J. Blaisdell, 'Calvin's Letters to Women: The Courting of Ladies in High Places', *Sixteenth Century Journal* 13: 3 [1982] 71) insisted that even if a Protestant wife was brutally beaten by her Catholic husband, she must not leave him unless she is convinced her life is in danger.

83. Cf. T.P. Considine, 'The Pauline Privilege', *ACR* 40 (1963) 110–13.

84. Barr, *Semantics*, 100. See esp. pp. 100–60.

85. Ibid., 113.

86. Lövestam, 'Divorce and Remarriage', 65.

87. See chap. 1 n.8 and n.56.

88. J.A. Fischer, '1 Cor. 7: 8–24 – Marriage and Divorce', *BR* 23 (1978) 27.

89. K. Ritzer ('Secular Law and the Western Church's Concept of Marriage', *Concilium* 55 [1970] 69) notes that 'Pope Innocent I (401–17) stressed the ruling that anyone must also be reckoned a bigamist who had already been married as a pagan and then contracted a second marriage as a Christian. "For baptism does indeed wash away sins, but not a number of wives."'

90. For the meaning of 2 Cor. 5: 17, see Ladd, *Theology of the NT*, 479–94.

91. See above n.66.

92. A. Peters, 'St. Paul and Marriage: A Study of I Corinthians Chapter Seven', *AfER* 6 (1964) 218–19; J.M. Ford, 'Levirate Marriage in St. Paul (1 Cor. vii)', *NTS* 10 (1964) 361–2; E. Arens, 'Was St. Paul Married', *TBT* 66 (1973) 1188–91; E.M. Yamauchi, 'Cultural Aspects of Marriage in the Ancient World', *BSac* 135 (1978) 250.

93. Fee, '1 Corinthians 7: 1', 307–12.

94. Ibid., 308–9.

95. Ibid., 311, 314.

96. Ibid., 312.

97. C. Brown, '*Chōrizō*: Divorce, Separation and Remarriage', *NIDNTT* 3 (1978) 537. Brown has inserted his view of 1 Cor. 7: 27–8 in two or three other articles in the *NIDNTT*.

98. Robertson and Plummer, *First Corinthians*, 158–60; R. Kugelman, '1 Cor 7: 36–38', *CBQ* 10 (1948) 63–71.

99. H. Achelis, 'Agapētae', *ERE* 1: 179; R.H. Seabolt, 'Spiritual Marriage in the Early Church: A Suggested Interpretation of 1 Cor. 7: 36–38', *CTM* 30 (1959) 103–19, 176–89; Stauffer, *TDNT* 1: 652 and n.24; A. Oepke, *'Gynē'*, *TDNT* 1 (1964) 785; G. Schrenk, *'Thelēma'*, *TDNT* 3 (1965) 60–1; G. Delling, *'Parthenos'*, *TDNT* 5 (1967) 836; possibly J. Gager, 'Functional Diversity in Paul's Use of End Time Language', *JBL* 89 (1970) 330–3; Hurd, *1 Corinthians*, 169–80.

100. Ford, 'Levirate Marriage', 361–5; 'The Rabbinic Background of St. Paul's Use of *hyperakmos* (1 Cor. vii: 36)', *JJS* 17 (1966) 89–91.

101. See above n.67. Also S. Belkin, 'The Problem of Paul's Background', *JBL* 54 (1935) 49–52; W.F. Beck, '1 Corinthians 7: 36–38', *CTM* 25 (1954) 370–2; H. Chadwick, '"All Things to All men" (1 Cor, ix. 22)', *NTS* 1 (1954–5) 266–8 (Chadwick may well be correct in saying that the question addressed to Paul came from engaged couples who had come under the ascetic teaching current in Corinth.); C.S.C. Williams, 'I and II Corinthians', *PCB* §834e; BDF §101 (*gamein*); MHT 2: 409–10.

102. Paul's next statement in 1 Cor. 7: 27 is, 'Are you released from a wife (*lelysai apo gynaikos*)? Do not seek a wife'. *Lelysai* is most likely a present perfect in which the verb *lyō* expresses a state or condition of singleness (cf BDF §341). The *NIV* translation, 'Are you unmarried?' is correct if 'unmarried' means 'never before married'. The *NEB* translation, 'Has your marriage been dissolved?' is way off the mark. The meaning of vv. 27–8 is not solved on a grammatical level, but on the contextual level. At v.25 Paul turns to the previously unmarried.

103. There is a knotty textual and punctuation problem at the beginning of v. 34. Elliott ('Paul's Teaching on Marriage', 221) adopts the reading of p^{15} BP 104, 365, etc. Though similar to the *RSV* and *NIV* translation, he feels the single woman and betrothed girl are here differentiated. We would adopt the reading of D F G Ψ and the majority of MSS (cf. p^{46} א A 33, etc.) and place a full stop at the end of v. 33, nothing after *memeristai* in v. 34 and a semicolon after *hē gynē*. This maintains parallelism with vv. 32b–3. Cf. F.L. Godet, *Commentary on First Corinthians* (Edinburgh: T. & T. Clark, 1889; reprint ed., Grand Rapids: Kregel, 1977) 381–4.

104. G.R. Dunstan, 'Hard Sayings – V. 1 Cor. 6: 16', *Theol* 66 (1963) 491. See also J.I. Miller ('A Fresh Look at I Corinthians 6. 16 f.', *NTS* 27 [1980] 125–7) who argues that 'relationships and loyalties are at stake in this passage, but not the union of man and wife, with which Paul is not, at the moment, mainly concerned' (126).

105. BAGD, *'pas'*, 1αβ. But some have argued that the adversative *de* can signify an exceptive contrast and thus justify the interpolation of 'other' in the general statement.

106. C.F.D. Moule, *An Idiom Book of New Testament Greek* (2nd ed.;

Cambridge: Univ. Press, 1959) 196. J. Murphy-O'Connor ('Corinthian Slogans in 1 Cor. 6: 12–20,' *CBQ* 40 [1978] 391–6), as far as we know, is the most recent survey of this understanding. In addition to showing that v. 13a *and* v. 13b form part of the Corinthian slogan, he attempts to show that 'there can be little doubt that [v. 18b] also must be attributed to the Corinthians' (395). *Sōma*, he adds, carries its normal physical (not holistic, with Moule and others) sense.

107. R.H. Gundry, *SŌMA in Biblical Theology with an Emphasis on Pauline Anthropology* (SNTSMS 29; Cambridge: Univ. Press, 1976) 69.

108. M. Barth, *Ephesians* (AB; 2 vols; Garden City, NY: Doubleday, 1974) 640–1. Cf. G.R. Dunstan, 'The Marriage Covenant', *Theol* 78: 659 (1975) 244–52.

Chapter 7

1. Cf. A. Mahoney, 'A New Look at the Divorce Clauses in Mt 5, 32 and 19, 9', *CBQ* 30 (1968) 29–38. Possibly J.J. O'Rourke, 'A Note on an Exception: Mt 5: 32 (19: 9) and 1 Cor 7: 12 Compared', *HeyJ* 5 (1964) 299–302.

2. J. Bonsirven, *Le divorce dans le Nouveau Testament* (Paris: Desclée, 1948); H. Baltensweiler, 'Die Ehebruchsklauseln bei Matthäus zu Matth. 5: 32; 19: 9', *TZ* 15 (1959) 340–56; *Die Ehe im Neuen Testament* (ATANT 52; Zürich: Zwingli Verlag, 1967). Cf. Dupont's review of and response to Bonsirven's arguments in *Mariage et divorce dans l'évangile* (Bruges: Desclée, 1959) 107–14.

3. W.K. Lowther Clark, 'The Excepting Clause in St Matthew', *Theol* 15 (1927) 161–2; F. Gavin, 'A Further Note on *PORNEIA*', *Theol* 16 (1928) 102–5; F.F. Bruce, *Commentary on the Book of Acts* (NICNT; Grand Rapids: Eerdmans, 1954) 315 and n.52; C.C. Ryrie, *The Place of Women in the Church* (New York: Macmillan, 1958) 43–8; H.J. Richards, 'Christ on Divorce', *Scr* 11 (1959) 22–32; M. Zerwick, *Biblical Greek* (trans. and adapted from 4th Latin ed. by J. Smith; Rome, 1963) p. 43 n.8 and §442; B. Vawter, *The Four Gospels: An Introduction* (Garden City, N.Y.: Doubleday, 1967) 273–6; 'The Biblical Theology of Divorce', *PCTSA* 22 (1967) 223–43, esp. p. 235 nn.30–1; D. Crossan, 'Divorce and Remarriage in the New Testament', in *The Bond of Marriage* (ed. W.W. Bassett; Notre Dame: Univ. Press, 1968) 1–33; R.P. Martin, 'St. Matthew's Gospel in Recent Study', *ExpTim* 80 (1969) 136; J.P. Meier, *Law and History in Matthew's Gospel: A Redactional Study of Mt. 5: 17–48* (AnBib 71; Rome: Biblical Institute Press, 1976) 140–50 (and see p. 147 n.54 for others associated with this view); J.A. Fitzmyer, 'The Matthean

Divorce Texts and Some New Palestinian Evidence', *TS* 37 (1976) 197–226; J.C. Laney, *The Divorce Myth* (Minneapolis, Minn.: Bethany, 1981) 62–81.

4. Bonsirven (*Le divorce*, 46–60) understands *porneia* in the Jerusalem decree and the Matthean texts in a wider sense than the forbidden unions of Lev. 18: 6–18. 'Concubinage' is the word he would suggest: any marriage unlawful in Jewish law would be included. Cf. R.A. Dyson and B. Leeming, 'Except It Be for Fornication?' *Scr* 8 (1956) 75–82.

5. Bonsirven (*Le divorce*, 46), Dyson and Leeming ('Except', 81), and Ryrie and Laney believe the exception clauses were spoken by Jesus.

6. F.J. Moloney, 'Matthew 19, 3–12 and Celibacy: A Redactional and Form Critical Study', *JSNT* 2 (1979) 42–60.

7. *APOT* 2: 58 n.7. Tobit 4: 12 possibly refers to marriages with foreigners.

8. Cf. J. Milgrom, 'The Temple Scroll', *BA* 41 (1978) 115. The scroll is dated about the second half of the second cent. BC. On the extension to all the people, see D. Daube, *The New Testament and Rabbinic Judaism* (London: Athlone, 1956) 86; G. Vermes, *The Dead Sea Scrolls in English* (Middlesex, Eng.: Penguin Books, 1968) 216.

9. Cf. B.H. Streeter, *The Four Gospels: A Study of Origins* (London: Macmillan, 1936) 16, 500–28; Meier (*Law and History*, 9) reminds us that Ignatius of Antioch is the first to quote Matthew.

10. F.F. Bruce, *New Testament History* (N.p.: Thomas Nelson, 1969; reprint ed., Garden City, N.Y.: Doubleday, Anchor, 1972) 286.

11. Ibid., 287. A valuable unpublished work on the text and meaning of the decree is W.A. Brindle, 'The Apostolic Decree of Acts 15' (Th.M. thesis, Dallas Theological Seminary, Dallas, Texas, 1973).

12. Cf. G.J. Wenham, *The Book of Leviticus* (NICOT; Grand Rapids: Eerdmans, 1979) 32–7; M. Barth, *Ephesians* (AB; 2 vols.; Garden City, N.Y.: Doubleday, 1974) 2: 590–1.

13. Bruce, *NT History*, 287–8.

14. Fitzmyer, 'Matthean Divorce Texts', 209. Cf. Richards, 'Christ on Divorce', 29–30; Crossan, 'Divorce and Remarriage', 23; F. Hauck and S. Schulz, '*Pornē ktl.*', *TDNT* 6 (1968) 593.

15. Cf. Isaksson, *Marriage and Ministry in the New Temple* (trans. N. Tomkinson with J. Gray; ASNU 24; Lund: Gleerup, 1965) 131.

16. Cf. J.D. Eisenstein, 'Incest: In Rabbinical Literature', *JE* 6: 574; Ben-Zion Schereschewsky, 'Marriage, Prohibited', *EncJud* 11: 1052.

17. Laney, *Divorce Myth*, 75. Cf. Dyson and Leeming, 'Except', 81–2; Mahoney, 'A New Look', 33.

18. Bruce, *NT History*, 28; R. Banks, *Jesus and the Law in the Synoptic Tradition* (SNTSMS 28; Cambridge: Univ. Press, 1975) 158; H. Hoehner, *Herod Antipas* (Cambridge: Univ. Press, 1972; reprint ed.,

Grand Rapids: Zondervan, 1980) 139 n.2; W.L. Lane, *The Gospel according to Mark* (NICNT; Grand Rapids: Eerdmans, 1974) 353–4; R.W. Herron, Jr., 'Mark's Jesus on Divorce: Mark 10: 1–12 Reconsidered', *JETS* 25 (1982) 273–81.

19. Crossan, 'Divorce and Remarriage', 24.
20. Richards, 'Christ on Divorce', 31. Cf. Dupont, *Mariage et divorce*, 88–91; S.S. Smalley, 'Redaction Criticism', in *New Testament Interpretation* (ed. I.H. Marshall; Grand Rapids: Eerdmans, 1977) 185–6, 190.
21. Banks, *Jesus and the Law*, 153 n.1.
22. Richards, 'Christ on Divorce', 31–32.
23. Fitzmyer, 'Matthean Divorce Texts', 220–21.
24. See chap. 6 n.57.
25. *The Institutes of Gaius* (with trans. and commentary by F. DeZulueta; 2 vols; Oxford: Clarendon, 1946–53) 1: 18–23.
26. Ibid., 2: 31.
27. G. Rawlinson, *Ezra and Nehemiah: Their Lives and Times* (New York: Randolph, [1890]) 42. Cf. *The Oxford Annotated Bible with the Apocrypha* (eds H.G. May and B.M. Metzger; New York: Oxford Univ. Press, 1965) 584 n. at Ezra 10: 2.
28. Though Ezra knows of and uses the 'normal' Hebrew verb for 'to marry' (*lāqaḥ*, cf. Ezra 2: 61), he uses other terms when he says they 'took' (*nāśā* in 9: 2, 12; 10: 44) some of the daughters of the land, or 'gave a dwelling to' (*yāšab* in 10: 2, 10, 14, 17–18) 'foreign women'. The former verb is used elsewhere in the OT of 'to take as a wife' in Ruth 1: 4; 2 Chr. 11: 31; 13: 21; 24: 3; the three instances in Ezra, and Neh. 13: 25. Each of these references has foreign women, multiple wives and/or concubines as the object. The latter term is used only in Ezra and Nehemiah (13: 24, 27) and the accusative is always foreign women. The LXX uses *kathizō* (to sit down, settle, live) to translate this word, and *kathizō* is never used to translate any of the other 'usual' words for marriage (i.e., *lāqaḥ*, *bā'al*, or *nāśā'*).
29. Ezra uses *yāṣā'* (of 'putting away' wives and children in 10: 3, 19 in the Hiphil; cf. Qal in Deut. 24: 2), and elsewhere in the OT *gāraš* is used passively only of divorced women in Lev. 21: 7, 14; 22: 13; Num. 30: 9; and Ezek. 44: 22 (BDB, p. 176); and *šālaḥ* means to 'send away, dismiss' (= divorce) with acc. of wife in Deut. 22: 19, 29; 24: 1, 3, 4; Jer. 3: 1, 8; Mal. 2: 16 (all Piel), and fig. in Isa. 50: 1 (Pual). W.R. Eichhorst ('Ezra's Ethics on Intermarriage and Divorce', *Grace Journal* 10: 3 [1969] 23) thinks that Ezra also carried out this divorce action 'according to the law' (10: 3) and followed Deut. 24: 1–4. This not only misunderstands Deut. 24: 1–4, but it fails to see that 'the law' according to which they should 'put away' their women refers to that law in 9: 1–2, 10–12 and 14 which Ezra was confessing: 'shall

we again break *Thy commandments* and *intermarry* with *the people* who commit these abominations'. The law in view is Deut. 7: 3 and Exod. 34: 16, *not* Deut. 24: 1–4.

30. For a possible explanation of this incident, see G.E. Mendenhall, *Tenth Generation: The Origins of the Biblical Tradition* (Baltimore: John Hopkins Univ. Press, 1973) 105–21.

31. R. Yaron, 'Aramaic Marriage Contracts from Elephantine', *JSS* 3 (1958) 12, 23, 26–7, 39.

32. G.D. Fee, '*Eidōlothyta* Once Again: An Interpretation of 1 Corinthians 8–10', *Bib* 61 (1980) 172–97.

33. Ibid., 186. Cf. Eph. 5: 3, 5; Gal. 5: 19, 20; Col. 3: 5.

34. Ibid., 183.

35. Cf. C. Rabin, ed. and trans., *The Zadokite Documents* (2nd rev. ed.; Oxford: Clarendon, 1958) 16–19.

36. See chap. 6 n.47. Against this, see Dyson and Leeming, 'Except', 77–8; Isaksson, *Marriage and Ministry*, 90–1.

37. E. Lövestam, 'Divorce and Remarriage in the New Testament', in *JLA* 4 (ed. B.S. Jackson; Leiden: Brill, 1981) 56.

Chapter 8

1. J. Murray, *Divorce* (Phillipsburg, NJ: Presbyterian & Reformed, [1953]) 34 n.4. H. Montefiore's ('Jesus on Divorce and Remarriage', in *Marriage, Divorce and the Church* [London: SPCK, 1971]86) criticisms of the betrothal view either betray his misunderstanding of the authoritative presentation of this view or that he has not read it.

2. A. Isaksson, *Marriage and Ministry in the New Temple* (trans. N. Tomkinson with J. Gray; ASNU 24; Lund: Gleerup, 1965). In this study Isaksson preferred his view over six others. He appears not to have considered the preteritive view. Evangelicals appear to be largely unaware of Isaksson's book, and though many reviews of it have appeared, we have found none in traditionally evangelical journals. J.D.M. Derrett, for instance, wrote of Isaksson's study: 'No short review can do justice to the wealth of material and argument, presented always cogently and often brilliantly' (*JBL* 85 [1966] 98). Cf. the reviews by J.A. Fitzmyer, *TS* 27 (1966) 451–4; J.M. Ford, *JTS* 18 (1967) 197–200.

3. Cf. B. Drachman, 'Betrothal', *JE* 3: 125; M. Mielziner, *The Jewish Law of Marriage and Divorce* (Cincinnati, Ohio: Block, 1884) 76–7.

4. E. Neufeld, *Ancient Hebrew Marriage Laws* (London: Longman's, Green & Co., 1944) 142–3. For a quite extensive study on betrothal in Biblical and Talmudic Law, see B. Cohen, 'On the Theme

of Betrothal in Jewish and Roman Law', *PAAJR* 18 (1948) 67–135.

5. G.F. Moore, *Judaism in the First Centuries of the Christian Era* (3 vols in 2; n.p.: Harvard Univ. Press, 1927–30; reprint ed., New York: Schocken, 1971) 2:121. Cf. R. de Vaux, *Ancient Israel* (2 vols; New York: McGraw Hill, paperback ed., 1965) 1:36; G. Delling, '*Parthenos*', *TDNT* 5 (1967) 835 n.59; Λ. Phillips, 'Another Look at Adultery', *JSOT* 20 (1981) 11; and many others.

6. Neufeld, *Hebrew Marriage Laws*, 143–4. Cf. Drachman, *JE* 3:126; Mielziner, *Jewish Law*, 82.

7. Cf. N. Lathrop, 'The Holy Scriptures and Divorce', *BSac* 56 (1899) 266–77; E.G. Selwyn, 'Christ's Teaching on Marriage and Divorce: A Reply to Dr. Charles', *Theology* 15 (1927) 88–101; W. Fisher-Hunter, *The Divorce Problem* (Waynesboro, Penn.: MacNeish, 1952); J.M. Boice, *The Sermon on the Mount* (Grand Rapids: Zondervan, 1972) 134–41; C.C. Ryrie, *You Mean the Bible Teaches That?* (Chicago: Moody, 1974) 45–56; M. Geldard, 'Jesus' Teaching on Divorce: Thoughts on the Meaning of *porneia* in Matthew 5:32 and 19:9', *ChM* 92 (1978) 134–43; J.D. Pentecost, *The Words and Works of Jesus Christ: A Study of the Life of Christ* (Grand Rapids: Zondervan, 1981) 354–58. C.-D. Stoll, *Ehe und Ehescheidung: Die Weisungen Jesu* (Giessen: Brunnen Verlag, 1983) 28. Cf. I.H. Marshall ('*Apostasion*', *NIDNTT* 1 [1975] 506) mentions this view. For other proponents of this view, see J. Dupont, *Mariage et divorce dans l'évangile* (Bruges: Desclée, 1959) 108 n.3.

8. Isaksson, *Marriage and Ministry*, 139.

9. As for the original form and content of Jesus' divorce saying, Isaksson competently surveys the whole scholarly debate of form and content (66–74), the Synoptic problem (93–115), the external and internal evidence raised against the authenticity of the Matthean exception clause (75–87), as well as the reasons suggested for the inclusion of the clauses (87–92), yet concludes that there are no decisive arguments that can be put forward against the authenticity of the clauses: they may well go back to Jesus Himself.

10. Ibid., 140.

11. Ibid., 140–1.

12. Ibid., 126.

13. Cf. E.D. Burton, 'The Purpose and Plan of the Gospel of Matthew', *Biblical World* 11 (1898) 37–44; R.P. Martin, 'St. Matthew's Gospel in Recent Study', *ExpTim* 80 (1969) 132–6.

14. I. Abrahams, *Studies in Pharisaism and the Gospels* (2 vols in 1; Cambridge: Univ. Press, 1917–24; reprint ed., New York: KTAV, 1967) 73. Cf. Moore, *Judaism*, 2:125.

15. Abrahams, *Pharisaism and the Gospels*, 70.

16. Cf. A.N. Sherwin-White, *Roman Society and Roman Law in the New*

Testament (Oxford: Univ. Press, 1963; reprint ed., Grand Rapids: Baker, 1978) 21 n.3 and pp. 41–2.

17. A. Tosato, 'Joseph, Being a Just Man (Matt 1: 19)', *CBQ* 41 (1979) 548.

18. Ford, 'Review', 198.

19. Cf. J.D.M. Derrett, *Law in the New Testament* (London: Darton, Longman & Todd, 1970) 156–88; F.F. Bruce, *New Testament History* (N.p.: Thomas Nelson, 1969; reprint ed., Garden City, NY: Doubleday, Anchor, 1972) 180–81; L. Morris, *The Gospel according to John* (NICNT; Grand Rapids: Eerdmans, 1971) 884–91; S.A. James, 'The Adulteress and the Death Penalty', *JETS* 22 (1979) 45–53; Z.C. Hodges, 'The Woman Taken in Adultery (John 7: 53 – 8: 11): Exposition', *BSac* 137 (1980) 51 n.12.

20. Consider that Matthew is recording events and sayings from the life of Jesus in Jewish Palestine around AD 30, yet he is writing a Greek document (?) for a Greek-speaking community in and around Antioch anywhere from 30 to 40 years later (in the opinion of most scholars). That Matthew is faithful to record sayings of Jesus that may have no direct application for his readers is evident from passages like Matt. 5: 23–6. Cf. R.T. France, 'The Authenticity of the Sayings of Jesus', in *History, Criticism and Faith* (ed. C. Brown; Inter-Varsity, 1977) 101–41.

21. Isaksson is most likely wrong when he states that Joseph *should have* 'accused Mary in court and thus have shamed her publicly' (*Marriage and Ministry*, 138). He understands the *kai* in this verse adversatively (BDF § 442, 1): 'Her husband Joseph was a just man *and yet* would not put her to open shame . . .'

22. Ibid., 139.

23. Ibid., 39–40.

24. See the chap. on 'Home and Family' in *The Jewish People in the First Century* (eds S. Safrai and M. Stern; 2 vols; Compendia Rerum Iudaicarum ad Novum Testamentum; Assen/Amsterdam: Van-Gorcum, 1974–6), 2: 728–92. Also, Cohen, 'On the Theme of Betrothal', and Moore, *Judaism*, 119–40.

25. C.F. Keil and F. Delitzsch, *The Pentateuch* (trans. J. Martin; 3 vols in 1; Commentary on the Old Testament; n.p.: reprint ed., Grand Rapids: Eerdmans, (1978), *Exodus*, 124.

26. R. Brown, *The Gospel according to John* (AB; 2 vols; Garden City, NY: Doubleday, 1970) 1: 357. For a more complete discussion of this, see R. Schnackenburg, *The Gospel according to John* (3 vols; New York: Seabury, 1968–82) 2: 212.

27. Isaksson, *Marriage and Ministry*, 134–5.

28. Cf. end of chap. 7.

29. R. Banks, *Jesus and the Law in the Synoptic Tradition* (SNTSMS 28; Cambridge: Univ. Press, 1975) 155. Cf. Derrettt, 'Review', 98.

30. Isaksson, *Marriage and Ministry*, 134 n.1.
31. E. Lövestam, 'Divorce and Remarriage in the New Testament', in *JLA* 4 (ed. B.S. Jackson; Leiden: Brill, 1981) 57.
32. Ibid., 58.
33. Isaksson, *Marriage and Ministry*, 141.
34. *The Apostolic Fathers* (trans. K. Lake; LCL; 2 vols; London: Wm. Heinemann, 1912–13) 1: 273.
35. Isaksson, *Marriage and Ministry*, 141–2.
36. E. Schillebeeckx, *Marriage: Human Reality and Saving Mystery* (trans. N.D. Smith; New York: Sheed and Ward, 1965) 245. Cf. pp. 344–5.

Chapter 9

1. Criticised by F. Hauck and S. Schulz, '*Pornē ktl.*', *TDNT* 6 (1968) 592 n.75; M.J. Harris, 'Prepositions and Theology in the Greek New Testament', *NIDNTT* 3 (1978) 1195; B. Vawter, 'The Divorce Clauses in Mt 5, 32 and 19, 9', *CBQ* 16 (1954) 160–2.
2. W.L. Lane, *The Gospel according to Mark* (NICNT; Grand Rapids: Eerdmans, 1974) 173. Cf. C.E.B. Cranfield, *The Gospel according to Mark* (CGTC; Cambridge: Univ. Press, 1977) 154–5; 'St. Mark 4. 1–34', *SJT* 4 (1951) 398–414; T.F. Torrance, 'A Study in New Testament Communication', *SJT* 3 (1950) 298–313.
3. Vawter, 'Divorce Clauses', 155–6. Hauck and Schulz (*TDNT* 6: 591 n.71) agree: 'The addition of *kata pasan aitian* in Mt. (19: 3) is a hit at the lax view of the school of Hillel.'
4. Vawter, 'Divorce Clauses', 166.
5. Cf. J.P. Arendzen, 'Re-Writing St. Matthew', *Exp* 93 (1918) 366–71; 'Another Note on Matthew xix, 3–12', *Clergy Review* 21 (1941) 23–6; Vawter, 'Divorce Clauses', 163–7; T.V. Fleming, 'Christ and Divorce', *TS* 24 (1963) 106–20; R. Banks, *Jesus and the Law in the Synoptic Tradition* (SNTSMS 28; Cambridge: Univ. Press, 1975) 146–59. Fleming would translate Matt. 19: 9, 'not because of *adultery*', and states that Christ rules out all other causes for divorce but refuses to discuss the case of adultery (110–12).
6. Vawter, 'Divorce Clauses', 166.
7. Ibid., 164.
8. So Arendzen, 'St. Matthew', 368, 'Matthew xix, 3–12', 24 6; and Fleming, 'Christ and Divorce', 109. R.H. Gundry (*Matthew: A Commentary on His Literary and Theological Art* [Grand Rapids: Eerdmans, 1982] 381), like Arendzen, feels that there is enough evidence to warrant saying that the form of the exception clause in Matt. 5: 32 might be the correct reading for 19: 9 also.
9. C.F.D. Moule, *An Idiom Book of New Testament Greek* (2nd ed.;

Cambridge, Univ. Press, 1959) 86. A.T. Robertson (*GGNT*, 646) says *parektos* with the gen. means 'without'. Cf. BAGD.

10. Supported by B D $f^1 f^{13}$ 33 a number of Old Latin and Vulgate MSS, bo and sa. Cf. chap. 1 n.36.

11. *Didache* 6.1 ('See "that no one make thee to err" from this Way of the teaching, for he teaches thee *without* God', trans. by K. Lake, *The Apostolic Fathers*, LCL 1: 319) and *The Testimony of the Twelve Patriarchs* Zebulun 1.4 ('I am not conscious that I have sinned all my days, *save* in thought', *APOT* 2: 328). Arendzen ('Matthew xix, 3–12', 25) discusses these two passages.

12. Banks, *Jesus and the Law*, 156.

13. Vawter, 'Divorce Clauses', 164.

14. Of the 124 uses of *epi* in Matthew, 18 are followed by the dat., 37 are followed by the gen., and 69 are followed by the acc.

15. Cf. M. Zerwick, *Biblical Greek* (adopted and trans. from 4th Latin ed. by J. Smith; Rome, 1963) §126. Cf. Matt. 7: 28; 14: 14; 18: 5, 13; 19: 9; 22: 33. Robertson (*GGNT*, 646) feels the notion of basis is also found in Matt. 4: 4; 24: 5.

16. See chap. 4 n.11.

17. Vawter, 'Divorce Clauses', 164; Banks, *Jesus and the Law*, 156. Banks adopted Vawter's position. However, as of 1967, Vawter has basically adopted the unlawful marriages view, and thinks Dupont's and Quesnell's understanding of the eunuch-saying makes very good sense (cf. 'Divorce and the New Testament', *CBQ* [1977] 528–42).

18. Banks, *Jesus and the Law*, 156. Harris (*NIDNTT* 3: 1195) says literally this is 'not on the basis of immorality', then later mentions the exceptive character of the clause. Augustine (*Adulterous Marriages* 1.10.11 [FC 27: 74]) notes a number of textual variants for Matt. 19: 9 which he was aware of, and feels the better reading of the Greek is 'without the cause of immorality' (1.11.12) as C.T. Huegelmeyer translates it.

19. Cf. Fleming, 'Christ and Divorce', 118 n.33; Banks, *Jesus and the Law*, 156 n.2.

20. Banks, *Jesus and the Law*, 156.

21. See the excellent summary of these terms by Vawter, 'Divorce and the New Testament', 536–7 n.16.

22. J.B. Hurley (*Man and Woman in Biblical Perspective* [Grand Rapids: Zondervan, 1981] 103 n.12) makes the statement that 'had Matthew wanted to uphold Shammai's view, he would have chosen *aschēmon pragma* (shameful thing)'. Though we agree with him that Matthew does not adopt Shammai's view, his statement appears to be ill informed.

23. See chap. 6 n.47. Also, J.J. Rabinowitz, 'The Sermon on the Mount and the School of Shammai', *HTR* 49 (1956) 79; G. Kittel, '*Legō*',

TDNT 4 (1967) 105 n.143; E. Lövestam, 'Divorce and Remarriage in the New Testament', in *JLA* 4 (ed. B.S. Jackson; Leiden: Brill, 1981) 58 n.59.

24. B. Cohen, 'On the Theme of Betrothal in Jewish and Roman Law', *PAAJR* 18 (1948) 127 n.336. Cf. Lövestam, 'Divorce and Remarriage', 54–8.

25. Ibid., 60.

26. Ibid., 61.

27. Banks, *Jesus and the Law*, 157.

28. Cf. J. Behm, '*Exō*', *TDNT* 2 (1964) 576. As we noted in chap. 2, those who cannot accept Jesus' precept on divorce (Matt. 19: 9) in Matt. 19: 11a are the Pharisees and unbelievers. Jesus is not talking about two classes of Christians in Matt. 19: 11, but about true and false disciples.

29. Note for example: Matt. 13: 10–17, 34–6; 15: 10–20; 17: 19–20; 19: 10–12; 20: 17–19; Mark 4: 10–12, 33–4; 7: 17–23; 9: 28–9, 33–7; 10: 10–12, 23–31; Luke 8: 9–10, 18; 9: 18–27, 43–5; 10: 21–4; 18: 31–4.

30. Another parallel that seems to display a lack of understanding on the part of the disciples over a public situation was their inability to cast the demon out of the epileptic boy (Matt. 17: 14–20//Mark 9: 14–29).

31. For what this means, see Cranfield, *Gospel according to Mark*, 148–9, 154–5; Lane, *Mark*, 156–9, 172–3.

32. C.G. Montefiore, *The Synoptic Gospels* (2nd ed.; 2 vols; London: Macmillan, 1927) 1: 233.

33. Cf. D. Daube, *The New Testament and Rabbinic Judaism* (London: Athlone, 1956) 147–8. Most of Daube's criticisms of the secondary character of Matthew's account vanish with a careful reading of Matt. 19: 10–12.

34. (1) The question of paying tribute to Caesar (Matt. 22: 15–22) and (2) the question about the resurrection by the Sadducees (Matt. 22: 23–33). The critical questioning over the origin of Jesus' authority in Matt. 21: 23–7 is an example of where Jesus stalemated the religious leaders with His retort. The only instance where Jesus appears to answer a question that one of the religious leaders addressed to Him is in Matt. 22: 23–40. It appears to be a non-hostile question and probably an honest one.

35. H.J. Richards, 'Christ on Divorce', *Scr* 11 (1959) 26. Richards discusses these 'trick questions' in Matthew on pp. 26–7.

36. Banks, *Jesus and the Law*, 158. If by 'Mosaic commandment' Banks means Deut. 24: 1, then he too misses the remarriage legislation import of this passage which only comes in v. 4.

37. See the commentaries on Mark's gospel by Cranfield and Lane.

38. Cf. Daube, *NT and Rabbinic Judaism*, 'Public Retort and Private Explanation', 141–50.

39. See chap. 6 n.13. Note that BAGD ('*mē*') list Matt. 19: 9 under AI1 (= a negative particle, negativing clauses, in conditional clauses) and Matt. 26: 5 is placed under AIII6 (= in a prohibitive sense in abrupt expressions without a verb).

40. Zerwick, *Biblical Greek*, §442. Zerwick adopts the unlawful marriages view. Cf. 'De matrimonio et divortio in Evangelio', *Verbum domini* 38 (1960) 193–212.

Chapter 10

1. E. Stauffer, '*Gameō*', *TDNT* 1 (1964) 650 n.14. Stauffer adds: 'These casuistic clauses can hardly derive from Jesus and were obviously not known to Pl. in 1 C. 7: 10 ff.' Cf. T.W. Manson, *The Teaching of Jesus: Studies of Its Form and Content* (2nd ed.; Cambridge: Univ. Press, 1935) 200 n.5; W.D. Davies, 'The Moral Teaching of the Early Church', in *The Use of the Old Testament and Other Essays* (ed. J.M. Efird; Durham, N.C.: Duke Univ. Press, 1972) 324–5.

2. W.C. Allen, *A Critical and Exegetical Commentary on the Gospel according to S. Matthew* (3rd ed.; ICC; Edinburgh: T. & T. Clark, 1912) 201–2.

3. Ibid., 52. Contrast our understanding of this at the end of chap. 2.

4. Ibid., 203. Cf. R. Bultmann, *The History of the Synoptic Tradition* (trans. J. Marsh; rev. ed.; New York: Harper & Row, paperback ed., 1976) 26–7, 132; G. Bornkamm, *Jesus of Nazareth* (trans. Irene and Fraser McLusky with J.M. Robinson; New York: Harper & Row, 1960) 99; G. Bornkamm, G. Barth, and H.J. Held, *Tradition and Interpretation in Matthew* (trans. P. Scott; Philadelphia: Westminster, 1963) 25–6, 94, 158; W.D. Davies, *The Setting of the Sermon on the Mount* (Cambridge: Univ. Press, 1964) 388, 396–8; D.W. Shaner, *A Christian View of Divorce according to the Teachings of the New Testament* (Leiden: Brill, 1969) 54, 68, 79; P. Hoffmann, 'Jesus' Saying about Divorce and Its Interpretation in the New Testament Tradition', *Concilium* 55 (1970) 59–60; W. Harrington, 'Jesus' Attitude towards Divorce', *ITQ* 37 (1970) 203–6; L. Sabourin, 'The Divorce Clauses (Mt 5: 32; 19: 9)', *BTB* 2 (1972) 81.

5. D.R. Catchpole. 'The Synoptic Divorce Material as a Traditio-Historical Problem', *BJRL* 57 (1974) 95. Cf. Allen, *Matthew*, 205–6.

6. Sabourin, 'Divorce Clauses', 85. Cf. Harrington, 'Jesus' Attitude', 199–209. Harrington has since adopted Derrett's no further relations view (cf. 'The New Testament and Divorce', *ITQ* 39 [1972] 178–86). For another Catholic writer who feels that Matthew's exception is evidence of the Church's authority to express the mind

of Christ and permit divorce and remarriage in the case of adultery, see J.N.M. Wijngards, 'Do Jesus' Words on Divorce (Lk. 16: 18) Admit of No Exception?' *Jeevadhara* 4 (1975) 399–411. Another traditio-historical proponent is R.N. Soulen, 'Marriage and Divorce: A Problem in New Testament Interpretation', *Int* 23 (1969) 439–50.

7. For example, Catchpole believes that Matt. 19: 10–12 is unrelated to vv. 3–9 and he finds confusion in v.3 ('Synoptic Divorce Material', 95, 101). For further discussion of the principles of tradition criticism see Catchpole's essay on 'Tradition History', in *New Testament Interpretation* (ed. I.H. Marshall; Grand Rapids: Eerdmans, 1977) 165–80. Catchpole has been criticised by G.R. Osborne, 'The Evangelical and *Traditionsgeschichte*', *JETS* 21 (1978) 128.

8. Cf. R.H. Stein, 'Is it lawful for a man to divorce his wife?' *JETS* 22 (1979) 115–21. It is surprising that Stein, in choosing to believe that the exception clauses were never uttered by Jesus but inserted by Matthew, should then insist on maintaining the Erasmian interpretation. Why should Erasmus's reading of a difficult saying be allowed to establish the meaning of other texts which are clear and unambiguous? Stein gives two reasons for believing that Jesus' words on divorce in Mark and Luke are an overstatement (the harmonisation of the NT divorce sayings is thus a hermeneutical problem): (1) the Erasmian interpretation of Matt. 19: 9; and (2) an interpretation of 1 Cor. 7: 15 that permits remarriage. In the light of our study, both of these examples are misinterpreted by Stein and thus provide little basis for understanding Mark 10: 11–12 and Luke 16: 18 as overstatement.

9. Catchpole, 'Synoptic Divorce Material', 99.

10. Ibid., 99–100.

11. Ibid., 100.

12. Josephus *Antiquities* 15. 259–60 (15.7.10); 18. 136 (18.5.4)

13. Catchpole, 'Synoptic Divorce Material', 111–12.

14. Ibid., 105–7.

15. Cf. E. Lövestam, 'Divorce and Remarriage in the New Testament', in *JLA* 4 (ed. B.S. Jackson; Leiden: Brill, 1981) 60; A.M. Rabello, 'Divorce of Jews in the Roman Empire', in *JLA* 4 (1981) 92–3.

16. Catchpole, 'Synoptic Divorce Material', 100–27.

17. Cf. B.H. Streeter, *The Four Gospels: A Study of Origins* (London: Macmillan, 1936) 259. See the quite good review of this question in D.L. Dungan, *The Sayings of Jesus in the Churches of Paul* (Philadelphia: Fortress, 1971) 102–22. Cf. chap. 8 n.9.

18. Q. Quesnell, '"Made Themselves Eunuchs for the Kingdom of Heaven" (Mt 19, 12)', *CBQ* 30 (1968) 335–58.

19. B. Vawter, 'The Divorce Clauses in Mt 5, 32 and 19, 9', *CBQ* 16 (1954) 159.

20. A. Isaksson, *Marriage and Ministry in the New Temple* (trans. N. Tomkinson with J. Gray; ASNU 24; Lund: Gleerup, 1965) 72.
21. Ibid., 73.
22. Ibid., 73–4. Cf. pp. 85–7.
23. Quoted in Dungan, *Sayings*, 105–6. The italics are Dungan's.

Chapter 11

1. Cf. W.J. Bartling, 'Sexuality, Marriage, and Divorce in 1 Corinthians 6: 12 – 7: 16 – A Practical Exercise in Hermeneutics', *CTM* 29 (1968) 355–66; R.A. McCormick, 'Notes on Moral Theology: April–September, 1970', *TS* 32 (1971) 107–22 covers 'Theology and Divorce'; C.E. Curran, 'Divorce: Catholic Theory and Practice in the United-States – Part One', *AER* 168 (1974) 3–34; 'Part Two', 75–95; W. Schrage, 'Ethics in the NT', *IDBSup*, 281–9.
2. Compare *heneken emou* (because of Me) in Matt. 16: 25 with *dia tēn basileian* (because of the kingdom) in Matt. 19: 12 (cf. 19: 29).
3. See chap. 5.
4. G. Bromiley, *God and Marriage* (Grand Rapids: Eerdmans, 1980) 40–1. Other pastoral considerations along these lines may be found in J.C. Laney, *The Divorce Myth* (Minneapolis, Minn.: Bethany, 1981) 115–49; P.E. Steele and C.C. Ryrie, *Meant to Last* (Wheaton, Ill.: Victor Books, 1983).
5. Bromiley, *God and Marriage*, 47.

SELECTED BIBLIOGRAPHY

Adams, Jay E. *Marriage, Divorce and Remarriage in the Bible*. Phillipsburg, New Jersey: Presbyterian & Reformed Publishing Co., 1980.

Amram, David W. *The Jewish Law of Divorce according to Bible and Talmud*. London: Nutt, 1897.

Arendzen, J.P. 'Another Note on Matthew xix, 3–12'. *Clergy Review* 21 (1941): 23–6.

———. 'Ante-Nicene Interpretations of the Sayings on Divorce'. *Journal of Theological Studies* 20 (1919): 230–41.

———. 'Re-Writing St. Matthew'. *Expositor* 93 (1918): 366–71

Arens, Eduardo. 'Was St. Paul Married?' *The Bible Today* 66 (1973): 1188–91.

Atkinson, David. *To Have and To Hold: The Marriage Covenant and the Discipline of Divorce*. London: Collins, 1979.

———. 'A Response [to G.J. Wenham's review of *To Have and To Hold*]'. *Churchman* 95 (1981): 162–3.

Attfield, D.G. 'Hard Sayings [1 Cor. 6: 16]'. *Theology* 67 (1964): 117–18.

Audet, Jean-Paul. 'Love and Marriage in the Old Testament'. Translated by F. Burke. *Scripture* 10 (1958): 65–83.

Bacon, B.W. 'The Apostolic Decree Against ΠΟΡΝΕΙΑ'. *Expositor* 7 (1914): 40–61.

Bailey, Kenneth E. 'Paul's Theological Foundation for Human Sexuality: 1 Cor. 6: 9–20 in the Light of Rhetorical Criticism'. *Theological Review* 3 (1980): 27–41.

Balch, D.L. 'Backgrounds of I Cor. vii: Sayings of the Lord in Q; Moses as an Ascetic θεῖος ἀνήρ in II Cor. iii'. *New Testament Studies* 18 (1972): 351–64.

Balducelli, Roger. 'The Decision for Celibacy'. *Theological Studies* 36 (1975): 219–42.

Baltensweiler, Heinrich. 'Current Developments in the Theology of Marriage in the Reformed Churches'. Translated by Lucinde Tieck. In *Concilium*. Vol. 55: *The Future of Marriage as Institution*, pp. 144–51. New York: Herder and Herder, 1970.

————. 'Die Ehebruchsklauseln bei Matthäus. zu Matth. 5, 32; 19, 9'. *Theologische Zeitschrift* 15 (1959): 340–56.

————. *Die Ehe im Neuen Testament. Exegetische Untersuchungen über Ehe, Ehelosigkeit und Ehescheidung*. Abhandlungen zur theologie des Alten und Neuen Testaments. Vol. 52. Zürich/Stuttgart: Zwingli Verlag, 1967.

————. Review of *Marriage and Ministry in the New Temple*, by Abel Isaksson. *Theologische Zeitschrift* 23 (1967): 356–8.

Banks, Robert. *Jesus and the Law in the Synoptic Tradition*. Society for New Testament Studies Monograph Series. Vol. 28. Cambridge: University Press, 1975.

Barber, Cyril J. 'What Is Marriage?' *Journal of Psychology and Theology* 2 (1974): 48–60.

Barré, Michael L. 'To Marry or to Burn: πυροῦσθαι in 1 Cor 7: 9'. *Catholic Biblical Quarterly* 36 (1974): 193–202.

Bartling, Walter J. 'Sexuality, Marriage, and Divorce in 1 Corinthians 6: 12 – 7: 16 – A Practical Exercise in Hermeneutics'. *Concordia Theological Monthly* 29 (1968): 255–66.

Bassett, W.W. 'Divorce and Remarriage – The Catholic Search for a Pastoral Reconciliation: Part I'. *American Ecclesiastical Review* 162 (1970): 20–36; 'Part II', pp. 92–105.

————. 'The Marriage of Christians – Valid Contract, Valid Sacrament?' In *The Bond of Marriage*, pp. 117–69. Edited by W.W. Bassett. Notre Dame: University of Notre Dame Press, 1968.

Bevilacqua, Anthony J. 'History of the Indissolubility of Marriage'.

Proceedings of the Catholic Theological Society of America 22 (1967): 253–308.

Blevins, James L. 'The Age of Marriage in First-Century Palestine'. *Biblical Illustrator* 7 (1980): 65–7.

Boice, James Montgomery. 'The Biblical View of Divorce'. *Eternity*, December 1970, pp. 19–21.

Bontrager, G. Edwin. *Divorce and the Faithful Church*. Scottdale, Penn.: Herald Press, 1978.

Bromiley, Geoffrey W. *God and Marriage*. Grand Rapids: Wm. B. Eerdmans Publishing Co., 1980.

Brueggemann, Walter. 'Of the Same Flesh and Bone (Gn 2, 23a)'. *Catholic Biblical Quarterly* 32 (1970): 532–42.

Burrows, Millar. *The Basis of Israelite Marriage*. New Haven, Conn.: American Oriental Society, 1938.

Byron, Brian. 'The Brother or Sister Is Not Bound: Another Look at the New Testament Teaching on the Indissolubility of Marriage'. *New Blackfriars* 52 (1971): 514–21.

––––––. '1 Cor. 7: 10–15: A Basis for Future Catholic Discipline on Marriage and Divorce?' *Theological Studies* 34 (1973): 429–45.

––––––. 'General Theology of Marriage in the New Testament and 1 Cor. 7: 15'. *Australian Catholic Record* 49 (1972): 1–10.

Campbell, Robert C. 'Teaching of the Old Testament concerning Divorce'. *Foundations* 6 (1963): 174–8.

––––––. 'Teachings of Jesus concerning Divorce'. *Foundations* 6 (1963): 265–9.

––––––. 'Teachings of Paul concerning Divorce'. *Foundations* 6 (1963): 362–6.

Cartlidge, David R. '1 Corinthians 7 as a Foundation for a Christian Sex Ethic'. *Journal of Religion* 55 (1975): 220–34.

Catchpole, David R. 'The Synoptic Divorce Material as a Traditio-

Historical Problem'. *Bulletin of the John Rylands University Library* 57 (1974): 92–127.

Caverno, Charles. 'The Divorce Problem: A Rational Religious View'. *Bibliotheca Sacra* 69 (1912): 242–68.

Charles, R.H. *The Teaching of the New Testament on Divorce*. London: Wms. & Norgate, 1921.

Clark, Elizabeth A. 'John Chrysostom and the *Subintroductae*'. *Church History* 46 (1977): 171–85.

Cohen, Boaz. 'Concerning Divorce in Jewish and Roman Law'. *Proceedings of the American Academy for Jewish Research* 21 (1952): 3–34.

————. 'On the Theme of Betrothal in Jewish and Roman Law'. *Proceedings of the American Academy for Jewish Research* 18 (1948): 67–135.

Coiner, H.G. 'Those "Divorce and Remarriage" Passages (Matt. 5: 32; 19: 9; 1 Cor. 7: 10–16) – With Brief Reference to the Mark and Luke Passages'. *Concordia Theological Monthly* 29 (1968): 367–84.

Coleman, Gerald D. 'Pastoral Theology and Divorce'. *American Ecclesiastical Review* 169 (1975): 256–69.

Collins, Raymond F. 'The Bible and Sexuality'. *Biblical Theology Bulletin* 7 (1977): 149–67.

————. 'The Bible and Sexuality II'. *Biblical Theology Bulletin* 8 (1978): 3–18.

Colson, F.H. 'The Divorce Exception in St Matthew'. *Expositor* 11 (1916): 438–46.

Condon, Kevin. 'Apropos of the Divorce Sayings'. *Irish Biblical Studies* 2 (January 1980): 40–51.

Considine, Thomas. '"Except It Be for Fornication"'. *Australian Catholic Record* 33 (1956): 207–23.

————. 'The Pauline Privilege'. *Australian Catholic Record* 40 (1963): 107–19.

Corbett, P.E. *The Roman Law of Marriage*. Oxford: Clarendon Press, 1930.

Crater, Tim. 'Bill Gothard's View of The Exception Clause'. *Journal of Pastoral Practice* 4: 3 (1980): 5–12.

Crossan, Dominic. 'Divorce and Remarriage in the New Testament'. In *The Bond of Marriage*, pp. 1–33. Edited by W.W. Bassett. Notre Dame: University of Notre Dame Press, 1968.

Crouzel, Henri. *L'église primitive face au divorce du premier au cinquième siècle*. Paris: Beauchesne, 1971.

―――. 'Le texte patristique de Matthieu v. 32 et xix. 9'. *New Testament Studies* 19 (1972): 98–119.

―――. 'Quelques remarques concernant le texte patristique de Mt 19, 9'. *Bulletin de Littérature Ecclésiastique* 82 (1981): 83–92.

―――. 'Remarriage After Divorce in the Primitive Church: A Propos of a Recent Book'. *Irish Theological Quarterly* 38 (1971): 21–41.

Curran, Charles E. 'Divorce: Catholic Theory and Practice in the United States – Part One'. *American Ecclesiastical Review* 168 (1974): 3–34.

―――. 'Divorce: Catholic Theory and Practice in the United States – Part Two'. *American Ecclesiastical Review* 168 (1974): 75–95.

Daniel, Constantin. 'Esséniens et Eunuques (Matthieu 19, 10–12)'. *Revue de Qumran* 6 (1968): 353–90.

Daube, David. 'Concessions to Sinfulness in Jewish Law'. *Journal of Jewish Studies* 10 (1959): 1–13.

―――. 'The New Testament Terms for Divorce'. *Theology* 47 (1944): 65–7.

DeHaan, Richard W. *Marriage, Divorce and Re-Marriage*. Grand Rapids: Radio Bible Class, 1979.

Delling, Gerhard. 'Das Logion Mark. x 11 [und seine Abwandlungen] im Neuen Testament'. *Novum Testamentum* 1 (1956): 262–74.

―――. Review of *Marriage and Ministry in the New Temple*, by Abel Isaksson. *Theologische Literaturzeitung* 92 (1967): 276–7.

Derrett, J. Duncan M. *Law in the New Testament*. London: Darton, Longman & Todd, 1970.

————. Review of *Marriage and Ministry in the New Temple*, by Abel Isaksson. *Journal of Biblical Literature* 85 (1966): 98–9.

Dodd, C.H. 'New Testament Translation Problems II [1 Tim. 3:2, 12; Titus 1:6]'. *Bible Translator* 28 (1977): 101–16.

Drinkard, Joel F., Jr. 'Eunuchs in the Ancient Near East'. *Biblical Illustrator* 8:2 (1982): 39–41.

Dulau, Pierre. 'The Pauline Privilege: Is It Promulgated in the First Epistle to the Corinthians?' *Catholic Biblical Quarterly* 13 (1951): 146–52.

Dungan, David L. *The Sayings of Jesus in the Churches of Paul*. Philadelphia: Fortress Press, 1971.

Dunstan, Gordon R. 'Development of the Theology of Marriage in the Churches of the Anglican Communion'. *Concilium* 55 (1970): 133–43.

————. 'Hard Sayings – V. 1 Cor. 6:16'. *Theology* 66 (1963): 491–3.

————. 'The Marriage Covenant'. *Theology* 78 (1975): 244–52.

Dupont, Jacques, *Mariage et divorce dans l'évangile. Matthieu 19, 3–12 et parallèles*. Desclée de Brouwer, 1959.

Duty, Guy. *Divorce & Remarriage*. Minneapolis: Bethany Fellowship, 1967.

Dyson, R.A. and Leeming, Bernard, 'Except It Be for Fornication?' *Scripture* 8 (1956): 75–82.

Ehrlich, R.H. 'The Indissolubility of Marriage as a Theological Problem'. *Scottish Journal of Theology* 23 (1970): 291–311.

Eichhorst, Wm. R. 'Ezra's Ethics on Intermarriage and Divorce'. *Grace Journal* 10:3 (Fall 1969): 16–28.

Elliott, J.K. 'Paul's Teaching on Marriage in 1 Corinthians: Some Problems Considered'. *New Testament Studies* 19 (1973): 219–25.

Ellisen, Stanley A. *Divorce and Remarriage in the Church*. Grand Rapids: Zondervan Publishing House, 1977.

Ellison, H.L. 'The Message of Hosea in the Light of His Marriage'. *Evangelical Quarterly* 41 (1969): 3–9.

Epstein, Louis. *Marriage Laws in the Bible and Talmud*. The Harvard Semitic Series. Vol. 12. Cambridge, Mass.: Harvard University Press, 1942.

―――. *Sex Laws and Customs in Judaism*. N.p.: American Academy of Jewish Research, 1948; reprint ed., Introduction by Ari Kiev. New York: KTAV Publishing House, 1967.

Fee, Gordon D. '1 Corinthians 7: 1 in the *NIV*'. *Journal of the Evangelical Theological Society* 23 (1980): 307–14.

Field, David. 'Talking points: The divorce debate – where are we now?' *Themelios* 8: 3 (1983): 26–31.

Finkelstein, J.J. 'Sex Offenses in Sumerian Laws'. *Journal of the American Oriental Society* 86 (1966): 355–72.

Fischer, James A. '1 Cor. 7: 8–24 – Marriage and Divorce'. *Biblical Research* 23 (1978): 26–36.

Fisher-Hunter, W. *The Divorce Problem*. Waynesboro, Penn.: MacNeish Publishers, 1952.

Fitzmyer, Joseph A. 'The Matthean Divorce Texts and Some New Palestinian Evidence'. *Theological Studies* 37 (1976): 197–226.

―――. Review of *Marriage and Ministry in the New Temple*, by Abel Isaksson. *Theological Studies* 27 (1966): 451–4.

Fleming, T.V. 'Christ and Divorce'. *Theological Studies* 24 (1963): 106–20.

Ford, J. Massingberd. 'Levirate Marriage in St Paul (1 Cor. vii)'. *New Testament Studies* 10 (1964): 361–5.

―――. 'The Meaning of "Virgin"'. *New Testament Studies* 12 (1965–6): 293–9.

―――. 'The Rabbinic Background of St. Paul's Use of ὑπέρακμος (1 Cor. 7: 36)'. *Journal of Jewish Studies* 17 (1966): 89–91.

―――. Review of *Marriage and Ministry in the New Temple*, by Abel Isaksson. *Journal of Theological Studies* 18 (1967): 197–200.

―――. 'St Paul, the Philogamist (1 Cor. vii in Early Patristic Exegesis)'. *New Testament Studies* 11 (1965): 326–48.

Friedman, Mordechai A. 'Israel's Response in Hosea 2: 17b: "You Are My Husband"'. *Journal of Biblical Literature* 99 (1980): 199–204.

Galot, Jean. 'La motivation évangélique du célibat'. *Gregorianum* 53 (1972): 731–57.

Gangel, Kenneth O. 'Toward a Biblical Theology of Marriage and Family Part One: Pentateuch and Historical Books'. *Journal of Psychology and Theology* 5 (Winter 1977): 55–69.

————. 'Toward a Biblical Theology of Marriage and Family Part Two: Poetical and Prophetical Books'. *Journal of Psychology and Theology* 5 (Spring 1977): 150–62.

————. 'Toward a Biblical Theology of Marriage and Family Part 3: Gospels and Acts'. *Journal of Psychology and Theology* 5 (Summer 1977): 247–59.

————. 'Toward a Biblical Theology of Marriage and Family Part 4: Epistles and Revelation'. *Journal of Psychology and Theology* 5 (Fall 1977): 318–31.

Gavin, F. 'A Further Note on ΠΟΡΝΕΙΑ'. *Theology* 16 (1928): 102–5.

Geldard, Mark. 'Jesus' Teaching on Divorce: Thoughts on the Meaning of *porneia* in Matthew 5: 32 and 19: 9'. *Churchman* 92 (1978): 134–43.

Giblin, Charles H. '1 Corinthians 7 – A Negative Theology of Marriage and Celibacy?' *The Bible Today* 41 (1969): 2839–55.

Glassock, Ed. '"The Husband of One Wife" Requirement in 1 Timothy 3: 2'. *Bibliotheca Sacra* 140 (1983): 244–58.

Gordon, Cyrus H. 'A Marriage of the Gods in Canaanite Mythology'. *Bulletin of The American Schools of Oriental Research* 65 (1937): 29–33.

Greengus, Samuel. 'Old Babylonian Marriage Ceremonies and Rites'. *Journal of Cuneiform Studies* 20 (1966): 55–72.

————. 'The Old Babylonian Marriage Contract'. *Journal of the American Oriental Society* 89 (1969): 505–32.

Greeven, D.H. 'Ehe nach dem Neuen Testament'. *New Testament Studies* 15 (1969): 365–88.

Grelot, Pierre. 'The Institution of Marriage: Its Evolution in the Old Testament'. *Concilium* 55 (1970): 39–50.

Hansen, Paul G.; Feucht, Oscar E.; Kramer, Fred; and Lueker, Erwin. *Engagement and Marriage: A Sociological, Historical, and Theological Investigation of Engagement and Marriage.* Marriage and Family Research Series. St Louis: Concordia Publishing House, 1959.

Harrington, Wilfred J. 'Jesus' Attitude towards Divorce'. *Irish Theological Quarterly* 37 (1970): 199–209.

———. 'The New Testament and Divorce [A Summary of J.D.M. Derrett's Interpretation]'. *Irish Theological Quarterly* 39 (1972): 178–86.

Harris, Rivkah. 'The Case of Three Babylonian Marriage Contracts'. *Journal of Near Eastern Studies* 33 (1974): 363–9.

Herron, Robert W., Jr. 'Mark's Jesus on Divorce: Mark 10: 1–12 Reconsidered'. *Journal of the Evangelical Theological Society* 25 (1982): 273–81.

Heth, William A. 'Another Look at the Erasmian View of Divorce and Remarriage'. *Journal of the Evangelical Theological Society* 25 (1982): 263–72.

———. 'The Meaning of Divorce in Matthew 19: 3–9'. *Churchman* (forthcoming).

Hobbs, T.T. 'Jeremiah 3: 1–5 and Deuteronomy 24: 1–4'. *Zeitschrift für die alltestamentliche Wissenschaft* 86 (1974): 23–9.

Hodges, Zane C. 'The Woman Taken in Adultery (John 7: 53 – 8: 11): The Text'. *Bibliotheca Sacra* 136 (1979): 318–32.

———. 'The Woman Taken in Adultery (John 7: 53 – 8: 11): Exposition'. *Bibliotheca Sacra* 137 (1979): 41–53.

Hoffmann, Paul. 'Jesus' Saying about Divorce and its Interpetation in the New Testament Tradition'. *Concilium* 55 (1970): 51–66.

Holzmeister, U. 'Die Streitfrage über die Ehescheidungstexte bei Matthäus 5, 32, 19, 9'. *Biblica* 26 (1945): 133–46.

Hughes, J.J. Review of *L'église primitive face au divorce*, by Henri Crouzel. *Journal of Ecclesiastical History* 24 (1973): 60–3.

Hurley, James B. *Man and Woman in Biblical Perspective*. Grand Rapids: Zondervan Publishing House, 1981.

Isaksson, Abel. *Marriage and Ministry in the New Temple. A Study with Special Reference to Mt. 19. 13 [sic]–12 and 1. Cor. 11. 3–16*. Translated by Neil Tomkinson with the assistance of Jean Gray. Acta Seminarii Neotestamentici Upsaliensis. Vol. 24. Lund: Gleerup; Copenhagen: Munsgaard, 1965.

James, Stephen A. 'The Adultress and the Death Penalty'. *Journal of the Evangelical Theological Society* 22 (1979): 45–53.

Jensen, Joseph. 'Does *Porneia* Mean Fornication? A Critique of Bruce Malina'. *Novum Testamentum* 20 (1978): 161–84.

Job, John. 'The Biblical view of marriage and divorce 4 – New Testament teaching'. *Third Way*, November 17th, 1977, pp. 13–14.

Jossua, J.P. 'Moral Theological Forum: The Fidelity of Love and the Indissolubility of Christian Marriage'. *Clergy Review* 56 (1971): 172–81.

Joyce, George H. *Christian Marriage*. 2nd ed. London: Sheed and Ward, 1948.

Kempthorne, R. 'Incest and the Body of Christ: A Study of 1 Corinthians vi. 12–20'. *New Testament Studies* 14 (1968): 568–74.

Kilgallen, John J. 'To what are the Matthean Exception-Texts (5, 32 and 19, 9) an Exception?' *Biblica* 61 (1980): 102–5.

Kleist, James A. 'Eunuchs in the New Testament'. *Catholic Biblical Quarterly* 7 (1945): 447–9.

Knox, L. Mason. 'Divorce in the Roman Catholic Church: An Ecumenical Evaluation'. *American Ecclesiastical Review* 169 (1975): 341–58.

Kodell, Jerome. 'The Celibacy Logion in Matt. 19: 12'. *Biblical Theology Bulletin* 8 (1978): 19–23.

Kubo, Sakae. 'I Corinthians vii. 16: Optimistic or Pessimistic?' *New Testament Studies* 24 (1978): 539–44.

Kugelman, R. '1 Cor. 7: 36–8'. *Catholic Biblical Quarterly* 10 (1948): 63–71.

Kuntz, J.M. 'Is Marriage Indissoluble?' *Journal of Ecumenical Studies* 7 (1970): 333–7.

de Labriolle, Pierre. 'Le "Mariage Spirituel" dans l'antiquité chrétienne'. *Revue Historique* 137 (1921): 204–25.

Lake, Kirsopp. 'The Earliest Christian Teaching on Divorce'. *Expositor* 10 (1910): 416–27.

Laney, J. Carl. *The Divorce Myth.* Minneapolis: Bethany House Publishers, 1981.

———. 'Paul and the Permanence of Marriage in 1 Corinthians 7'. *Journal of the Evangelical Theological Society* 25 (1982): 283–94.

Lathrop, Noah. 'The Holy Scriptures and Divorce'. *Bibliotheca Sacra* 56 (1899): 266–77.

Lehmann, Manfred 'Gen. 2: 24 As the Basis for Divorce in Halakah and New Testament'. *Zeitschrift für die alttestamentliche Wissenschaft* 72 (1960): 263–7.

Lightman, Majorie and Zeisel, Wm. 'Univira: An Example of Continuity and Change in Roman Society'. *Church History* 46 (March 1977): 19–32.

Lipinski, E. 'The Wife's Right to Divorce in the Light of an Ancient Near Eastern Tradition'. In The *Jewish Law Annual* 4: 9–27. Edited by B.S. Jackson. Leiden: E.J. Brill, 1981.

Loewenstamm, S.E. 'The Laws of Adultery and the Murderer in Biblical and Mesopotamian Jurisprudence'. *Beth Hamiqra* 13 (1962): 55f.

Lövestam, Evald. 'Divorce and Remarriage in the New Testament'. In *The Jewish Law Annual* 4: 47–65. Edited by B.S. Jackson. Leiden: E.J. Brill, 1981.

Lowther Clarke, W.K. 'The Excepting Clause in St Matthew'. *Theology* 15 (1927): 161–2.

McEachern, Alton H. 'Divorce Laws in First-Century Palestine'. *Biblical Illustrator* 7 (Fall 1980): 68–9.

McKeating, Henry. 'Sanctions Against Adultery in Ancient Israelite Society, with Some Reflections on Methodology in the Study of the

Old Testament'. *Journal for the Study of the Old Testament* 11 (1979): 57–72.

McNeile, A.H. Review of *Christ's Teaching on Divorce*. A sermon preached by R.H. Charles. *Theology* 1 (1920): 95–8.

MacRory, J. 'Christian Writers of the First Three Centuries and St. Matt. xix. 9'. *Irish Theological Quarterly* 6 (1911): 172–85.

―――. 'The Teaching of the New Testament on Divorce'. *Irish Theological Quarterly* 5 (1910): 80–95.

―――. 'The Teaching of the New Testament on Divorce: A Critical Examination of Matt. xix. 9'. *Irish Theological Quarterly* 6 (1911): 74–91.

Mahoney, Aidan. 'A New Look at the Divorce Clauses in Mt 5, 32 and 19, 9'. *Catholic Biblical Quarterly* 30 (1968): 29–38.

Malina, Bruce. 'Does *Porneia* Mean Fornication?' *Novum Testamentum* 14 (1972): 10–17.

Maly, Eugene H. 'Celibacy'. *The Bible Today* 34 (1968): 2392–400.

Margoliouth, D.S. 'Christ's Answer to the Question about Divorce'. *Expository Times* 39 (1927–8): 273–5.

Martin, James D. 'The Forensic Background to Jeremiah III 1'. *Vetus Testamentum* 19 (1969): 82–92.

Matura, Thaddée. 'Le célibat dans le Nouveau Testament d'après l'exégèse récente'. *Nouvelle Revue Théologique* 97 (1975): 481–500; 593–604. ['Celibacy in the NT'. *Theology Digest* 24 (Spring 1976): 39–45.]

Meeks, Wayne A. 'The Image of the Androgyne: Some Uses of a Symbol in Earliest Christianity'. *History of Religions* 13 (1974): 165–208.

Meier, John P. *Law and History in Matthew's Gospel. A Redactional Study of Mt. 5: 17–48.* Analecta Biblica. Vol. 71. Rome: Biblical Institute Press, 1976.

Meier, Paul D. *You Can Avoid Divorce.* Grand Rapids: Baker Book House, 1978.

Mendelsohn, Isaac. 'The Family in the Ancient Near East'. *Biblical Archaeologist* 11 (May 1948): 24–40.

Mielziner, M. *The Jewish Law of Marriage and Divorce in Ancient and Modern Times, and Its Relation to the Law of the State.* Cincinnati: Block Publishing & Printing Co., 1884.

Miller, J.I. 'A Fresh Look at I Corinthians 6. 16f'. *New Testament Studies* 27 (1980): 125–7.

Moloney, Francis J. 'Matthew 19, 3–12 and Celibacy: A Redactional and Form Critical Study'. *Journal for the Study of the New Testament* 2 (January 1979): 42–60.

Montefiore, H. 'Jesus on Divorce and Remarriage'. In *Marriage, Divorce and the Church*, pp. 79–95. London: SPCK, 1971.

Moore, George Foot. *Judaism in the First Centuries of the Christian Era: The Age of the Tannaim.* 3 vols in 2. N.p.: Harvard University Press, 1927–30; reprint ed., New York: Schocken Books, 1971.

Moran, W.L. 'The Scandal of the "Great Sin" at Ugarit'. *Journal of Near Eastern Studies* 18 (1959): 280–1.

Mueller, James R. 'The Temple Scroll and the Gospel Divorce Texts'. *Revue de Qumran* 38 (1980): 247–56.

Murphy, J. Joseph. 'The Gospels and Divorce: A Theological Study'. *Clergy Review* 23 (1943): 441–9.

Murphy-O'Connor, Jerome. 'Corinthian Slogans in 1 Cor. 6: 12–20'. *Catholic Biblical Quarterly* 40 (1978): 391–6.

Murray, John. *Divorce.* Phillipsburg, NJ: Presbyterian & Reformed Publishing Co., [1961].

Neal, Marshall. 'The Christian and Marriage'. *Biblical Viewpoint* 7 (1973): 97–105.

Nembach, U. 'Ehescheidung nach alttestamentlichem und jüdischem Recht'. *Theologische Zeitschrift* 26 (1970): 161–71.

Neufeld, E. *Ancient Hebrew Marriage Laws: With Special References to General Semitic Laws and Customs.* London: Longman's, Green & Co., 1944.

Noonan, John T., Jr. 'Indissolubility of Marriage and Natural Law'. *Theology Digest* 19 (Spring 1971): 9–15.

————. 'Novel 22'. In *The Bond of Marriage*, pp. 41–90. Edited by W.W. Bassett. Notre Dame: University of Notre Dame Press, 1968.

O'Callaghan, Denis. 'Theology and Divorce'. *Irish Theological Quarterly* 37 (1970): 210–22.

O'Connor, W.R. 'The Indissolubility of a Ratified, Consummated Marriage'. *Ephemerides theologicae lovanienses* 13 (1936): 692–722.

Olsen, V. Norskov. *The New Testament Logia on Divorce: A Study of their Interpretation from Erasmus to Milton*. Beiträge zur Geschichte der biblischen Exegese 10. Tübingen: J.C.B. Mohr (Paul Siebeck), 1971.

Oppenheimer, Helen. 'Is the Marriage Bond an Indissoluble "Vinculum"?' *Theology* 78 (1975): 236–44.

O'Rourke, John J. 'Does the New Testament Condemn Sexual Intercourse Outside Marriage?' *Theological Studies* 37 (1976): 478–9.

————. 'Hypotheses Regarding 1 Corinthians 7, 36–8'. *Catholic Biblical Quarterly* 20 (1958): 292–8.

————. 'A Note on an Exception: Mt. 5:32 (19:9) and 1 Cor. 7:12 Compared'. *Heythrop Journal* 5 (1964): 299–302.

————. 'The Scriptural Background of Canon 1120'. *Jurist* 15 (1955): 132–7.

Orr, Wm. F. 'Paul's Treatment of Marriage in 1 Cor. 7'. *Pittsburgh Perspective* 8:3 (1967): 5–22.

Osburn, Carroll D. 'The Present Indicative in Matthew 19:9'. *Restoration Quarterly* 24 (1981): 193–203.

O'Shea, Wm. J. 'Marriage and Divorce: the Biblical Evidence'. *Australian Catholic Record* 47 (1970): 89–109.

Palmer, Paul F. 'Christian Marriage: Contract or Covenant?' *Theological Studies* 33 (1972): 617–65.

Paterson, John. 'Divorce and Desertion in the Old Testament'. *Journal of Biblical Literature* 51 (1932): 161–70.

Paterson, W.P. 'Divorce and the Law of Christ'. *Expositor* [Seventh Series] 10 (1910): 289–305.

Peters, A. 'St Paul and Marriage: A Study of 1 Corinthians Chapter Seven'. *African Ecclesiastical Review* 6 (1964): 214–24.

Peters, G.W. *Divorce and Remarriage*. Chicago: Moody Press, 1972.

Phillips, Anthony. 'Another Example of Family Law'. *Vetus Testamentum* 30 (1980): 240–5.

———. 'Another Look at Adultery'. *Journal for the Study of the Old Testament* 20 (1981): 3–25.

———. 'Some Aspects of Family Law in Pre-Exilic Israel'. *Vetus Testamentum* 23 (1973): 349–61.

———. 'Uncovering the Father's Skirt'. *Vetus Testamentum* 30 (1980): 38–43.

Phipps, Wm. E. 'Did Jesus or Paul Marry?' *Journal of Ecumenical Studies* 5 (1968): 741–4.

Piattelli, Daniela. 'The Marriage Contract and Bill of Divorce in Ancient Hebrew Law'. In *The Jewish Law Annual* 4: 66–78. Edited by B.S. Jackson. Leiden: E.J. Brill, 1981.

Pilch, John J. 'Marriage in the Lord'. *The Bible Today* 102 (1979): 2010–13.

Pospishil, Victor J. *Divorce and Remarriage: Towards a New Catholic Teaching*. New York: Herder and Herder, 1967.

———. 'Divorce and Remarriage in the Early Church'. *Irish Theological Quarterly* 38 (1971): 338–47.

Powers, B. Ward. 'Divorce and the Bible'. *Interchange* 23 (1978): 149–74.

Quesnell, Quentin. '"Made Themselves Eunuchs for the Kingdom of Heaven" (Mt. 19, 12)'. *Catholic Biblical Quarterly* 30 (1968): 335–58.

Quinn, Jerome D. 'Celibacy and the Ministry in Scripture'. *The Bible Today* 46 (1970): 3163–75.

Rabello, Alfredo Mordechai. 'Divorce of Jews in the Roman Empire'. In *The Jewish Law Annual* 4: 79–102. Edited by B.S. Jackson. Leiden: E.J. Brill, 1981.

Rabinowitz, Jacob J. 'The "Great Sin" in Ancient Egyptian Marriage Contracts'. *Journal of Near Eastern Studies* 18 (1959): 72–3.

————. 'Marriage Contracts in Ancient Egypt in the Light of Jewish Sources'. *Harvard Theological Review* 46 (1953): 91–7.

Rex, H.H. 'An Attempt to Understand 1 Cor. 7'. *Reformed Theological Review* 14 (1955): 41–51.

Richards, H.J. 'Christ and Divorce'. *Scripture* 11 (1959): 22–32.

Richardson, Peter. ' "I say, not the Lord": Personal Opinion, Apostolic Authority and the Development of Early Christian Halakah'. *Tyndale Bulletin* 31 (1980): 65–86.

Roberts, R.L. 'The Meaning of *Chorizo* and *Douloo* in 1 Cor 7: 10–17'. *Restoration Quarterly* 3 (1965): 179–84.

Rordorf, Willy. 'Marriage in the New Testament and in the Early Church'. Translated by H.O. Old. *Journal of Ecclesiastical History* 20 (1969): 193–210.

Rousseau, Oliver. 'Divorce and Remarriage: East and West'. *Concilium* 24 (1967): 113–38.

Rowley, H.H. 'The Marriage of Hosea'. *Bulletin of the John Rylands University Library* 39 (1956–7): 200–33.

Ryrie, Charles C. 'Biblical Teaching on Divorce and Remarriage'. *Grace Theological Journal* 3 (1982): 177–92.

Sabourin, L. 'The Divorce Clauses (Mt 5: 32, 19: 9)'. *Biblical Theology Bulletin* 2 (1972): 80–6.

Safrai, S. and Stern, M., eds., in co-operation with D. Flusser and W.C. van Unnik. *The Jewish People in the First Century*. 2 vols Compendia Rerum Iudaicarum ad Novum Testamentum. Assen/Amsterdam: VanGorcum, 1974–6.

Sandmel, Samuel. 'Jewish and Christian Marriage: Some Observations'. *Heythrop Journal* 11 (1970): 237–50.

Saucy, Robert L. 'The Husband of One Wife'. *Bibliotheca Sacra* 131 (1974): 229–40.

Schaller, Berndt. ' "Commits Adultery with Her", Not "against Her",
Mk 10: 11'. *Expository Times* 83 (1972): 107–8.

Schillebeeckx, E. *Marriage: Human Reality and Saving Mystery*. Translated
by N.D. Smith. 2 vols in 1. New York: Sheed and Ward, 1965.

Schmemann, Alexander. 'The Indissolubility of Marriage: The Theo-
logical Tradition of the East'. In *The Bond of Marriage*, pp. 97–105.
Edited by W.W. Bassett. Notre Dame: University of Notre Dame
Press, 1968.

Schubert, K. 'Ehescheidung zur Zeit Jesu'. *Theologische Quartalschrift* 151
(1971): 23–7.

Seboldt, Roland H.A. 'Spiritual Marriage in the Early Church: A Suggested Interpretation of 1 Cor. 7: 36–8'. *Concordia Theological Monthly* 30
(1959): 103–19; 176–89.

Selwyn, E.G. 'Christ's Teaching on Marriage and Divorce: A Reply to Dr
Charles'. *Theology* 15 (1927): 88–101.

Shaner, Donald W. *A Christian View of Divorce according to the Teachings of
the New Testament*. Leiden: E.J. Brill, 1969.

Sheppard, W.T. Celestine. 'The Teaching of the Fathers on Divorce'.
Irish Theological Quarterly 5 (1910): 402–15.

Sherlock, J. Alex. Review of *L'église primitive face au divorce*, by Henri
Crouzel. *Theological Studies* 33 (1972): 333–8.

Sinks, Robert F. 'A Theology of Divorce'. *Christian Century*, April 20th,
1977, pp. 376–9.

Small, Dwight Hervey. 'The Prophet Hosea: God's Alternative to Divorce for the Reason of Infidelity'. *Journal of Psychology and Theology* 7
(1979): 133–40.

———. Review of *Marriage, Divorce and Remarriage in the Bible*, by Jay E.
Adams. *Eternity*, June 1981, pp. 44–5.

———. *The Right to Remarry*. Old Tappan, NJ: Fleming H. Revell Co.,
1975.

Smith, Harold. 'The Earliest Interpretations of Our Lord's Teaching On
Divorce'. *Expositor* 93 (1918): 361–6.

Soulen, Richard N. 'Marriage and Divorce: A Problem in New Testament Interpretation'. *Interpretation* 23 (1969): 439–50.

Stagg, Frank. 'Biblical Perspectives on the Single Person'. *Review and Expositor* 74 (1977): 5–19.

Stein, Robert H. 'Is it lawful for a man to divorce his wife?' *Journal of the Evangelical Theological Society* 22 (1979): 115–21.

Stock, Augustine. 'Matthean Divorce Texts'. *Biblical Theology Bulletin* 8 (1978): 24–33.

Stoll, C.D. *Ehe und Ehescheidung: Die Weisungen Jesu.* Giessen: Brunnen Verlag, 1983.

Stott, J.R.W. 'The Biblical Teaching on Divorce'. *Churchman* 85 (1971): 165–74.

Thompson, Thomas L. 'A Catholic View on Divorce'. *Journal of Ecumenical Studies* 6 (1969): 53–67.

Thurian, Max. *Marriage and Celibacy.* Translated by Norma Emerton. Studies in Ministry and Worship. Introduction by Roger Schutz. London: SCM Press, 1959.

Tosato, A. 'Joseph, Being a Just Man (Matt. 1:19).' *Catholic Biblical Quarterly* 41 (1979): 547–51.

Turner, Nigel. 'The Translation of Μοιχᾶται ἐπ' Αὐτήν in Mark 10: 11'. *Bible Translator* 7 (1956): 151–2.

van Selms, A. *Marriage and Family Life in Ugaritic Literature.* London: Luzac, 1954.

Vass, George. 'Divorce and Remarriage in the Light of Recent Publications'. *Heythrop Journal* 11 (1970): 251–77.

Vawter, Bruce. 'The Biblical Theology of Divorce'. *Proceedings of the Catholic Theological Society of America* 22 (1967): 223–43.

———. 'Divorce and the New Testament'. *Catholic Biblical Quarterly* 39 (1977): 528–42.

———. 'The Divorce Clauses in Mt 5, 32 and 19, 9'. *Catholic Biblical Quarterly* 16 (1954): 155–67.

Verhey, Allen. 'Divorce and the New Testament (1).' *Reformed Journal* 26 (May–June 1976): 17–19.

———. 'Divorce and the New Testament (2)'. *Reformed Journal* 26 (July-August 1976): 28–31.

Ward, Michael R. 'Once Married Always Married? – A Biblical Review and Synthesis'. *Churchman* 87 (1973) 190–7.

Wenham, Gordon J. '*Bᵉtûlāh* "A Girl of Marriageable Age"'. *Vetus Testamentum* 22 (1972): 326–48.

———. 'The biblical view of marriage and divorce 1 – cultural background'. *Third Way*, October 20th, 1977, pp. 3–5.

———. 'The biblical view of marriage and divorce 2 – Old Testament teaching'. *Third Way*, November 3rd, 1977, pp. 7–9.

———. 'The biblical view of marriage and divorce 3 – New Testament teaching'. *Third Way*, November 17th, 1977, pp. 7–9.

———. 'Clarifying divorce'. *Third Way*, December 29th, 1977, pp. 17–18.

———. 'Gospel Definitions of Adultery and Women's Rights'. *Expository Times* (forthcoming).

———. 'The Marriage Bond and the Church: A Summary and Evaluation of the Recent Church of England Report on Divorce and Remarriage'. *Third Way*, June 1st, 1978, pp. 13–15.

———. 'Matthew and Divorce: An Old Crux Revisited'. *Journal for the Study of the New Testament* (forthcoming).

———. 'May Divorced Christians Remarry?' *Churchman* 95 (1981): 150–61.

———. 'The Restoration of Marriage Reconsidered [Deut. 24: 1–4]'. *Journal of Jewish Studies* 30 (1979): 36–40.

——— and McConville, J.G. 'Drafting Techniques in Some Deuteronomic Laws [Deut. 22: 13–29]'. *Vetus Testamentum* 30 (1980): 248–52.

Wiebe, P.H. 'The New Testament on Divorce and Remarriage: Some Logical Implications'. *Journal of the Evangelical Theological Society* 24 (1981): 131–8.

Wijngards, J.N.M. 'Do Jesus' Words on Divorce (Lk 16: 18) Admit of No Exception?' *Jeevadhara* 4 (1975): 399–411.

Wilson, Clifford H. 'Marriage Contracts in Mesopotamia and Genesis'. *Buried History* 6 (1970): 119–22.

Winter, Paul. 'Genesis 1: 27 and Jesus' Saying on Divorce'. *Zeitschrift für die alttestamentliche Wissenschaft* 70 (1958): 260–1.

Yadin, Yigal. 'L'Attitude essénienne envers la polygamie et le divorce'. *Revue Biblique* 79 (1972): 98–9.

Yamauchi, Edwin M. 'Cultural Aspects of Marriage in the Ancient World'. *Bibliotheca Sarca* 135 (1978): 241–52.

Yaron, R. 'Aramaic Marriage Contracts from Elephantine'. *Journal of Semitic Studies* 3 (1958): 1–39.

——. 'On Divorce in Old Testament Times'. *Revue Internationale des Droits de l'Antiquité* 3 (1957): 117–28.

——. 'The Restoration of Marriage [Deut. 24: 1–4]'. *Journal of Jewish Studies* 17 (1966): 1–11.

Zakovitch, Yair. 'The Woman's Rights in the Biblical Law of Divorce'. In *The Jewish Law Annual* 4: 28–46. Edited by B.S. Jackson. Leiden: E.J. Brill, 1981.

INDEXES

INDEX OF AUTHORS

SELECTED SCRIPTURE INDEX

Old Testament

New Testament